WHEELS OUT OF GEAR

2
TONE

THE SPECIALS

and a world in flame

By Dave Thompson

First edition published in 2004 by
Helter Skelter Publishing
South Bank House, Black Prince Road,
London SE1 7SJ

Copyright 2004 © Dave Thompson

All rights reserved
Cover design by Bold
Typesetting by Caroline Walker
Printed in Great Britain by CPI, Bath

All lyrics quoted in this book are for the purposes of review, study or criticism.

The publishers would like to thank Bleddyn Butcher for his help with this project.

A CIP record for this book is available from the British Library

ISBN 1-900924-84-6

WHEELS OUT OF GEAR

2
TONE

THE SPECIALS

and a world in flame

By Dave Thompson

Helter Skelter Publishing

CONTENTS

ACKNOWLEDGEMENTS

Thanks to everybody who helped and encouraged as this book took shape: the musicians, the producers, club owners, label heads, and everybody else who spared the time to remember those tumultuous days: Steve Ashley, Dicky Barrett, Boz Boorer, Mark Brennan, Pam Cross, Judge Dread, Ian Dury, Micky Fitz, Ray Fenwick, Chris Gilbey, Lynval Golding, Martin Gordon, Brian James, Pauline Murray, Brian Perera, Peter Purnell, Roddy Radiation, Tom Robinson, Ranking Roger, Dave Ruffy, Seggs, TV Smith, Neville Staples, Joe Strummer, Suggs, Dave Treganna, and the legendary AN Other.

Also to Jo-Ann Greene, for opening her private archive of period ephemera, and pointing out so many fresh directions; Amy Hanson, for enthusiasm and encouragement in the face of some deafening bass lines; Mike Scharman, for sharing the greatest Mod collection in town; and to Sean Body and all at Helter Skelter for making it all happen.

And finally, Batears and the family, Barb East, Ella, K-Mart (not the store!), Geoff Monmouth, Nutkin, Orifice, Julian Paul, Snarleyyowl the Cat Fiend, Sprocket, sundry Schecklers, Thompsons and Duas, and the Gremlins who live, as always, in the furnace.

A WORD IN ADVANCE

The years immediately following the Punk explosion of 1976-78 rank among the most fascinating, and fascinatedly convoluted eras in the history of British rock'n'roll, a period during which everybody seemed to be searching for the Next Big Thing, while studiously ignoring the fact that the Biggest Thing was already with us.

It was called Hopelessness, and there was a lot of it around. Every time another black family's house was firebombed, every time another breadwinner was laid off work, every time another innocent kid was arrested on SUS, every time another nuclear missile was pointed to the sky, every time Margaret Thatcher appeared on television to tell us that everything was fine. Hopelessness.

But despair is only as dark as the dreams that turn to nightmares at its touch; and, for all the passing Punks who still took solace from the Sex Pistols' insistence that there really was No Future, there were others who grasped salvation wherever it was presented, and hauled themselves... if not *above* it all, then at least to a place where it didn't look so bad. And that, it turned out, was the key.

If you can see the problem, then you can see the solution and, from the grip of the darkest days Britain had known in more than two generations, an entire new generation set itself to righting the wrongs that had become a way of life.

Music had, of course, collided with politics before – what was Punk, after all, if not an uprising of sorts against the status quo? And a decade earlier, American rock burned with righteous indignation, as the country's government led its youth through the fires of Vietnam.

The difference was, those past insurrections had challenged the Powers That Be, the governments of the day. The uprising that began in 1978, with the first brickbats of discontent on the streets of Britain's inner cities, and climaxed in 1981 with a summer of unprecedented riot, went beyond those petty aims, to challenge institution itself, to take on an engrained way of thinking, a physical way of life.

Poverty, unemployment, racism, sexism, militarism – the fighters on the frontlines could pick their target as easily as they picked up a brick; and, whether their hair was long or short, their outfit Punk or Mod, their mindset Skin or Rasta, still they fought as one, for everyone. And, though one might never say they won the war, neither did they lose it.

Britain's blacks never were repatriated by a hate-filled right wing government. Britain's unemployed were never dragged from the dole queues to the army camps, and thence to the gas chambers. And Britain itself was never evaporated in the hiss of nuclear armageddon. Indeed, today it seems crazy that there ever was a time when people thought those things were even vaguely possible. And even crazier to think that it was pop music that got a lot of them through it.

That is what this book is about – that four year period, 1978-1981, during which music not only took a stand against inevitability (for that was nothing new), but when it actually succeeded in that quest.

As such, it is not a biography of any one band, nor even of one movement. Of course, several groups – most notably the Specials – do receive considerable documentation within. For the most part, however, their story is told only in as much as it applies to the events unfolding around it. When the action ends, in summer 1981, so does the story.

Neither is it the saga of any one genre although, again, the Specials' 2-Tone ska revival certainly occupies a prominent place herein. But any one of a dozen groups, and half a dozen musical stylings, could have taken similar prominence, without changing either the tone or the terminology of this book in the slightest. From the Ruts and the Tom Robinson Band, to the Angelic Upstarts and the 4-Skins, the heroes here are all equally heroic, just as the villains are all equally villainous. And the memories themselves seem all the more incredible for having sat down to recall them.

INTRODUCTION

Britain gives her best... general unrest
Houses burning down
We've got a new shanty town

Wheels out of gear – what's the sense in living here?
Make us cheap and you'll pay very dear
Wheels out of gear

Wheels out of gear – Britain says it can't happen here
But it can happen anywhere
Wheels out of gear

TV Smith: 'Wheels Out Of Gear' (lyrics by permission of TV Smith, 1981)

A snapshot of Britain during the second-half of the 1970s would be remarkable as, quite possibly, the first and only time a Tory opposition actually told the unvarnished truth about the incumbent government: Labour wasn't working.

In 1976, unemployment passed the one million mark; the following year, it was inching towards 1.5. Nor did employment itself guarantee a living wage; in 1977, the government fixed pay increases at a maximum of 10 percent, which meant they just kept pace with inflation. *Just.*

When Britain's firemen walked out on strike in November 1977, after their demands for a 30 percent increase were thrown in their faces, the country itself did *not* go up in flames as predicted. But the last shred of optimism that clung to Jim Callaghan's embattled and increasingly embittered Labour government, and the final hope that they might be able to pull the country out of the abyss, those things were not so lucky.

Of course, we now know that labour would be working even less by the time the Tories had been in office for a while. In January 1982, less than three years after Margaret Thatcher moved into No. 10, British unemployment topped three million for the first time since the Depression of the 1930s. The newly-appointed Labour leader Michael Foot could afford to reflect almost fondly upon his own party's record: "When Mrs Thatcher came into office, there were five people chasing each job and that was bad enough. Today there are 32 people chasing every vacancy and in some parts of the country, it's double that."

In 1978, that horror had still to unfold – but things were already bad enough without sitting around worrying that they might get worse.

There was nothing to look forward to. Three summers running, Britain had bathed in novelties that the old folk couldn't compare with some mythic, halcyon past. 1975 basked beneath a Riviera-like heat wave that broke every record in the land; 1976 brought another, as those temperatures, too, were routinely shattered and water rationing brought standpipes back to street corners all over the country. And, if 1977 saw the summer swoop back to normal, at least there was the Jubilee to maintain some sense of occasion. How could 1978 hope to compete with all that? And would it bother, even if it wanted to?

A World Cup was looming, but England had long since lost interest in that, falling out of a qualifying group that was weighted against them from the moment it was drawn. Wearily, the nation turned its support to Scotland instead: they had pulled through and were busy predicting they were going to win the whole thing.

Of course, they didn't. Staked out in the Argentinean sun, one win, one loss, and a crippling draw with the minnows of Iran sent the Scots hobbling home just a few days after star player Willie Johnstone himself was sent packing after failing a drug test. The fact that the banned substance was, in fact, a prescribed asthma medication only heightened the despair that was to be the year's most lasting memory.

Music did offer some diversion. Still sparking from the insurgencies of the previous year's Punk, the charts continued throwing up the odd little shocker to make it worth watching *Top Of The Pops*: the Adverts, the Tom Robinson Band, Nick Lowe, the Boomtown Rats, Patti Smith… It wasn't all Brian and Michael and 'You're The One That I Want' – even if that's all you ever heard on the radio.

Live, it was even more open. Less than a quid got you in to most pubs and clubs, hand over two and the world was your oyster. A few nights in London in early August alone could leave future name-droppers reeling with nostalgic amazement: John Otway at the Red Cow, the Slits at the Music Machine (opening for Steve Gibbons! Now there's a mismatch to savour!), the UK Subs at the Forrester Arms and the Members at the Windsor Castle. Something to tell the grandkids about.

But there were other things afoot as that summer dragged on. The 1977-78 re-emergence of Britain's Skinhead culture after half a decade in the shadows was, in retrospect, inevitable. Punk, after all, was already tamed and, just as society always needs a scapegoat, anti-society always needs a focus.

In truth, only the most bigoted opponent would conclude that the simultaneous resurgence of the early-70s style Skinhead movement and the National Front (the public face of right-wing extremism and, for a short time in the mid-late 1970s, a potential force in British politics) was anything but coincidental. But it was those 'bigoted opponents' upon whom the Front fed, painting anyone who opposed them as precisely the kind of blinkered lefty liberals who would most benefit from a taste of the Fascist whip, and confronting them with the snarling, shaven face of nationalistic hatred.

Formed in 1967 from the union of the earlier League of Empire Loyalists, the British National Party, the Racial Preservation Society and the Greater Britain Movement, the Front grew slowly: in 1973, it could claim no more than 17,000 members nationwide. The worsening economy of the mid-1970s, however, proved a fertile breeding ground for the Front, not merely as a racist organisation, but also as a Fascist-style solution to all of Britain's ailments – other NF platforms that received growing support included withdrawing Britain from the EEC, and stronger criminal legislation.

In a 1976 by-election at Leicester, the Front received 15,340 votes; in local elections the following year, leader John Tyndall scooped 19 percent per cent of the vote in Hackney South and Bethnal Green, while the party attracted 200,000 votes nationwide. Neither was the Front at all shy about canvassing for new members, moving into the inner cities, leafleting and fly-postering and pitching itself at those elements which, to put it bluntly, 'respectable' society would have no problem in identifying on the street: the weird-looking kids who now hung about on every street corner.

The Front's early attempts at allying itself with the Punk movement failed dismally: an especially ill-advised effort at lining up alongside the Sex Pistols, unequivocally Punk's pacesetters, prompted Johnny Rotten to label the party as "loathsome slugs." The Skinhead movement, on the other hand, had no single definable leader and, unlike the Punks, no immediately identifiable credo. And those that were sucked in instantly became the media's favourite Face Of Hate. Nobody has ever published a reliable estimate of exactly how many Skinheads were drawn into the National Front's ranks. But even if it was just a couple of percent of the organisation's overall force, who would be the most visible figures on the Fascist frontline? An army of middle-aged men in jeans, suits or donkey jackets? Or a handful of Skins with shaven skulls, braces and boots?

Discussing the audience that grew up around the Oi! scene of 1980-81, but with words that apply across the Skinhead movement of the late 1970s, journalist Gary Bushell vouchsafes the sheer apoliticality of the movement. "Beyond the sense of voting Labour (if they bothered to vote at all) out of a sense of tradition, [only] a tiny percentage [of the movement's following] was interested in the extremes of either right or left."

He continues, "They looked good and dressed sharp. It was important not to look like a scruff or a student." But he also acknowledges that violence was a vital component in the mix: "As a breed they were natural conservatives. They believed in standing on their own two feet. They were patriotic, and proud of their class and their immediate culture. The young men oozed machismo, but some of the women were just as tough." And therein lay the premise upon which the Front recruiters relied, for when you wrap that toughness in a Union Jack tattoo, at a time when the Union Jack itself had been hijacked as the fascist's most potent symbol, there was only one conclusion for the knee-jerk millions to draw: 'Cropped-head + Bovver Boots = A Damned Good Kicking For Some Poor Sod,' with the poor sod, nine-times-out-of-ten expected to be black.

Tarring all Skinheads with the same racist brush is a feat of stereotyping that, in any other application, would turn liberal knees to jelly; denying that there is a deal of truth in that stereotype is, similarly, an historical absurdity.

Far more Skinhead musicians and fans allied themselves with the Socialist Workers' Party and similarly themed leftist organisations than ever linked with the Front and the allied British Movement. Even more turned out in staunch support of Rock Against Racism, an SWP offshoot designed specifically to focus musical attention on the problems facing British youth, black *and* white. From that focus came new direction, in the form of the two most important musical forces of the immediately-post-Punk era: Oi! and 2-Tone. If they were musically incompatible, they were irrevocably symbiotic.

Oi! took its name, according to some sources, from nothing more challenging than the choruses of 'oggie-oggie-oggie...' that rose spontaneously from the terraces of the Football League. Both within and without the hooligan culture that today permeates almost all recollections of sporting life throughout that decade, Skinhead culture had continued to breed on the terraces through its recession of the early-mid-1970s, and at least two of the new movement's most powerful bands, the pioneering Sham 69 and the later Cockney Rejects, were deeply steeped in football culture – Sham even took their name from a piece of footballing graffiti, a spray painted reminder of singer Jimmy Pursey's hometown Hersham's most successful year, 1969. A few of the letters had worn away by the time Pursey chanced upon them – so he adapted the rest to his own purposes.

In terms of etymology, 2-Tone was the polar opposite to Oi!, the product of study rather than a stain on the wall, a conscious creation rather than an organic explosion. Yet, what began as a record label – founded by Specials vocalist Jerry Dammers as an outlet for his own assemblage's then-unique brand of Ska-Punk – became a way of life so swiftly that, by the time the label released its first single, the Specials' 'Gangsters', 2-Tone was already a definable brand name. Arthur Kay's Originals and Madness were both gloriously underway, the Selecter, the Beat and Bad Manners weren't far behind them.

Yet, without 2-Tone, and the rest of the Ska-Punk half-breed which history now lumps under that one, convenient banner, Oi! could never have flourished as it did. The headlines, of course, concentrated on the trouble that attended certain Skinhead gatherings, zeroing in on the bad apples who sided with the hateful Front, delighting in tales of unquestionable racist violence. But that coverage missed countless corollaries. That was where 2-Tone came in, redressing the balance. And then upsetting it entirely.

2-Tone exerted a peculiar influence over its audience. Outside shows, it was the Skins who harassed passers-by with NF leaflets and chants. Inside, however, it was the Skins who gave the performers the most encouragement, transforming entire theatres into vast, swirling celebrations of fashion, dance and, most of all, unity. Colour became irrelevant, dress became incidental. For however long the euphoria lasted, the audience was, indeed, 2-Toned.

The climate into which 2-Tone stylishly skanked was a weird one: Oi! was rising from the ashes of Punk but 1979 was also the summer of Mod, a ghost laid to rest in the mid-1960s, but reawakened by Paul Weller's slavish obsession with his old Who and Small Faces records and the Who's own revitalization around the movie version of their last decent LP, *Quadrophenia*.

Even at its peak, modern Mod possessed little to call its own. Jolly bandwagoning concerns like the Merton Parkas (whose pianist, Mick Talbot, would later join both Dexy's Midnight Runners and Weller's miscalculated Style Council), the Purple Hearts and Secret Affair all flirted with what could be called a generic Mod sound, but simply reiterated old Motown and Who (again) singles. It was the mood that mattered, the fact that once again, youth had a reason to dress up and feel cool.

2-Tone, too, traced its antecedents back to the first Mod era, but with an added 'something', a socio-political edge apparent in both the participants' own music and the cover versions they chose. When the Specials revived Dandy Livingstone's laconic 'A Message To You, Rudy', they revived the emotions that made the song so important when it was first released, appealing to a new generation whose own social prospects were as appalling as the original Rude Boys. And it offered them an escape route.

Caught between the existing menace of an incumbent government that had lost its direction years ago and the imminent peril of Margaret Thatcher's fundamentalist conservatism, British youth stared into a bleak no-future that even the Sex Pistols could not have envisaged. The only real dilemma was what they were going to do about it?

What made Punk so exceptional as a cultural force was that it came out of nowhere. It had no precedent, no past and, in the eyes of authority, no parallel. Once it was accepted, however, although its absorption into the musical mainstream was only ever a process of trial and error, it could be trained.

2-Tone, Mod and Oi! were different. They actively sought out the mainstream so that they could do their damage from within. When Skins, Mods and Rude Boys clashed in battle, the tabloids were appalled, the police were merciless. But the authorities? They rather seemed to enjoy it.

"The establishment like these divisions," Sham's Jimmy Pursey once mused. "That there's Teds [Teddy Boys] fighting the Hell's Angels fighting the Skinheads fighting so-and-so. If they ever thought the kids didn't care what they wore or thought, but were just one against one thing – them – they'd be really scared. This way, with 27 identities, they know they've got us beat."

In 1977-78, he was correct. By 1979-80, however, those identities had blended – not, perhaps, into a wholly amorphous mass, but into something whose borders were sufficiently blurred to make snap judgements seem awkward. Is it a Mod? Is it a Skin? Is it a Rude Boy? No, it's Super-cult, and all the Kryptonite in the world wasn't going to stop it.

CHAPTER ONE

The son of a clergyman, Gerald 'Jerry Dammers' Dankey arrived in England in 1956, a two-year-old whose father was working in India when the boy was born. Living first in the steel town of Sheffield, then the sewing machine capital of Coventry, the young Dammers tore through adolescence, sloughing off identities like snakeskin: "I used to be a Mod, a mini-Mod. Then I grew my hair longer [and lived for two weeks in] a sort of hippy commune. I came back [and] freaked out completely. I got into this suedehead type of thing. I was about 17... badly into drink and vandalism." Just another product, in other words, of what was then still a functioning welfare state.

In keeping with the latest fashion with which he had aligned himself, Ska and Reggae formed the soundtrack to Dammers' teenaged years, providing the sounds that he dreamed of embedding himself within. An aspirant songwriter from his early teens, the rough skank of 'Little Bitch', a somewhat loveless paean to teenaged hopelessness, was written when he was just 15. The contraceptive caution 'Too Much Too Young' was also written early, as Dammers watched girls in his own social circle fall prey to teenaged pregnancies. (The suggestion in other chronicles that the song was a rewrite of Jamaican singer Lloyd Terrill's 'Birth Control' is so ridiculous that one can only assume the writer knew nothing more of the latter song than its title. As a bemused Neville Staples remarked, "I can't imagine where he got *that* from!")

Precious little, then, of Dammers's lyricism fed into any Jamaican concerns. Extricating his vision from the sun-drenched beaches and crime-ridden shanties that were the traditional haunt of white Reggae songs, he transplanted his protagonists into the dire heart of early 1970s Britain and, doubtless, was stunned when his youthfully earnest politicising fell far from the requirements of the other musicians he hung with as the decade rambled on.

Whiling away his school years, the organ-playing Dammers ran through a bunch of teenaged triers; a student at Lanchester Poly, he followed up with a variety of early-twenties aspirants. Few of them were any more serious than their names suggested – you were never going to hear anybody announcing Peggy Penguin & the Southside Greeks on *Top Of The Pops*, while the Sissy Stone Soul Band was simply the kind of sprawling soul and pop covers group that every inner-city nightclub seems to attract. He also had a stint with the ever-changing Ray King Soul Band, a veteran Coventry act whose leader's reputation and repertoire alike ranked him alongside the likes of Geno Washington on the circuit.

It was a tough apprenticeship, spent winding around a Midlands live circuit that, by the mid-1970s, was contracting as quickly as Coventry itself. But simply bumping into the same people at every show forged bonds between the musicians that hindsight, at least, could paint as the foundations for some kind of local scene.

By the time Punk hit Coventry, Dammers was already 23, singing with a soul act called the Night Train, and heading for Boring Old Fartdom. But he was never going to sit still for that. Neol Davies, the Night Train's guitarist (and another graduate of the Ray King Soul Band), was already making noises about forming a new band of his own, recording demos with Dammers' flat mate, drummer John Bradbury.

Davies' career interconnects many of the Coventry musicians who would subsequently emerge in the 2-Tone vanguard. His first serious line-up, the Reggae group Chapter Five, was formed in 1973 with drummer Silverton Hutchinson (who became the Specials' first drummer), bassist Charley Anderson (in Jamaica, a schoolmate of Mikey Dread), vocalist Arthur Henderson and keyboard player Desmond Brown. All of them would later join Davies in The Selecter.

From there, Desmond and Silverton linked with another soon-to-be Special, Jamaican-born guitarist Lynval Golding and another future member of the Selecter, bassist Charley 'H' Bembridge, in Pharaoh's Kingdom, who changed their name to 'Earthbound' whenever Davies sat in on their performances. Davies and Bradbury were also planning their own new band, the Transposed Men, with a line-up that would reunite them with Chapter Five's Desmond Brown, future Swinging Cats guitarist Steve Vaughan and bassist Kevin Harrison.

That scheme was still in the formative stages, though, whereas Dammers already seemed to have something in mind. Setting up a Revox in his front room, he began pouring his excess energies into making demos, a scratchy hybrid of Reggae and Punk which, if nothing else, might appeal to the people who shared his new-found love for the Clash.

The relationship between Punk and Reggae, hallowed though it is, was in fact little more than a marriage of convenience, the chance meeting of two musical forms thrust together via the outlaw status the mainstream accorded them. Punk, after all, was the musical consequence of ingredients drawn not only from across the rock'n'roll spectrum, but also from the cultural microcosms which comprised contemporary British society. The Jamaican community, with its focal points in the underprivileged underbellies of the country's biggest cities and its long established principles of righteous rebellion, would inevitably become drawn into the stew.

All that was needed now was for somebody, or several somebodies, to fuse the two.

There were no shortage of pioneers. Joe Strummer and Mick Jones, middle class white boys slumming it in the shadow of the Westway as they pieced together the Clash, were a common sight on the straggling street market of Portobello Road, cutting through the heartland of west London's West Indian neighbourhood, thumbing through the racks of Jamaican imports. Johnny Rotten, the iconoclastic frontman of the Sex Pistols, was a known dub freak. When the Pistols signed to Virgin Records in the spring of 1977, the label's support of Reggae was a key element in the decision. Chelsea's Gene October used to haunt the Rasta record store underneath Ladbroke Grove tube station. The Adverts' TV Smith was mail-ordering I-Roy and Dillinger albums down to his north Devon home.

Still, when Punk's own Mecca – the Roxy Club in Covent Garden – first launched in January 1977, it was chance, not design, that brought Reggae onto the dancefloor. "When the Roxy started," DJ Don Letts reflected, "there were literally no Punk records to play... so I had to play something I liked, which was Reggae. I guess I did turn a few people onto it. The crowd wanted to hear more Reggae. We turned each other on through our different cultures. They liked me because I gave them access to Jamaican culture, and they turned me on to a white culture that didn't fucking exist before they came along."

Close to 25 years later, Letts pulled together a 'typical' evening's entertainment for the *Dread Meets Punk Rockers Uptown* CD compilation – King Tubby, Big Youth, Junior Byles, Horace Andy, Lee Perry, Culture – and reminisced further. "The Third World DIY approach to creating the Reggae sound was something... the Punks could relate to. It was a culture that spoke in a currency they could identify with."

The Clash were the first Punks to try and clash those cultures, when they cut a cover of Junior Murvin's 'Police And Thieves': "Now I think what a bold brass neck we had to cover it," vocalist Strummer marvelled years later. "But I'm glad we did, because... it led onto great things in the future with Lee Perry and Bob Marley hearing it, and being hip enough to know we'd brought our own music to the party.'

Built around a dramatic Mick Jones rearrangement, with two guitars playing the on *and* off-beats ("any other group," explained Strummer, "would've played on the offbeat [alone], trying to assimilate Reggae"), 'Police And Thieves' almost didn't make it onto the Clash's debut. In the event, it emerged the most important track on the entire record. Before the end of the year, Perry himself would be producing the Clash's next single, 'Complete Control'. No sooner had he completed that than he was excitedly telling Bob Marley all about it. The pair promptly recorded their own 'Punky Reggae Party', a celebration that united black and white, Punk and Rasta with an inseparability that survives to this day.

Reggae was breaking out everywhere. Producer Adrian Sherwood took the first tentative steps on the journey which would establish his On-U dub sound among the primal forces of the next decade. Dennis Bovell's Matumbi, already seven-year veterans of the British reggae scene, were determinedly pushing their way onto Punk club bills – appropriately,their name meant "reborn" in the Yoruba language. Southall-based Reggae band Misty In Roots proved the traffic was not all one way by using their own label, People Unite, to launch the Ruts, the most accomplished Punk/Reggae crossover of them all. And poet Linton Kwesi Johnson burst through with a succession of commentaries destined to rewrite the cultural and political map.

In 1974, Johnson's *Voices of the Living and the Dead*, a slender collection of writings about life in black Britain, introduced a local London-Jamaican patois never before seen in print. By the time of 1975's *Dread Beat And Blood* collection, Johnson's journalism was appearing in the music papers (he was Reggae correspondent for the *New Musical Express* and *Black Music*) and the cultural press (the *Race Today* co-operative newspaper).

Now, he moved up a notch. Johnson was long accustomed to giving readings at parties, meetings and rallies; beginning in late 1976, he moved onto a wider stage, assembling a backing band and performing his poetry to music. By the end of 1977, he was recording his first album, *Dread Beat an' Blood*, credited to Poet & The Roots; by the dawn of the 1980s, Johnson was drawing as much attention to the injustices of the day as any media-appointed spokesguru.

"What Linton Kwesi Johnson did was very important," the Selecter's Compton Amanor explains. "For a start, recognising that there were kids [in England] who were here to stay. We're born here, we live here, we're British. The Rasta things always had to encircle itself with the myth of Roots which, in the end, takes your identity away even more, gives you more hang-ups. You talk to kids, say 'Where are you from?' and they say 'Africa' – but they were born here. It doesn't really mean anything. Linton Kwesi Johnson brought

Reggae into a British culture. Before that, Reggae bands over here were playing Jamaican music in a British society."

Before the end of 1977, midlanders Steel Pulse, the Cimarrons, the Reggae Regulars and Aswad had all followed Matumbi and Misty's evolution onto the Punk scene, instigators of a truly British Reggae consciousness. From Jamaica via New York City, Tapper Zukie erupted through the patronage of Patti Smith. In the clubs and pubs, Dillinger's 'Cocaine On My Brain' was positively endemic.

The importance of this cross-fertilization, as Marley and Perry were among the first to appreciate, lay in the fact that Punk was not simply a musical phenomenon. At its heart, music was simply the vehicle by which more pressing social and political concerns were being aired.

It was that which led the authorities to strive so ferociously to suppress Punk's first stirrings, banning the bands, closing their clubs, arresting its icons. Punk was, first and foremost, the sound of the rebellious streets. If its blood ties with Reggae were forged through a mutual distrust of the establishment, they were cemented by the establishment's heavy-handed attempts at repression. Young Rastas were an easy target for opportunistic police harassment. Now Punks joined them on the wanted list. As Don Letts explained, the establishment never had any problem in alienating him: "I was a first generation British born black, I was already pissed off." What he found remarkable was the fact that "by the mid-seventies, the establishment had managed to alienate its own white youth."

For Jerry Dammers, that conjoined alienation became a guiding spirit. Turning down an offer from guitarist Mark Byers to join the Wild Boys, a Lou Reed/David Bowie-flavoured combo that was probably the hottest live act in Coventry at that time, Dammers began seeking out musicians who might share… if not his musical tastes, then at least his musical ambitions.

At a club one night, Dammers ran into one of his Polytechnic acquaintances, Horace Panter, bassist with the soul act Breaker. The self-styled Sir Horace Gentleman had never tried to play Reggae before, but he was sufficiently impressed by Dammer's excitement that he twisted his style around its rhythms regardless.

"I'd played sort of R&B, Booker and the MGs kind of soul kind of stuff. I'd never played Reggae before," Sir Horace confessed. "I used to have Lynval [Golding] and Desmond [Brown] come round and give me Reggae lessons. They used to say, 'No, you don't play it like this, you play it like THIS and the bass goes like this,' and I'd sit there going, 'What? This doesn't sound right at all.' But, after several beatings, then I learned how to play it, and it's reasonably natural to play it now. It's good, because it was a learning process for everybody. I learned to play Reggae, [they] learned about Punk, and whatever, and it all sort of found its own level."

Other musicians passed through the ranks. By summer 1977, the line-up had stabilised: vocalist Tim Strickland was lifted from Dave & the Ravers (an unusual outfit which paired heavily Lou Reed-influenced rock quartet with a sax, a trombone and a flute player); Pharaohs' Kingdom provided drummer Silverton Hutchinson and guitarist Lynval Golding. With the addition of a jack-of-all-trades roadie, Neville Staples, the Automatics emerged.

Born in Jamaica, Staples had lived in England since he was 12. He was not a musician *per se*. His musical interests lay in dancing and DJ-ing. He'd set up his own sound system while still in his teens and was a familiar face around the local clubs, both with his own turntables and as an adjunct to fellow DJ (and future producer) Pete Waterman's popular Monday night roadshow at the Coventry Locarno.

Owner of one of the hippest record shops in town, the subterranean Soul Hole that specialised in the kind of music more mainstream (and above-ground) stores rarely carried, Waterman's DJ sets were as eclectic as his stock. Staples led a dance troupe called Neville and the Boys: "I used to dance to 'The Horse' by the Versatiles."

Among the multitude of duties that Staples would assume for the Automatics, spinning records before the show and operating the mixing desk throughout were those that made the greatest use of his talents. But he turned his hand to everything, including wrestling Dammers' keyboard out of his apartment and through the protesting doorways of the rehearsal room, a small staged area at the Heath Hotel on Foleshill Road. Finally, he suggested they cut it in half, a trick that Deep Purple's Jon Lord had discovered in his own career's infancy. Still, there was no way it would fit on the hotel's tiny stage. The band wound up rehearsing with their leader on the floor, directing events like an orchestral conductor.

The Automatics played their first show at the Heath Hotel in autumn 1977. Vocalist Strickland insists, "I couldn't sing. I thought it would be funny and Punk to read the lyrics (not mine, of course, but Jerry's) off sheets of paper, I would sit down during the instrumental bits. On one occasion I went to the bar and bought a pint during the set."

Further shows followed at the Heath. From there, the party graduated to Mr George's, opening for the Certified. There, they cut a distinctive shape; the first time Terry Hall, vocalist with another local band the Squad, heard them, he was impressed enough to describe them as "the Stranglers with Reggae overtones." But Strickland remained a weak link. By December, Dammers was looking to replace him... with Terry Hall.

At 18, Hall was several years younger than the rest of the Automatics and, according to Strickland, "loads better than me and almost as dour and miserable as I was." He was also a lot more active. The Squad were regular openers for the Wild Boys, and Mark Byers' brother, Roddy 'Radiation' remembered: "[Terry] used to be hilarious. [He] used to jump into the audience, spitting at people." His bandmates, meanwhile, would content themselves with borrowing the Wild Boys' PA, "and knacking up all the mikes before we went on."

Hall brought that same sense of chaos to the Automatics and, with it, an excitement Strickland had never been able to muster. "I was gone and bore no resentment," the deposed vocalist shrugged – although he does admit that, one night at Tiffany's, a few weeks after his departure, he walked to the front of the stage while the Automatics were playing and threw half a pint over his replacement. "It was one of those inexplicable moments, which didn't last." (Years later, Strickland went to work for the managers of Hall's mid-1980s project, Colourfield.)

The Automatics quickly found themselves making a mark, firmly establishing themselves as Coventry's premier punky-reggae combo. "We used to support bands all around the Midlands," says Neville Staples. "XTC came to the Locarno, the Damned came up there, Ultravox at Tiffanies. We were just starting… not just starting, but just starting to get known and get supports. Then we'd go out on our own in different towns. It just started growing slowly."

Dammers, however, was forever on the lookout for ways in which to accelerate that growth and, early into the New Year, he found a great one.

CHAPTER TWO

The legend, gleefully embroidering the truth in almost everything but its outcome, goes like this: On January 18, 1978, Johnny Rotten revealed to the world that he had walked out of the Sex Pistols two days earlier, and would not be going back. It was a stunning turn of events... hadn't the Pistols just completed a triumphant, headline-hogging tour of the American South? Jerry Dammers had an idea – quite possibly the most audacious one he'd ever had. Why not offer Rotten a gig with the Automatics?

Heading down to London, Dammers began to infiltrate the circle of associates that surrounded the ex-Pistol. He got as far as another Coventry lad, Clash roadie Steve Connolly, before realising that this was probably the closest he'd get. Handing over a tape of a recent Automatics rehearsal, he asked if it could be passed along to Rotten. In fact, the tape never made it further than the Clash's manager, Bernie Rhodes. That was far enough. By the time Dammers returned to Coventry, he'd landed the Automatics a gig opening for the Clash at Birmingham's Barbarellas, on January 24.

Nobody had expected the Clash to be gigging until the spring, by which time their much-anticipated second album would be on the streets. It was problems in the studio that sent the group back out onto the road, apparently in a last-ditch attempt to show American producer Sandy Pearlman the kind of sound they wanted – as distinct from the glossy Americanisms that he appeared intent on imposing.

The ploy may nor may not have worked. *Give 'Em Enough Rope* emerged as a schizophrenically lukewarm hiccup. The three shows that the band played for Pearlman's benefit (the others were in Dunstable and Coventry) are best remembered for the American getting decked by one of the Clash's roadcrew, when he tried to pop backstage to say hello.

For the Automatics, on the other hand, every moment they spent in the company of the Clash was magical. "The Clash IS my all-time favourite band!" raves Neville Staples. "The Clash performed with so much energy!

Unlike any band I've seen then or now. I used to watch them every night when we supported them and I can't say that about any other band (except for The Specials) that I worked with, past or present, in all my years of touring."

Birmingham not only offered the Automatics the chance to play alongside their heroes, it introduced them to a Mr Fix-It of their own, someone whose belief in the group, based on just one sighting of their live show, was almost as profound as their own.

Chris Gilbey was an Australia-based Brit whose personal track record reached back to the late 1960s, when he played guitar for Kate, one of the many psych-pop hopefuls swirling around London in the aftermath of the Summer of Love. They released a couple of singles, and briefly enjoyed the wild publicity of having former Pretty Things drummer Viv Prince on board, but Kate went nowhere. Gilbey emigrated to Australia, where he turned his attention to management.

He'd been on board for the first years of AC/DC's rise to stardom and was now looking to bring the same rewards to the Saints, a brutal Brisbane R&B act that somehow got scooped up into the Punk bag, then spent their entire career trying to get out of it again. Even at home, they were scarcely the kind of band you'd want to try and quantify.

Nick Cave, one of their most devoted acolytes, reminisces: "[The Saints] would come down to Melbourne and play these concerts which were the most alarming things you've ever seen, just such anti-rock kind of shows, where the singer [Chris Bailey] wouldn't come on stage. When he did, he was this fat alcoholic. It was so misanthropic, it was unbelievable, and the whole band was like that. They were so loud!"

With Gilbey in tow, the Saints relocated to London in 1976. Two years later, both he and they were nearing the end of their love affair with the English capital. But Gilbey was still on the lookout for new and intriguing unknowns. He was already considering taking a drive up to Birmingham to see the Clash when a friend, promo man Peter Davies, recommended that he make a point of catching the support band. Davies himself hailed from Coventry and, like most people on the local scene, was already well-acquainted with Jerry Dammers. It was time, he believed, that the rest of the country was given a chance to catch on.

Acting on Davies' enthusiasm, Gilbey "went up to see them in Birmingham with a friend of mine from advertising, Nick Fairhead. I thought they were pretty interesting and arranged a support gig for them, at the Marquee with the Saints [on Easter Sunday, March 26, 1978]."

Gilbey also persuaded a few record company reps to attend the show. "Most of them said, 'No thanks'. But there was a guy from Polygram, who said he would put up some money for demos.' Though the Marquee gig was so under-attended that the Automatics actually had to borrow ten pounds to get themselves back to Coventry, they did so in the knowledge that, the next time they visited London, it would be to record.

As the session date approached, Dammers began looking to add a new guitarist to the group, to free Lynval Golding up for more vocal work – and, again, he had eyes for just one player, the Wild Boys' Roddy Radiation.

The son of a soul trumpeter, Radiation's first instrument was trombone, before he switched to guitar at 13, and began the traditional apprenticeship through the youth club circuit. He'd known Dammers since the early 1970s – according to Radiation, they met when Dammers turned up to audition as drummer for a band that the guitarist was then putting together. He failed the audition ("the worst drummer I've ever heard in my life"), but the pair remained friends. As the Wild Boys' own career began winding down, Dammers began a slow courtship.

The pair were drinking at the Domino when Dammers finally popped the question. "He said that they were going to London the next day to record some demos, and did I want to play guitar at the session? I said 'yes', got drunk, went home and forgot all about it – until they turned up at my house the next morning, banging on the front door while I was still in bed. 'Fuck me! They meant it!'"

The Automatics were booked into Berwick Street Studios, a modest operation just around the corner from the Marquee. They were accompanied by Pete Waterman, now adding record production to his parallel careers in DJ-ing and A&R. At the time, he was awaiting the outcome of his most recent project, selecting the songs which one of his clients, actor John Travolta, would be performing in the forthcoming movie *Grease*.

The Automatics recorded 13 songs in that session, blitzing through their entire live repertoire with little sense of finesse. Listening back to the tapes, clearly they found it exciting enough simply to be in a proper studio. The niceties of texture and ambience were the furthest things from their minds. Polygram took one listen to the tape, sniffed and sent the Automatics on their way.

Since released as the *Dawn Of A New Era* album, the failings of the recordings are immediately apparent. Essentially, they were the sound of a group of players with varied musical inspirations, trying to bring them all to the fore at once, while clinging to the none-too-focussed notion that they're playing Reggae. Rockabilly riffs vie with big rock lead guitar flourishes; of the songs that would, in later years, become a national obsession, few are recognisable.

'Nite Klub' was much slower than its familiar romp, powered by an almost 'Tiger Feet'-ish bass stomp; but 'Blank Expression' was a lot faster, despite the Reggae riffs that try and weigh it down. 'Concrete Jungle', a song that Roddy Radiation brought from the Wild Boys' repertoire, retained that band's Punkish sensibilities, but 'It's Up To You' looked even further afield, towards the post-Punk icicle chainsaws of Siouxsie and the Banshees and the like. Finally, 'Jay Walker' even toyed with funk, to wrap up a schizophrenic mish-mash that did the Automatics few favours.

Nevertheless, word of the group's existence had leaked into the mainstream – or, at least, far enough in that another bunch of Automatics got wind of them.

London-based, these namesakes had been around since the end of 1976, when frontman Dave Philp left the transitory gaggle of players destined to become power-pop maestros the Boys. Since then, the Automatics had opened for the Runaways at Hammersmith Odeon and stopped the traffic on the King's Road by playing on the back of a moving truck. They'd also just signed with Island Records. But, while their output is best remembered by something Jim Kerr (of all pots) once sniffed, bemoaning the perceived lack of substance involved in the Automatics' 'When The Tanks Roll Over Poland Again' single, their claim on the name 'Automatics' was not something Dammers and co could overlook.

"[They] were a great group," Philp reflected of his band's nomenclatural rivals. "It was just luck of the draw. We got the record deal first and the lawyers made them change their names." Dammers' band's fans were less open to change. When the Automatics visited Coventry for the first time after the squabble, Philp recalled, "We got some shit for it, but the group themselves were gracious."

They were also a little perplexed. New names don't grow on trees... at least, good ones don't. The newly ex-Automatics had a terrible time coming up with a new identity. They toyed, for a time, with the Jay Walkers, lifted from the song of the same name; they thought seriously about the Hybrids. Neither went much further than any of the other suggestions. A straightforward switch to the Coventry Automatics seemed worse than having no name at all.

And they needed a new name quickly: the group had just been offered another show – another string of shows, in fact – with the Clash.

Bernie Rhodes hadn't really given the Automatics a second thought since the Birmingham gig in January. Joe Strummer, on the other hand, was thoroughly enthused. "They were rough, but I really enjoyed their energy," he reflected years later. "You could tell they had something going, even if they weren't sure what it was. A lot of bands were doing the Punk-Reggae thing at that time, us included, but they were taking it all very seriously, very rootsy. The Automatics, though, had a really different approach, which was down to a lot of things, but mainly, I think, Terry's voice. He didn't have a Reggae voice, and he didn't even try. He sounded so English, and that was the difference."

Keen to hear more of this startling hybrid, Strummer insisted that the Automatics be added to the bill.

The first show, at Aylesbury Friars on June 28, was just days away when Dammers finally unveiled the band's new name – the Special A.K.A. The Automatics. Too long. Four hours before the first show, they became the Special A.K.A.; days later, noting that most people had shortened it further, they became the Specials – "a sort of in-joke," laughs Radiation, "as we weren't special yet."

The earliest of the Clash shows were a disaster. There were nights when even the second-billed Suicide, the minimalist American electro-duo whose show was habitually hounded by abuse and bottles, fared better than the Specials. But Joe Strummer's enthusiasm remained undimmed. Rhodes' insistence that the group play only the first few shows of the two-week tour was quickly over-ridden; his original payment of just £25 a night, too, was soon doubled. One of the most important developments of the entire outing, however, occurred on just the second night, at Leeds' Queen's Hall on June 29.

The gig was already underway, and the Specials were ploughing through one of the Reggae instrumentals that were then a feature of the set, when suddenly a voice came floating in from the soundboard, where roadie Neville Staples was wrestling with the hall's acoustics. "I was at the mixing desk and I picked the talk-back mike up and was DJ-ing from the desk and the crowd loved it. They turned the spotlight round on me, and I just ran onstage and started DJ-ing from there. The band had no idea I was going to do that... I had no idea I was going to do that! It was just a vibe." Before the night was over, however, he'd been pulled out of the roadcrew and elected a full member of the group.

The Specials were on their own when it came to both travelling between shows, and finding accommodation in every new town. At first, they spent their nights either crushed together inside their battered Dormobile van or, if they were lucky enough, crashing on somebody's floor. After a few nights, however, the Clash's road crew took pity on them and lent them a tent. "When we pulled into a town for a gig," Clash roadie Johnnie Green wrote later, "we all kept a look-out for the Specials' encampment on the outskirts."

The tour climaxed at the Music Machine in London; then, off the road in mid-July, Bernie Rhodes offered the group a place under his own wing. It was too good an opportunity to turn down, of course – like his one-time partner, Malcolm MacLaren, Rhodes was widely regarded among the most influential entrepreneurs in the entire Punk spectrum. Unfortunately, he was also one of the most mercurial, rarely juggling less than a bucketload of projects at any one time.

The Subway Sect, the jazz-Punk hybrid Black Arabs and a French act called the Lous were also on his mind presently. The Specials quickly found themselves doing nothing more than waiting for his mind to flash around to them. Sequestered in the Chalk Farm warehouse where the Clash rehearsed, sleeping seven-to-a-room and dutifully following Rhodes' demand that they keep practising, morale began to dip.

To turn things around, or maybe just to get the band off his back, Rhodes decided to send them to Paris – "to get our act together," as Lynval Golding puts it. The trip was ill-starred from the moment Rhodes dropped the musicians and one roadie, Mickie Foot, at the ferry terminal. The channel crossing passed off uneventfully but, no sooner had the party set foot on French soil, than Silverton Hutchinson was making his way home, refused entry by immigration officials who didn't like the look of his Barbados passport. Things became even more surreal when Jerry Dammers stepped forward to try and negotiate the drummer's reprieve. He forgot he was holding all the band's cash in one hand – and was almost hauled away himself, on a charge of attempted bribery.

Rhodes had arranged for someone to meet the group at Calais; unfortunately, he hadn't told them just how many people, or how much equipment, needed a ride to Paris. Terry Hall, Roddy Radiation, Jerry Dammers and Sir Horace spent their first day in France hitch-hiking to the capital; Golding and Neville Staples, meanwhile, travelled in the back of a van that was barely big enough for the drum kit and keyboards.

Meeting up in Paris, with Hutchinson now restored to their ranks, the Specials discovered that their problems had only just begun. The last British group to stay at their hotel, the Damned, had apparently not treated the establishment too well, but bolted before they could be handed the bill. Apparently reasoning that one British pop group was the same as any other, the hotel landlady now presented it to the Specials, and impounded Radiation and Golding's guitars, just to make sure they knew she meant business. According to Golding, "there was a big argument. We got pushed downstairs, and the woman decided to throw us out of the hotel, so we got down to the lobby and there was a big argument, pushing around until the glass door to the hotel got smashed."

Finally, the cavalry arrived, in the form of the promoter. Golding continues, "The guy from the club arrived and started talking to the woman and he told us to go to the club. It took us about 10 minutes to walk there – all the way I was screaming at passers-by, 'I want my guitar back!' By the time we got to the club the guitars and all equipment was there. I thought, 'Wow, these guys are wicked. How did they do it?' They just pulled guns and demanded all the guitars and everything, and there we are!!! – so 'GANGSTERS!'" A line from the still unwritten song of the same name immortalizes the incident for all time: "Can't interrupt while I'm talking, or they'll confiscate all your guitars."

Little else that occurred in Paris was of interest. Radiation remembers members of Ian Dury's Blockheads dropping by to watch them play one night, and then reminding them of the fact a year later in London, but the trip passed by and the Specials returned to the UK no wiser, and certainly no richer for the experience.

Back at the warehouse, Rhodes continued dropping by to watch rehearsals, occasionally with a barely interested promoter or journalist in tow. But, when he offered the group a management contract, even a tempting £30 a week wage could not alleviate Dammers' disappointment at how matters had turned out. A contract was drawn up, but Dammers was resolute. "There were a lot of arguments about that... basically, we refused to sign [it]."

There were more arguments within the group itself. They were receiving little, if any, money and, finally, drummer Hutchinson reached the end of his tether. He quit and returned to Coventry – at which point, says Roddy Radiation, it finally began to dawn on the rest of the Specials precisely what Rhodes was trying to achieve.

He had already orchestrated the demise of the Subway Sect, another band who thought their big break was imminent when they toured with the Clash, only to have their ambitions rudely shattered when Rhodes sacked the entire line-up bar vocalist Vic Godard. The stunned singer was then introduced to the Black Arabs, a novelty combo best known today for their odd reinterpretations of sundry Sex Pistols classics on the Great Rock'n'Roll Swindle soundtrack. But the partnership never gelled, leaving Rhodes to seek out another new vocalist for the Arabs. He had settled on Terry Hall. "He likes to put musicians together like that," Roddy Radiation confirms. "Rhodes wanted to split us up. But you can't do that with people."

By early autumn 1978, the Specials bade Rhodes a none-too-fond farewell and returned to Coventry where a break-up was, indeed, on the cards. A year that had seen their hopes raised so high, so often, had ended with nothing more than a hole where the drummer used to be and the dawning realisation that the Punkified Reggae (or Reggae-fied Punk) wasn't happening. Rhodes had made the point on more than one occasion, with an insistence that finally prompted even Dammers to agree. "We had songs where part... was Reggae, then [it'd] go into a rock section, then perhaps into Reggae, and it would throw people off," he reflected. He was already aware that there were any number of other bands already working in the same vein. Now he was facing the fact that most of them were doing it on a lot better, as well.

CHAPTER THREE

"Do we have any foreigners in the audience tonight?" Eric Clapton took the stage drunk, and seemed progressively worse for wear as the evening progressed. "If so, please put up your hands. I think we should vote for Enoch Powell." Onstage at the Birmingham Odeon, in the immigrant heart of Britain's Midlands, the guitarist formerly known as God openly pledged his support to a right-wing politician best known for advocating the forced repatriation of Britain's black population.

It was August 5, 1976, and Clapton had inadvertently thrown another log onto the fires of the incipient Punk explosion. The very next week, all three major British music papers, *Sounds*, *Melody Maker* and the *New Musical Express*, carried a letter signed by Red Saunders, David Widgery and Syd Shelton, announcing the organization of "a rank and file movement against the racist poison in music. We urge support for Rock Against Racism." In the next seven days, the letter drew 140 responses from the public. Over the next seven years, it changed the face of Britain.

Rock Against Racism (RAR) remains the most single-minded and, in that single-mindedness, successful force for political change in the history of music. In allying itself so early and so potently, with the forces of Punk Rock, RAR became all but inseparable from that movement, a rallying point so powerful that, even when all the other Punk tenets had come crumbling down and it had become readily apparent that unemployment, poverty and hunger wouldn't be electric guitars, RAR remained triumphant. Maybe racism itself had not been destroyed. But the culture of ignorance that is its most fertile breeding ground was certainly given less raw material with which to work.

Clapton himself swiftly recanted. He was drunk, he said; he was joking. Eventually, even his fiercest detractors conceded that sometimes, one can say things which fall completely out of context, usually because one has not actually put them into context in the first place. Clapton was publicly reacting to a private incident (an Arab pinching his wife's bottom); but, when he admitted he was wrong, he never asked for forgiveness. For, in so brutally focussing attention upon an issue which had been smouldering beneath the surface of British society for 20 years, he helped society itself take a step which as many years worth of 'concerned citizenry' had never been able to put into action.

Rock Against Racism hosted its first concert at a London pub in November 1976, an affair characterised by a couple of unknown bands, a wall stacked with literature, leaflets and buttons, and an audience shuffling disjointedly around, not sure how to behave. Would there be speeches? Would there be hand-holding and massed choruses of 'We Shall Overcome'? Or would there simply be a lot of music, a little private discussion, and, for the first time in radical politics, an organisation that was content to let the people take action, while their leaders benignly looked on? Most people guessed the first two, a few held out hope for the third. The few were proven correct.

Initially by word of mouth, but later through its own *Temporary Hoarding* magazine, RAR cried out for political activism. But it did not preach, it did not bully and it did not argue. Like the Trotsky-ite Socialist Workers Party (SWP) upon which it was most obviously modelled, RAR's tactics were simple – focussing attention upon struggles and issues, then using those struggles to built support for itself. You were either for or against. What you did next was your own concern.

Of course, not everybody supported such methods, particularly when it became apparent that the new operation had borrowed more than method from the SWP. RAR operated out of SWP-owned premises and was frequently featured in the pages of the party's *Socialist Worker* newspaper. Inevitably, the right wing drew neat conclusions and condemned the whole thing as a leftist plot, a full-scale Communist take-over of the nation's confused youth.

In fact, RAR had little patience for party politics, seeing in the machinations of even liberal government policies further barriers against the progress of its own issues. 'Other battles are fought with ballots and bullets,' the audience at one RAR pub gig was told. 'Ours is fought with Belts And Braces,' and out came the band of the same name, fervent supporters of the RAR cause. As RAR co-founder Widgery explained, "the music came first and was more exciting. It provided the creative energy and the focus in what became a battle for the soul of young working class England."

The almost wholly ideological agenda set out at RAR's founding conference was to change little over the next five years. Quoted by latter-day RAR historian Dave Renton, 19-year-old London squatter Caroline Harper spoke for many of the organisation's followers when she admitted that she was initially attracted by the music, and the anti-establishment feel of her first RAR concert. "We naturally identified with other people getting harassed by the police. It didn't matter if you had green hair or were black, you would be stopped by the police, for any reason. We felt like victims of an authoritarian state."

That intimidation was only heightened by the growing strength of the National Front. Across the country, most prominently in areas which previous waves of immigration had designated racial melting pots, the Front was conducting a campaign which sought to indoctrinate great swathes of British youth, its tactics wavering between simple intimidation and outright physical damage.

Asian and black households were being targeted constantly, with graffiti and stones, with punches and bottles, sometimes even with firebombs. Not, of course, by the Front's members – they were far too smart for such criminal activities. It was the people their message spread to: the teenage workers canned from their jobs 'because a black would do it for half the wage'; the blue collar home-owners whose property values had plummeted 'because a Pakistani family had moved in down the block'; the Skinhead kid whose sister had been knocked up by a Rasta. They were the ones who heard the Front's rhetoric, and translated it into action with knuckleheaded ease.

Such attacks were rarely reported in the media or, if it could be helped, to the police. If you can't trust your own neighbours, how could you trust your neighbours' police force? Better to try to sort yourself. So fear bred ferocity, beatings bred belligerence.

"Before the Rock Against Racism thing really got going," says Chelsea vocalist Gene October, "if you were white, there were parts of town you simply didn't go into, because the blacks would kick the shit out of you, not because they were racist, but because you might be. The black kids wanted to mix and later, after Punk happened and Rock Against Racism got going, they could. You'd walk past a bunch of Rastas and they'd be fine, 'How you going, mate?' You'd get black kids at Punk shows, Punk kids at Reggae shows. That simply couldn't have happened a year earlier. That's how much Rock Against Racism changed things."

In August, 1977, just a year after that first RAR missive appeared in the press, the movement was vast enough to mobilize, if not wholly organise, a massive army to block and harass a National Front march through predominantly black Lewisham, in south London. Inevitably, the event ended in vast numbers of arrests and injuries; inevitably, too, RAR were portrayed as troublemakers, storming an hitherto peaceful, legal and democratic exercise. But it was the marchers who went home bloodied and beaten, and the protestors who celebrated into the night.

Through 1977-78, RAR was everywhere. Allied, from summer 1977, with the Anti-Nazi League (an organisation formed after the Battle of Lewisham), its most important displays were the vast rallies which transformed entire city blocks into semi-carnivals, as thousands of marchers moved through some of London's most racially sensitive areas *en route* to free concerts featuring the cream of the Punk and Reggae community. The April 1978 march, which ended with a massive festival in Victoria Park, Hackney, was the largest event of its type ever staged in the UK. The concert itself, featuring performances from Tom Robinson, Steel Pulse, X-Ray Spex and Sham 69's Jimmy Pursey, is a central element in the headlining Clash's *Rude Boy* movie.

Other, similarly vast extravaganzas followed. A carnival in Manchester attracted 35,000 people; there were 8,000 in Edinburgh; 5,000 in Cardiff; 2,000 in Harwich. A second London event, in south London's Brockwell Park on September 24, proved even bigger than the first, with even a simultaneous Front rally just down the road failing to dampen the sense that Rock Against Racism was triumphing over its foe.

Those were the events that received the major headlines. Smaller-scale benefits were being staged on a weekly basis, some featuring genuinely exciting headline material: Aswad and Matumbi, the Tom Robinson Band, Elvis Costello, Stiff Little Fingers; others offering little more than what was, at the time, considered standard pub-and-club fare: the Enchanters, the Carol Grimes Band, Milk, the unknown infant Ruts. Some raised money, some raised hackles – the National Front regularly picketed such events. But all raised awareness.

The Front tried to fight back, fire with fire. But few bands would openly align themselves with the movement. Those that did – Skrewdriver were among the first – frequently found themselves unwelcome anywhere else. Attempts by the Front to claim the Sex Pistols for their own were fiercely denounced by

Johnny Rotten. A more plausible claim on the likes of Sham 69 and Cock Sparrer, whose partisan Skinhead following really did seem the Front's natural constituency, was likewise exploded when Sham vocalist Jimmy Pursey became one of RAR's most vociferous supporters, even as Sham's own gigs becoming a veritable magnet for Front-themed chanting and violence, both inside and out.

From the moment that they

appeared, crop-topped bovver boys up from the 'burbs, with their post-Slade guitars and the rabble-riling songs that sprayed like spit and graffiti, Sham 69 spread their message like the plague was out of fashion. 'Since I was a kid,' Jimmy Pursey explained, 'I used to go to the discos regular. Then when I was about 14, I got really drunk and crawled up onstage and mimed to a couple of Stones songs. Well, the geezer who ran the gaff really liked it, so...' – so, it became a regular gig and, in late 1976, Pursey joined his first band, 'local mates playing up a dead end. They were terrible before I joined. Hadn't a clue what was going on." But they quickly learned.

Having launched themselves onto a Punk scene that was already in full swing, the original Sham line-up splintered in June, 1977, after just a handful of shows, but with their subsequent Skinhead legacy already firmly in place. With bassist Albie Slider alone surviving the split, in came drummer Mark Cain and guitarist Dave Parsons to take up the role of Pursey's songwriting partner, in which form, Sham and producer John Cale created the nihilistic snot classic 'I Don't Wanna,' for release on the indy infant Step Forward label.

Slider quit the music business in October, 1977; he was replaced by Dave Treganna, and the new-look Sham debuted on a rooftop in central London, celebrating the opening of the Vortex Club. Of course the police intervened and, when the band refused, in true blue Beatles fashion, to stop playing, Pursey was arrested. Rock's newest martyr got off with a thirty pound fine, but the exposure was priceless.

The Inner London Education Authority, planning a schools documentary on Punk, invited Sham to add two songs to Confessions of a Music Lover and, while the show never made it off the closed circuit educational broadcasting network, Polydor Records were sold. They signed the band in late 1977, and 'Borstal Breakout,' Sham's debut single, steamrollered into view in the new year.

Drawing their core audience from within the same amorphous anti-culture of soccer supporters that inspired the band's own songs, Sham were suddenly everywhere, the singing face of the Skinhead revival and a voice for downtrodden outcasts the country over – a role that the band took very seriously indeed. 'If the kids,' they insisted, 'are united (stomp stomp) they will never (stomp stomp) be divided.' And that was true. Unfortunately, the divisions had already begun to appear.

At the Roundhouse in February 1978, with their heroes opening for the Adverts, Sham-badged and T-shirted Skins not only made the dance floor and the corridors their own; they were also among the ringleaders of an audacious plot to break into the basement of the building, and storm the auditorium from beneath. On the tube home from Camden, however, there was not a Pursey poster-toting Skin to be seen among the posse of spikeytops who barged up and down the Northern Line, in search of suitable victims.

Pursey and bandmate Dave Parsons, speaking in 2004, confirm that Sham's own audience was essentially good-natured; and was certainly more sinned against (in the pages of the music press) than sinning. 'I think it was just a load of lost people looking for a place to go, and we were that closest thing to that council-house way of thinking,' Pursey said in 2004. 'Kids who never had anything before, apart from Saturday afternoon football and going out. They were lost at that time, coming out of the early to middle 70s with nothing to do and nowhere to go.'

Sham offered those kids an unconditional solution to both of those dead-ends. Unfortunately, the Front received the same open invitation. 'It was easy for those groups to infiltrate us,' Parsons told Record Collector magazine, 'because a lot of our fans were skinheads. And our skinheads were cool. There was no problem with the skinheads we had.' It was with those who gravitated to the fringe of the Sham army that the trouble began.

RAR flourished with unimagined ferocity. By mid-1978, *Temporary Hoarding* was selling over 12,000 issues a month. RAR was operating its own record label out of an address in Artesley, in rural Bedfordshire. The music press was unquestioningly supportive. The *New Musical Express* interviewed Red Saunders, and barely interrupted him once. *Sounds* ran a memorable feature reminding its readers that it wouldn't only be black entertainers who would suffer if the National Front ever got into power. Musicians as diverse as Joe Strummer (born in Ankara, Turkey), the Police's Stewart Copeland (Alexandria, Egypt), Freddie Mercury (Zanzibar), even perennial parental favourite, Cliff Richard (Lucknow, India), would come under fire as well.

But the organization was not resting on its laurels. In fact, RAR was girding itself for the biggest fight of its short life. At the 1974 General Election, the Front ran 54 candidates and came away with 3.3 percent of the vote. Now, with everybody anticipating a General Election in early 1979, the Front were threatening to field upwards of 300 potential Members Of Parliament. Few were likely to win election, but the implications were terrifying.

The primary battlefield in the ensuing contest was, of course, racial. But race was not the only issue at stake. RAR existed (or came to exist) as a means of highlighting all the other forms of injustice and prejudice that the Front's authoritarian principles were set to project. RAR's rallies and benefits provided an umbrella for dozens of other, ideologically-linked but otherwise unconnected organisations and concerns, from gay rights and homelessness through to what was rapidly becoming the largest problem facing any of the represented groups, the increasingly heavy-handed behaviour of the police force.

The Tom Robinson Band's 'Glad To Be Gay' – with its ironic insistence that "the British police are the best in the world", a hit single in early 1978 and a live favourite for a full year before that – offered the first significant rallying point for everyone who – unlike the song's protagonist – had no problem whatsoever in believing "the stories I've heard."

The Leyton Buzzards, one of the classiest of the bands to emerge from the post-Punk ferment, weighed in with their own brutal, lightly Reggae'd account of a police raid on a party, 'British Justice (It Don't Exist)'. Linton Kwesi Johnson and Matumbi's Dennis Bovell weighed in with 'Doun Di Road', a smouldering study of inter-community violence, while Johnson also drew attention to the plight of George Lindo, a Bradford black set up for a robbery he could never have committed, and which, years later, it was shown he hadn't.

But it was a then-unknown Punk group from Sunderland, the somewhat Sham 69-y Angelic Upstarts, who pushed the issue of police brutality into its most glaring prominence, and who suffered at length for the consequences.

In 1976, Liddle Towers, an amateur boxer and nightclub bouncer from Birtley, near Chester-le-Street, was arrested outside the local Key Club following an argument with some passing police. Charged drunk and disorderly, Towers was taken into custody – and never emerged. The following morning, he was dead, killed by the savage beating meted out to him in the cell. An inquest returned the seemingly laughable verdict of justifiable homicide, establishing that Towers' own behaviour was so violent that the lawmen had no alternative but to restrain him to the best of their abilities.

However, Towers' killing was not an isolated incident and became a focal point for the growing number of voices speaking out against what Private Eye dryly termed 'the increasing slaughter of persons helping police with their inquiries.' By the end of the decade, the entire issue of suspects' rights would come under the scrutiny of a Royal Commission on Criminal Procedure. For now, however, there seemed little redress for any of the constabulary's purported victims.

In June 1978, the Angelic Upstarts' own Dead label released the foreboding 'Who Killed Liddle Towers?'. It was the first of several records to comment upon the incident: Dave Goodman & Friends' 'Justifiable Homicide', the Tom Robinson Band's 'Blue Murder' and folkie Martin Carthy's 'Rigs Of The Time' soon followed. All passed by unnoticed in the corridors of local power. The Upstarts, however, plied their trade just miles from the scene of the non-crime. For any cop bent on avenging the slight, the band was a sitting duck.

While the local authorities openly contemplated bringing a charge of incitement to violence against the Upstarts (a process that seems only to have been halted when it was realised just how much press attention the group was now receiving), undercover officers secretly infiltrated the group's gigs, in search of the slightest excuse to break up the party.

Vocalist Thomas 'Mensi' Mensforth, a distinctively imposing Skinhead, found himself the target of almost daily Stop-And-Search encounters. When he claimed that he had all-but been given his own police 'tail', few disbelieved him. Nor, as more and more north-eastern venues closed their doors to the Angelic Upstarts, did anybody even suggest it might just be coincidence. In the eyes of local law enforcement, the band were marked men, and the depth of commitment that the Upstarts were able to bring to Rock Against Racism was born as much from experience as ideology.

Rock Against Racism was not alone in its fight against the resurgent right wing. Although its own policies were as much a part of the problem as anything that the Fascists promised, the Labour government continued to fight for its life, no matter how inevitable defeat now seemed. When comedian Peter Cook suggested that the only way Margaret Thatcher could fail to get elected was if she assaulted the Queen Mother, he wasn't even joking.

Nevertheless, on September 7, 1978, Prime Minister James Callaghan announced that he had no absolutely intention of calling an early election, declaring that his Labour government would remain in power for a fifth (and final) year. Broadcasting to the nation just weeks into what history records as the Winter Of Discontent, a season which saw strikes by lorry and tanker-drivers, water workers, hospital porters and dustmen paralyse so much of the country, Callaghan insisted there were no instant solutions to the domestic problems Britain was facing. Especially not those being proposed by the opposition Conservatives and Liberals.

"The government must and will continue to carry out policies that are consistent, determined, that don't chop or change and that brought about the present recovery in our fortunes. We can see the way ahead."

His opponents immediately retaliated. Thatcher, making a speech in Lichfield, described the government point-blank as "chickens" and chided, "The real reason [Callaghan] isn't having an election is because he thinks he'll lose." The Liberal Party's David Steel was no less scathing, describing Callaghan's statement as "quite astounding. Parliament is four years old and to breathe new life into it, we must have an election."

For the moment, Labour's supporters carried the day. In December 1978, a Vote of Confidence in the House saw the party carry the day by just ten votes, 300-290. But, when a smiling Callaghan flew back into London in the New Year, after attending a four-nation summit in Guadeloupe, his cheery greeting only served to further infuriate a public already seething at his decision to jet off into the sunshine while the country went to the dogs. "I promise if you look at [Britain today] from the outside," he announced, "I don't think other people in the world would share the view that there is mounting chaos." Or, as *The Sun* succinctly put it the following morning, "Crisis? What Crisis?"

On January 22, 1979, the biggest mass work stoppage since the General Strike of 1926 saw tens of thousands of public service workers walk out in support of their pay claims. A mass exodus of hospital porters, orderlies and cooks, ambulance drivers, rubbish collectors, school caretakers and canteen staff, lollipop ladies, gravediggers and airport baggage handlers brought all four of the United Kingdom's national capitals to a halt – and ensured that they remained there until mid-February when the Government finally began to negotiate a compromise.

Six weeks later, on March 28, Thatcher's Conservatives called for a second Vote of Confidence. This time, Callaghan lost, 311 votes to 310. It would be another few days before the date of the election, May 3, was officially announced but, from the moment the story broke, halfway through that evening's *News At 10*, the campaigning was underway – by the mainstream parties fighting for the country's votes and the fringe groups battling for its soul.

CHAPTER FOUR

On April 14, 1979, Rock Against Racism and the Anti-Nazi League combined to stage their biggest festival since Brockwell Park, an all-day event within the Victorian splendour of Alexandra Palace, London. The concert itself was the  culmination of the country-wide Militant Entertainment tour, and was one of a number of events, large and small, planned to take place around the country in the lead-up to the General Election.

With Belts & Braces, the Ruts, Stiff Little Fingers, Alex Harvey and a hybrid Generation X/Sham 69 line-up all set to play, Ally Pally bragged a stellar line-up; and still all eyes were on the evening's headliners, as the Tom Robinson Band made their first high-profile London appearance since the release, the previous month, of their distinctly disappointing second album, *TRB 2* – disappointing because, on the strength of their first and its attendant singles, TRB had a tighter grip on the mood of the nation than any other band of the age.

Today, Robinson himself has all-but retired from the music industry, preferring to concentrate on his career as a radio DJ, and his family: "The death of Joe Strummer brought home to me that we don't live forever," he explained in July 2003. "Family life and being a decent person is all that actually matters."

He is, in any case, "all talked out" – and no surprise. From the moment TRB broke through in late 1977 with the anthemic hit '2-4-6-8 Motorway', the radio-friendly camouflage for a fervently-held litany of gay rights, racial equality and brittle left wing politics, Robinson found himself appointed both the spokesman for every cause and agenda in the rock vocabulary, and their most powerful advocate. To the mortification of his label, EMI, the packaging for that second album even included a directory of country-wide activist groups.

Tom Robinson and drummer Mick Trevisick were originally members of Cafe Society, a faintly whimsical folky act which had a brief flirtation with King Kink Ray Davies' Konk label. It was not a happy liaison: Robinson complained (loudly) that Davies never gave the band the chance to show what it could do, Davies replied that they weren't good enough to do anything. With their one- and only album selling no more than 600 copies, a frustrated Café Society took to performing the Kinks' own 'Tired Of Waiting For You' and dedicating it to Davies; he, in turn, waited till Robinson himself was tasting stardom, before responding with the scathing 'Prince Of The Punks.'

Robinson was already preparing for his next move during the last days of Cafe Society, penning future favourites 'Martin', 'Grey Cortina', 'Motorway' and, perhaps most crucially, the nightmare prophecy of 'Long Hot Summer'. He told *Sounds* that, even then, "It seemed to me that '77 and '78 were going to be years of big trouble on the streets. And that's where the average music fan is. They're either still at school or just left school and are in a boring job. Whatever music you make, you've got to be in touch with their lives. I could see they were going to want much more basic, more simple hard-hitting rock music." Robinson was determined to provide that.

When Café Society broke up in late 1976, Robinson and Trevisick immediately recruited Anton Mauve, Bret Sinclair and Mark Griffiths, and debuted as the Tom Robinson Band at Islington's Hope & Anchor on November 28, 1976. For their second gig, at the Fulham Golden Lion on December 1, Sinclair and Griffiths were absent, replaced by one of Robinson's boyhood friends, Danny Kustow – the two met in what was, in the early 1970s, described as 'a home for maladjusted children' and, insisted Robinson, "it shows." So, that night, did the shifting mood of the times.

Earlier that evening, the Sex Pistols had made their infamous debut on primetime television, swearing up a storm on the London regional *Today* programme. Although the Golden Lion was at least half-full, it was like walking into a grave, as the audience tried to assimilate what they'd just witnessed. No more than three hours had passed since the Pistols went off the air, but already the paranoia was sparking. Few people, after all, denied that the Government only tolerated youth cults and cliques because they kept the kids from making serious trouble. The Pistols had finally stepped over the line. They *were* making trouble and, every time a panda car passed the pub with its sirens on, you could feel the tension rise.

Of course nothing happened in the end, but still it was apparent that a Rubicon of sorts had been crossed, between the say-nothing, do-nothing, think-nothing status quo of everyday life, and the need to stand up and make your voice heard. The blatantly political TRB, with songs like 'Glad To Be Gay', 'I'm Alright Jack' and 'Power In The Darkness' taking murderously accurate swipes at the establishment's greatest ingrained evils, were going to make sure that everybody knew which side they were on.

The 'classic' TRB – with Kustow now joined by keyboard player Mark Ambler and drummer Brian 'Dolphin' Taylor – debuted at a packed Sir George Robey in London's Finsbury Park in the New Year, before embarking upon a string of three- to four-week residences at any pub or club that would have them. But, despite the unassailable strength of TRB's show and the unquenchable rabidity of their following, few labels wanted to know.

Virgin and Stiff both passed on the chance to sign TRB, while the Jet label's interest was allegedly quashed by Robinson's ferocious gay stance. How ironic, then, that the one company that displayed no such squeamishness should be EMI, the label whose treatment of the Sex Pistols following the *Today* show shenanigans, sacking them with a King's ransom pay-off, had become synonymous with the anti-Punk.

Of course, it was impossible for anyone to object to TRB's choice for their debut single. '2-4-6-8 Motorway' was the greatest drive-time song any British songwriter has come up with, as good as anything anyone has accomplished; up there with 'Roadrunner' and 'Autobahn' and 'Motorbikin''. Indeed, if you overlooked the lyrics, Robinson's grasp on the mechanics of 'classic' rock was almost deliberately calculated to succeed. With the *New Musical Express* trumpeting TRB as "the most important new band in Britain," 'Motorway' roared to #5. Faster than a grey Cortina (another of Robinson's most cherished icons), TRB not only bridged the gulf between underground subversive and mainstream prophet, they also bespoke a fiercely parochial decline and fall that was all the more alluring for its cynical greyness.

If, as rock historians suggest, the Kinks of the late 1960s and the Blur-and-Oasis-led movement of the 1990s are the twin peaks of idealistic British Pop, TRB provide the doomladen trough: a post-apocalyptic universe in which carrion crows feed on corpses on the motorway ('You Gotta Survive'), the SAS have replaced the police on the beat ('The Winter Of 79'), and the rich are huddled in their country houses, waiting for the all-clear to sound ('I'm Alright Jack'). But, just

in case anyone was still missing the point; still thought of TRB as those cheery lads in old school ties who sang the song with all the numbers in it, the follow-up *Rising Free* EP hit the Top 20 in early 1978 and stripped away all the masks.

In a stark about-turn from customary practises, radio and TV both took to playing the *second* of the four songs on the EP, the hard-rocking call to disobedience, 'Don't Take No For An Answer'. Anybody buying the EP itself, however, quickly discovered that, in order to reach that track, they first had to negotiate 'Glad To be Gay', Robinson's second best-of-genre gesture, a song that not only rivalled 'Anarchy In The UK' and 'White Riot' as Britain's Alternative National Anthem, it went further than either as it reached out to its audience.

There were few sights stranger, at the time, than standing in the Marquee on a hot summer night, nervously eyeing the gang of tanked-up Skinheads hovering at the back, only to see the lot of them to break into an unironic chorus of 'Glad To Be Gay', cheering TRB to one of the most vociferously demanded encores of their career. Shortly after, Robinson was asked if he thought such audiences actually understood what they were singing. He replied that it didn't matter if they understood. What was important was, they thought about understanding. As with so many other prejudices, it is not hatred that is the enemy. It is ignorance.

"Motives don't matter," he explained. "It's the end result that matters. If you see a guy starving on the street and you give him a quid just to impress your girlfriend or boyfriend, it doesn't matter. 'cos at the end of the day that guy's still got the quid."

May 1978 brought TRB's third hit, 'Up Against The Wall', but it was with the release of *Power In The Darkness*, TRB's debut album, that all predictions of greatness were first proven, then surpassed. Eschewing all but the most recent of the band's singles, *Power In The Darkness* rose to #4. No matter how much turmoil consumed the group through the remainder of 1978 and early 1979, no matter how disappointing *TRB 2* turned out to be ("we had three years to write our first album," lamented Robinson, "and three months to write the second"), when TRB took the stage at Alexander Palace, their live set remained littered with first album highlights, the touchstones, prophecies and warnings that, more than any other repertoire of the age, summed up everything that the watching audience was up against that spring. And they closed the set with 'Power In The Darkness', just to drive the message home.

Both live and on record, 'Power In The Darkness' was (and is) a reminder that government is not the right of the minority to control the lives of the majority, and the fact that they are elected to a position which gives them that ability is no justification for abrogating their responsibilities. And when the needle first hits vinyl, it really seems little more than a tightly constructed rabble-rouser, built around a singalong chorus and verses that simply documents the freedoms that you endanger, every time you put an 'X' on a ballot sheet.

Midway through, however, the timbre changes: a radio news broadcast filters through the rock'n'roar, commenting on the latest bout of street rioting and the measures taken to quell it; to be succeeded, in turn, by what can only be described as a party political broadcast from whichever right wing demon you fear most.

An impassioned demand for a return to 'the traditional British values of obedience, discipline, morality and freedom' was standard rhetoric after all. But Robinson spoke the caveats that the politicians left unspoken – the litany of louts from whom we needed to be freed: "the Reds and the Pakis and the Unions, prostitutes, pansies and Punks, football hooligans, juvenile delinquents, lesbians and left-wing scum." Freedom, in other words, from just about everybody standing in front of the stage, listening to the song. Even more effectively, at Alexander Palace, the recitation was delivered by what looked like your average middle-class, middle-aged, smartly suited Conservative dickhead. It was only at the end that he tore off the mask, and stood revealed as a black Rasta – which probably sounds really limp today. But it was bloody effective on the night.

Alexandra Palace was TRB's last stand. A poorly attended UK tour was followed by visits to Japan and Norway, but the line-up – somewhat unstable for the best part of a year – was now in absolute flux. When Kustow quit in July 1978, Robinson finally folded the group – he was, he announced, "in no mood to carry on a Tom Robinson Band without any of the Tom Robinson Band in it."

Perhaps the group had already achieved everything it could, establishing a rock-political agenda which, no matter how hard sundry others tried, had simply never previously existed at anything but the most underground level before. It wasn't only the Skins singing 'Glad To Be Gay' that mattered, after all. It was everybody who heard TRB, listened to TRB and, however fleetingly, considered what the band's message meant to them.

Robinson's willingness to perform at rallies and benefits for any number of leftist causes undoubtedly reduced the group to the status of activist poster children for watching cynics (a popular badge of the day transposed the TRB's raised fist logo beneath the facetious 'Gay Whales Against The Nazis'). But, even if they arrived with no grander intention than hearing the hit singles, few of the people who actually attended those rallies ever left without at least a little something to think about.

The question was, who was going to make sure that they continued thinking now that Tom was gone?

CHAPTER FIVE

The Specials had made several appearances for Rock Against Racism in Coventry during their days as the Automatics. But when they rallied beneath the banner in London in March 1979, the group was utterly unrecognisable from the outfit that opened for the Clash nine months before.

Back in Coventry following their days in the London warehouse, the group came perilously close to splitting. Silverton Hutchinson had rejoined the line-up, but his enthusiasm for the project remained AWOL. Finally, after missing yet another rehearsal, he announced he was leaving. Standing in the unheated backroom in a pub near Coventry City football ground, most of his bandmates knew how he felt.

After many months of inactivity, during which the Specials' only purpose was to rehearse, the resumption of the same routine, four nights a week, every week, seemed futile. But, as Dammers countered on more than one occasion: what else were they going to do? Even with a drummer, the group was in no state to start gigging again – they'd already admitted that their music was going nowhere. They needed major surgery, a period during which they should shut their eyes and ears to everything going on around them and concentrate upon reshaping the Specials into something that was, indeed, special.

There were a few ideas floating around but the one that Dammers returned to again and again was to shift the Specials' repertoire away from Reggae, with all its rebel roots connotations, toward the music he himself had first started listening to and from which Reggae had developed: Ska. He'd already floated the idea once, during those unresolved rehearsals in London, but neither Hutchinson nor Radiation had gone along with it. Dammers had returned to the drawing board. Now with Hutchinson gone, he poached his more sympathetic flatmate, John Bradbury, from Neol Davies' Transposed Men, and returned to the subject.

On paper, the traditional resource for anybody wanting to trace the history of Jamaican music, the shift from Ska, through Rocksteady, to Reggae apparently required little more than fine-tuning the rhythms that got the dancehalls dancing. Laurel Aitken, one of the earlier music's most venerable statesmen, once opined, "Reggae and Ska are the same thing, except it's just a change of drum beat or a different drop of the bass." Musicologists, of course, will quibble with such glib summary ('what about the guitar riffs?' 'What about the production?' 'What about the politics?') but the only other difference was that one was now hip, and the other was old.

So much for paper. In the flesh, the two musics were chalk and cheese – the one scratchy, edgy, jumping and raw, the other (at least in the Roots incarnation that was so popular now) dark and booming, thoughtful and heavy. It was the difference between a handful of uppers and a bellyful of Quaaludes. And Dammers had had his fill of standing still.

Drawing on childhood memories and sitting up with Neville Staples and Lynval Golding and their own collections of classic Jamaican 45s, Dammers began piecing together fresh arrangements for songs already in the Specials' repertoire, finding fresh numbers to replace the oldies that would be swept away by the new regime.

It mattered not that little of what Dammers described as Ska would fit any purist's definition of the term – as, indeed, he was well aware. To attempt to peer microscopically into the musical and nomenclatural convolutions of the music at its source was both time-consuming and, ultimately, irrelevant. Beat-wise, after all, the Specials' sound would adhere closer to the loping tempos of rock-steady than to the oft-times frenetic energies of the original Jamaican Ska. They eschewed the horns that were an intrinsic element in classic Ska productions, while the vocals that Staples, Golding and Terry Hall wrapped around one another might have looked true to the music's traditional three piece format, but had precious little in common with the lush harmonies that were the hallmark of Ska's greatest exponents – the Wailers, the Maytals, the Dominoes and so forth.

The group's choice of covers, too, betrayed influences that dated back only as far as Dammers' own teenaged infatuation with Jamaican music, again nailing it firmly within late 60s rock-steady and early Reggae – "songs that said something," as Staples put it. 'Long Shot (Kick De Bucket)', 'The Liquidator', 'Monkey Man', the surging movie theme 'Guns Of Navarone' and the ubiquitous 'Skinhead Moonstomp' all dated from that period, and were cut (respectively, by the Pioneers, Harry J, the Maytals, a latter-day variant on the Skatalites and Symarip) strictly to the demands of Jamaican audiences that would no sooner listen to Ska, than a Punk crowd would sit through a Yes gig.

None of that mattered. Keep things simple, keep things short. 'Ska' was both of those things. When, in later years, purists questioned the Specials' hijacking of the term, the musicians' exasperation was never far from the surface.

Neville Staples yawns, "We used to listen to Ska, and that was our interpretation of it. Because, remember, we had white guys and black guys in the band. We all used to listen to Ska, Blue Beat, Prince Buster, but everyone's got to have a niche and that was ours. We used to listen to Ska music, we used to listen to a lot of the Trojan label stuff, 'Monkey Spanner'... and then it came to Reggae, 'Cocaine Running Around My Brain'... But why did we call our music Ska? I ain't got a fucking clue. For God's sake, man! We used to listen to Ska, that's all it was. I don't know it came about, I just know we used to listen to a lot of Ska. And Rocksteady. And Reggae.

"When you're doing music, you do it with your own interpretation. We had the influence of the people in the band. We had the Reggae influence, and I played Reggae guitar. Roddy played rock guitar. Horace would play kinda Reggae-come-rocky stuff, Brad would play Reggae mixed with rock. It was different, we just came up with that formula because of the people in the band. Before, the first demos we did, it was slow Reggae and that's how it was for us. Then it got more rocky with the Reggae in it. That was our version of the song, with what we had. Why have a horn section just because the original had one? We wanted to do it our way, not someone else's."

Terry Hall agreed. "It's not that we're just trying to revive Ska. It's using those old elements to try forming something new. In a way, it's all still part of Punk. We're not trying to get away from Punk. We're just trying to show some other direction. You've got to go back to go forward."

The music was only half the equation. Of all the lessons Dammers learned during the Specials' time with Bernie Rhodes, of all the mantras that were pounded into his head, perhaps the greatest was the importance of image. Rhodes, of course, was a past master. Instrumental in Malcolm MacLaren's shaping of the early Sex Pistols (or, at least, the public's perception of them), Rhodes then took his ideas a step further by adopting three more-or-less imageless would-be musicians and transforming them into the Clash – not by telling them what to wear or how to behave, but by instilling them with the confidence to make those decisions for themselves.

Dammers had the same confidence. Backstage at the Music Machine show with the Clash, Paul Simonon had been resplendent in a 60s-style Mod suit, topped with a distinctive pork pie hat. It was a look that Dammers hadn't seen in a decade – since it was, in fact, the height of Mod fashion. But it was one that he intuitively knew was 'right.'

There was another memory from the Clash tour, however, that he found hard to shake off: the Crawley show on July 8, when a gang of Skinheads climbed onstage during Suicide's set and physically attacked singer Alan Vega. According to Roddy Radiation, "they got a real beating, a lot of dodgy Skins. I didn't see it because I was getting changed, but I saw [Vega] backstage afterwards, covered in blood."

Laughing the incident off, Vega insisted it was nothing compared to some of the duo's New York shows, but still, Dammers told *The Guardian* in March 2002, that was the night that the concept of the Specials was born. "I idealistically thought, 'We have to get through to these people'." Remembering the halcyon days of his own adolescence, when white Skinheads happily danced to black music, he believed he'd discovered the formula that would accomplish that: "an integrated kind of British music, rather than white people playing rock and black people playing their music. [Our music] was an integration of the two."

Drawing from every source he could lay his hands on, from old newspaper articles and photographs, from record sleeves and his own teenaged memories, he first formulated, and then applied, the kind of image that he believed a modern Ska band should have. And finally, triumphantly, he was able to present his colleagues with a sketch of the finished item, the angular pop-art Dr Who whom he christened Walt Jabasco. Half Jamaican Rude Boy (Dammers' inspiration was a mid-1960s photograph of the Wailers' Peter Tosh), half London Skinhead; part Mod, part Punk, Jabasco would come to represent the Specials in every arena that they entered, and epitomise Ska-Punk to this day. Not so long ago, he was even seen stencilled on a wall in Seattle, with NO DOUBT FOREVER scrawled beneath him.

Where Jabasco pointed, the Specials followed.Scouring the second-hand and charity shops, the Specials accumulated the wardrobe necessary to live out the look: circles and arrows, pork-pie hats, 2-Tone tonics and mohair jackets, crombies, Harringtons, Ben Shermans, Doc Martens... half-a-bygone decade's worth of discarded youth fashion. Staples explains, "old people used to wear the suits and stuff, then we'd get them altered. Half the stuff wasn't even being made anymore. We made a mish-mash of black-and-white stuff... soon enough people were manufacturing it all again, but when we were first looking for it, second-hand stores were the only places you could find it."

But Dammers wasn't simply redesigning a band. He was designing a way of life, a musical force that would, in his mind, become as distinctive in its own world as Motown or Stax were in theirs'. Neither was it an idle dream, as the twenty-year-old example of the Blue Beat label proved. The prime source for Jamaican music in the UK throughout the early-mid 1960s, a label that churned out new releases as fast as the Jamaican studios could produce them, Blue Beat came to so dominate the British scene that nobody ever talked of Ska or Rocksteady, they simply talked of Blue Beat, as though the label itself was the music. And Dammers knew, if it had happened once, it could happen again.

Neither was Rhodes the only music biz veteran whose thoughts impacted upon Dammers' own plans. Chris Gilbey, the man who first took the Specials to London, had himself already faded from the scene, returning to Australia where he promptly scored a major hit as producer of Doug Mulray's 'I'm A Punk' before becoming involved with nascent new wavers The Church. Before he departed, however, he convened a last meeting with Dammers and co, and imparted two pieces of advice. The first, that they change their name, would soon become a fact of life – they were, of course, still the Automatics at this time. The second, however, had never seemed practical until now.

"I said they should put out their own single on their own label," recalls Gilbey. "Take it to radio and see what happens. Minimal risk to manufacture 500 singles and record two tracks. I think we talked about which tracks for the single and then I left the UK soon after that to return to Australia."

Gilbey had, in fact, already employed this same strategy when he was approached by Akron weirdies Devo in 1977. He had no interest in managing them, but he set them on their way regardless, as they followed his word and cut the 'Jocko Homo' single. Other, perhaps less well-connected, groups had made a similar leap-of-faith: earlier that same year, the Buzzcocks signed with UA at least partially on the strength of the self-produced and released *Spiral Scratch* EP; 999 kicked off on their own LaBritian label, while the Banned's 'Little Girl', one of the most distinctive power-pop hits of 1978, started life on the group's own Can't Eat Records. Close to a year after the idea was first planted in his mind, Dammers decided to give Gilbey's suggestion a go.

He named his label 2-Tone, a title that, of course, reflected the imagery he had so laboriously worked to perfect, but which had an alternate meaning, too. In the climate of the ever-worsening racial relations that, even without paying a moment's heed to the rhetoric of the Anti-Nazi League and the National Front, was spilling into every street in every city, 2-Tone spoke of the group's own wish – fulfilled in the line-up's very composition – for reconciliation. There was no black or white. Everything was 2-Tone.

Roddy Radiation explains, "because the band member's were black/white, politics were always important to the band. The rise of the right wing National Front and, later, the British Movement, was something that the Specials found very disturbing. Jerry was the most political member of the band. But we all had similar political feelings, even though our backgrounds were different (middle and working class)."

"Punk was dying, the Sex Pistols had split, the charts were full of second-division Punk bands and people were after something new," Sir Horace reminded *The Guardian* in 2001. "We were in the right place at the right time and we had the tunes."

Fiercely budgeting the Specials' own meagre resources, then topping up the kitty with a £700 loan from a businessman friend, Dammers led the Specials into the studio in late January, 1979. 'Gangsters', the song written following the band's return from their Parisian sojourn, was the obvious choice to record, an uncompromising reflection on the group's months under Bernie Rhodes' tutelage that was so firmly modelled on Prince Buster's beloved classic 'Al Capone' that the group thought nothing of lifting the opening sound of squealing brakes directly from the Buster record. Neither was anybody shy about letting the song's inspiration be named and shamed – live, Staples delighted in reiterating the demand "Don't call me Scarface, my name is... Bernie Rhodes!"

Finding a B-side was more problematic, however – *not* because the Specials didn't have enough material, but because they didn't actually have the money to record it. Finally, Dammers went back to the demos that he and Neol Davies had recorded, individually and collectively, back in 1977, and settled on an instrumental track, 'The Selecter', that Davies and, coincidentally, Specials drummer John Bradbury had recorded back then. With Bradbury's brother-in-law, Barrie Andrews, adding trombone, and with Davies himself musing aloud on the possibility of trying to put his own band together, it was agreed that 'The Selecter' would both back 'Gangsters' and, should Davies finally decide to go that particular route, debut his still-to-be-formed group.

In mid-February, Dammers was back in London, to meet with Rough Trade – at that time, the largest independent distributors in the UK, and also encouragingly economical when it came to such matters as manufacturing the actual record. Dammers himself had decided to press just 2,500 copies of the single, with costs being kept even lower by his request that the record be bagged in a plain white sleeve. He and his bandmates intended rubber-stamping the planned design, Walt Jabasco, themselves. Rough Trade, however, were convinced that, once word of the record got out, 2,500 copies would sell out in no time. It would work out cheaper in the long run, then, to double the initial pressing. Nervously, but confident in Rough Trade's own track record, Dammers agreed.

Other doors opened. One of Dammers' old lecturers at Lanchester Poly, Alan Harrison, had once shared a house with Rick Rogers, head of the Trigger PR company in Camden Town. The newly reformed Damned were numbered among his clients, and Harrison suggested that Dammers pay Rogers a visit.

By the time Dammers returned to Coventry, Trigger had added the Specials to their roster, and Rogers was established as the group's manager.

In the face of such rapid progress, and from whichever angle one looked at it, Dammers was convinced that the idea of launching his own record label was the right one. Controlling the label meant he would also be in control of his own marketing and financing, of course. Even more importantly, however, he would also control his own timing and that, as 1979 began to pick up speed, was suddenly becoming a crucial concern.

Everybody agrees that very few ideas can ever be said to be truly original – there is scarcely one modern innovation that cannot be claimed by at least two or three different inventors, all working in absolute ignorance of one another's travails. So it is in music.

But how coincidental was it that, just as Dammers and the Specials finally perfected their own recapitulation of suedehead chic in all its sartorial grandeur, east London's Leyton Buzzards should be stirring chartwards with their own glorious recounting of those same misty memories, not only namechecking the uniform that the Specials themselves had worked so hard to perfect – "mohawk suit, button-down shirt with a window-pane check, brand  new strides with a dog-tooth fleck" – but also throwing in a reference to one of the Specials' own proudest covers: "The Guns of Navarone." 'Saturday Night Beneath The Plastic Palm Trees' would climb no higher than #53, but it served notice of the storms to come regardless.

How coincidental, too, that just as the Specials put the finishing touches to their personal revision of the Ska that backdropped the Leyton Buzzards' dreamscape, down in the Kentish coastal town of Herne Bay, one Arthur

Kitchener was formulating more-or-less precisely the same musical brew as they were.

A genuine mid-60s South London Mod, Kitchener – or Arthur Kay, as he was better known – cut his musical teeth in a low-key soul act, the Next Collection, whose regular circuit frequently touched onto the fringes of the local West Indian community. It was there that Kay first heard Blue Beat music, although he later acknowledged that, if he'd missed it on that night, within a matter of weeks he'd be hearing it "pumping out of every street and every club in Brixton." Soon, the Next Collection's own repertoire had shifted almost wholly over to Ska, a transformation that quickly introduced them to one of the great legends of the authentic Jamaican scene, trombone player Rico Rodriguez, himself transplanted to London in 1962, and now keeping the music alive by gigging and guesting with every band he could.

Rodriguez played several shows with the Next Collection, but his patronage did them little good; by the end of the decade, the group had changed direction once again and, as the pop outfit Second Hand, was signing to Polydor. Kay, horrified by the switch, quit and moved into session work, most frequently at Chalk Farm Studios in north London, an outfit opened by Emil Shallit, the founder of the Blue Beat label. There he played on a string of low-key Anglo-Jamaican 45s but, as the early 70s Skinhead boom gave way to the less explosive age of glam, and record buyers began demanding something more than short, sharp skankers, Kay drifted away from music and, by 1978, he was working in a factory in Islington.

It was around the corner from there, one afternoon that summer, that he ran smack into a scene torn straight out of his own memory banks, a battalion of genuine Mod-accoutred scooters lined up outside Alfredo's café. This was no time-warp, however. Rather, director Francis Rodham was simply shooting scenes for the forthcoming movie version of the Who's *Quadrophenia*. But the sight and, as the movie moved closer to completion, the sheer buzz that surrounded the project reawakened every latent musical dream Kay had ever entertained.

Back in touch with some of his old associates, he learned that Mike Craig, the recording engineer at Chalk Farm Studios, was in the process of moving down to Herne Bay to help set up a new studio, Europa Sound. Asked down to help out on a session, Kay used some of the studio down-time to work on a song he'd written earlier in the year, a cunning clash between his own great love, Ska, and the nation's latest obsession, George Lucas' first sci-fi blockbuster... 'Ska Wars', of course. According to Kay, "we played it down a local disco and it went down really well, so we decided to release it on our own label, Red Admiral Records." It was late February, 1979.

Kay was still waiting for the single to return from the pressing plant when he heard about the Specials. Themselves just weeks away from the official release date of 'Gangsters', the band had returned to London for a burst of live shows around the capital's key pubs and clubs: the Nashville in West Kensington, the Moonlight in West Hampstead, University College and the Hope & Anchor in Islington.

Kay caught them at the Nash and, though history records his 'Ska Wars' ultimately beat 'Gangsters' to the streets by a matter of weeks, still he readily admits that the sight of a young new group playing his beloved Ska in concert "gave me the inspiration to form my own band, the Originals." It would be several months more, however, before that outfit was ready to hit the live circuit. In the meantime, the Specials encountered a far more immediate threat to their pioneering status when they arrived at the Hope & Anchor on March 18, for the first of two nights beneath the banner of Rock Against Racism – three representatives from a local band named Madness.

CHAPTER SIX

Keyboardist Mike 'Barso' Barson, bassist Carl 'Chas Smash' Smyth, drummer John 'Billy Whizz' Hasler, saxophonist Lee 'Kix' Thompson and guitarist Chris 'Chrissy Boy' Foreman, natives all of north London's Hornsey-Highgate-Hampstead triangle, had been kicking around the lowest levels of the London circuit since the last day of June 1977 when the North London Invaders, as they had just decided to call themselves, played their first-ever gig at a party thrown by friend Si Birdsall.

Barely rehearsed, and not exactly brimming with self-confidence either, the Invaders were an odd outfit by the standards of the day, a group whose need to form may have been drawn from the DIY ethics of Punk, but whose musical tastes strayed in other directions entirely. That night at Birdsall's house, their set comprised little more than a bunch of ragged rock'n'roll numbers, rendered even more clumsy by vocalist Dikron's failure to learn the words. The group wound up performing a set of instrumentals in the back garden – the party, on the other hand, spent much of its time indoors. It was not the most auspicious debut.

It would be eight months before the North London Invaders stepped out in public once again, by which time they had finally recruited a new vocalist, one Graham 'Suggs' McPherson, and nudged a few other members around. Bassist Gavin Rogers and saxophonist Lucinda Garland had now replaced Smash and Kix, although neither would stay long. Neither was Suggs' tenure likely to be less than limited – his habit of skipping off rehearsals to go and watch Chelsea ensured that the Invaders managed just one show, at the City & East in February 1978, before it was time for another change-around.

The Invaders' next gig did not materialise until the beginning of July, when they entertained the troops at the William Ellis Secondary School's end-of-year dance – new bassist Mark 'Bedders' Bedford was just concluding his education there, and had rangled them onto the bill. Drummer Hasler was pushed to the front of the stage: one of Bedders' friends, Garry Dovey took his place behind the drums; another, Daniel 'Woody' Woodgate, would replace him come autumn. Finally bringing this maddening roundabout of names and changes to an end, Suggs returned shortly before a show at the roller-blind factory where Bedders now worked; Kix came back a few weeks later and Hasler moved up to become the band's manager.

He did his job well. On November 10, the newly abbreviated Invaders opened for the Valves at Acklam Hall. It was a rough night, as the headlining Punks' crowd reacted none-too-kindly to the Invaders' still uncertain repertoire of covered rockers and gentle originals (under the pluralized title 'My Girls', the future hit 'My Girl' was already in the set, a somewhat mawkish ballad with little of its later bounce), but an educational one as well. As the crowd seethed before them, Madness spotted Chas Smash in the crowd, executing the wildly flailing dance that would soon become the band's own trademark.

There were further lessons to be drawn from another show, this time opening for the Tribesmen, another of the growing handful of British Reggae acts that had sprung up to challenge the hegemonies of Jamaican imports, with a worldview scratched directly from their own facts of life. Faced with Tribesman's own reggae-loving crowd, the Invaders decided to use the evening as an opportunity to road test a couple of covers that had recently crept into their repertoire, Prince Buster's 'Madness' and 'One Step Beyond'. The pair went down better than the rest of the set put together.

The Invaders' shift from rock'n'roll to Ska was Barso's doing. No less than some of the Specials' early excursions, his organ sound dominated the band, lending it a peculiarly carnival-like feel which in turn slipped easily into a syncopated dance beat. The enthusiasm that the group now perceived rising from the dancefloor went a long way towards persuading them that their search for a new musical direction, one that would finally allow them to put their rock'n'rolling days behind them, was over. Now their repertoire was dominated by the Ska sound, with deviations taking it only as far as a remodelled rendition of the Smokey Robinson hit 'Tears Of A Clown' and a couple of Ian Dury covers, 'Rough Kids' and 'Roadette Song'. Dury's visionary updating of Cockney Music Hall style and manner was to prove another of the group's longest-lasting influences. As Chas Smyth later reflected, "We also liked Roxy Music, early Roxy, Kilburn [and the] High Roads, which is Ian Dury's band. Alex Harvey... [the] Kinks... Ska was just a part of it."

Through the early New Year, the Invaders worked on the hybrid that they, innocent of developments anywhere else in the country, were convinced would mark them out. Punk had been crossed with a lot of other musical forces over the past couple of years. But no one had ever thought to mash it up with Ska. Or so they thought.

In early 1979, the Invaders – like the Automatics a year before them – discovered that it was time to change their name. Another Invaders had turned up, with a major label contract (with Polydor) and a countrywide tour aboard the Sham 69-sponsored Pursey's Package, alongside the Angelic Upstarts. Brainstorming, the north Londoners flicked through a succession of possible new names – the Big Dippers, the Soft Shoe Shufflers and Morris & The Minors were all considered, then consigned to the bin – before Chrissy Boy suggested Madness. The song was already in the repertoire, and dictated the group's direction. Why not elevate it to the status of the band's own anthem?

They became the Nutty Boys at the same time – not officially, but certainly as an alter ego whose presence was advertised on all their posters. Chas Smyth explains, "We were Madness, we were going against the grain. We were different to everyone else around, we started spraying and painting DMs before anyone else did. We had a different image. Lee wrote on the back of one of his Levi jackets in bleach, 'That Nutty Sound', [and it was] nice to be able to say that rather than 'we're Ska, we're this band, we're that band.' Kids used to come up to me and say, 'Oh, you're Mods and Skinheads, you know.' Who cares?"

After close to three months of seclusion, Madness resurfaced for their first show under their new name, and their first in their new guise, as the opening act at the Music Machine, on a bill topped by the now-sadly forgotten Sore Throat.

Gone was the ramshackle everyday-wear that had passed for stage gear in the Invaders days, replaced by their own charity-shop variant on the Specials' super-Mod glaze and surmounted by what would soon become their trademark pork-pie hats. Gone, too, was every last vestige of past musical identities, swept away by a Ska variation that, if anything, was even crazier than the Specials'. Chas Smash was back in the line-up, fully incorporated as the group's onstage dancer-come-Master of Ceremonies. And, though choreography would be far too strong a word for the other musicians' mannerisms, but there was a singularity to their movements anyway, a strength of purpose that would swiftly come to epitomise their Nuttiness.

By the time Suggs, Kix and Smash dropped by their local, the Hope & Anchor, on March 18, to catch a Rock Against Racism show, Madness' own musical direction – and nature – was already confirmed in the minds of the handful of concert-goers who had so far seen them. In their own minds, too, Madness were unique. One can only imagine the trio's surprise, then, when they found the event headlined by a group with precisely the same musical tastes as their own – the Specials.

Immediately after the show, the trio made their introductions, launching a conversation that continued on into the night, at Suggs' flat. There, Dammers outlined all he had already accomplished – the creation of 2-Tone, the imminence of 'Gangsters', the formulation of an entire musical movement that could rise up around the Specials. Already, he explained, Neol Davies was in the process of forming his own band, The Selecter, to parallel the Specials' own releases. The specific invitation may not have been made that same evening, but it was clear that he would welcome the chance to hear Madness, and maybe add them to the roster as well.

It was an exciting conversation, and an extraordinarily idealistic one. But, if anybody thought Dammers' head was maybe stuck up in the clouds someplace, a review in the following week's issue of *Sounds* quickly kicked away the cynicism. "The Specials can knock the shit out of the many great pretenders around," proclaimed Dave McCullough. "The songs, the power, the sense of a strong image, everything that counts is there." Only one issue bothered him. "Is the timing right? The divide between greatness and mere success is often elastic." But no matter. "The important thing is simply that the Specials are here."

The Specials continued gigging, in London and elsewhere, throughout the run-up to the release of 'Gangsters' in mid-April. For the most part, their attentions remained confined to the pub circuit, although it was rapidly becoming apparent that that circuit would not be able to hold them for long. On April 8, the Specials played their highest-profile show yet, as opening act for the Damned and the UK Subs – former Wild Boys drummer Pete Davies' latest band – at one of the London Lyceum's regular Sunday night showcases.

Unknown to most of the crowd when they took the stage, the Specials wound up their set as conquering heroes, with the applause still ringing even as the second-billed Subs came out. 'Gangsters' only added to the excitement. Reviews of the record were unanimously positive, while DJ John Peel immediately put his own weight behind it, airing it constantly and inviting the Specials in to record a session for his show less than a month later. (They recorded four songs, including what Radiation regards as the ultimate version of 'Gangsters'). The band also shot a video to accompany the single, stylishly powering through a staged 'live' performance and only increasing the edgy fission that fizzed around them. As the Specials prepared for their next major London performance, at the Music Machine in Camden Town on April 24, it was in the knowledge that they were hosting the hottest gig in town. And not only in terms of ticket demand.

In the two months since they began their London residency, the Specials had gathered up an audience that crossed so many tribal lines that the phrase '2-Tone' only began to describe it. The first few shows were unremarkable – outside of the cults that everyone remembers, a huge portion of a London audience was, basically, 'normal', with nothing more than maybe a badge or two to align them with any particular allegiance. As word began to spread, however, especially after the Lyceum show, the tribes converged: nascent Rude Boys who leaped wholeheartedly into Dammers' dream; Skinheads, who'd witnessed or simply heard about, the band that played all the old, great songs; Punks; Rastas... Anyone who fancied a good night out.

For most observers, however, it was the presence of the Skins that raised the most eyebrows and, in keeping with the mood of the times, sounded the first alarm bells. So far, the Specials' shows had passed off trouble-free. But they were one of the few bands who nurtured such an audience that could claim such a thing – even Sham were in turmoil, as Jimmy Pursey pleaded with his so-called fans to kindly stop kicking the crap out of one another. Who was to say the Specials' audience was not going to turn equally virulent?

Nobody; indeed, the voices (or, at least, suspicions) raised against the Specials' Skinhead following were only going to grow louder as the countdown to the General Election gathered pace, and the Anti-Nazi League prepared to draw the battle lines for the last major confrontation of the campaign. On April 23, St George's Day, just 24 hours before the Specials' Music Machine gig, the National Front would be staging a major campaign meeting in Southall, home to one of the largest Asian communities in the British Isles. The ANL, of course, would be there to greet them.

The crowds started gathering long before the meeting was scheduled to begin, only to find the entire area surrounding Southall Town Hall already sealed off by the police. As a legitimate political party, the Front's rally was, after all, a 'lawful' gathering – and it was the police's job to uphold that lawfulness. Or so their paymasters explained later on, as the entire country struggled to comprehend just what had led up to the beating-to-death – some called it murder – of 33-year-old New Zealand-born school teacher Blair Peach. A beating that was meted out by members of the police Special Patrol Group (SPG), armed not only with police issue batons, but also crowbars, sledgehammers and coshes – all of which were found in officers' lockers later.

Although many subsequent chroniclers have described the SPG as a 'recently formed' outfit, it had in fact been a part of the police force since 1961, when it emerged to provide a mobile, centrally based unit intended to combat problems that were beyond the abilities of the local force. What *was* recent was the alacrity with which the SPG was being called into service, and the agitation that their riot-suited and shield-toting presence generated within crowds that might otherwise have considered themselves wholly law-abiding. The Metropolitan Police themselves have since admitted that the presence of the SPG at large rallies and demonstrations 'sometimes came to assume unwanted symbolic significance.'

Southall was no exception. Some 3,000 protestors, the ANL and the Socialist Workers Party contingent swollen by the Southall Youth Movement and the Indian Workers' Association, gathered around the cordons, to be confronted by almost precisely as many police. The Met later revealed that no less than 2,756 officers were deployed that day, each of whom seemed convinced that violence was nothing less than inevitable.

They were, in fact, probably correct in that assumption. Simply by selecting Southall as the site of their meeting, the National Front was sending a very clear, very brutal, message to Britain's immigrant communities. But what message was being sent by the local authority that actually permitted the rally to take place? The previous year, a Front rally in Birmingham ended with scenes of such violence that many local councils began invoking the Public Order Act to prevent party supporters from even marching through their jurisdictions – the first use of that particular legislation, ironically enough, since the heyday of Oswald Mosley's British Union of Fascists, back before World War Two.

Tory Horace Cutler's Greater London Council, however, refused to employ those same powers, even after the Front admitted that their choice of venues was often decided in the spirit of deliberate provocation. And Blair Peach would pay for the city's recalcitrance.

From the moment the first confrontations between demonstrators and police erupted, it was apparent that the constabulary was not on duty simply to keep the peace. Rather, it was hard to shake the feeling that their primary concern was to crack some lefty skulls – to the point that even the steadfastly Conservative *Daily Telegraph*'s correspondent recorded actions far removed from the traditional image of the British Bobby. Reporters watched as crowds of protesters were systematically broken into small groups, cornered, subdued and then hauled off to waiting vans and coaches. "Nearly every demonstrator," the paper reported, "had blood flowing from some injury." There were over 300 arrests, but many eyewitnesses were convinced that the police were less concerned about taking into people custody than putting them in hospital.

The police, for their part, responded to criticism of their tactics by describing the demonstration as the most violent ever staged in London, surpassing the violence of the 1976 Notting Hill Carnival, the bloody 1977 anti-Fascist march in Lewisham, and even the vicious anti-Mosleyite rallies of the 1930s. Furthermore, they claimed, it was a tribute to the efficacy of their armour that police casualties were kept down to just 21, compared with 55 in Lewisham, and a sign of their restraint that, despite far higher figures appearing in the press, no more than another 20-or-so demonstrators were similarly reported as having been injured – again, compared with some 50 in 1977.

The difference was that nobody died at Lewisham.

Blair Peach was no stranger to demonstrations and rallies. A member of both the Socialist Workers Party and the Anti-Nazi League, he was a well-known activist in causes ranging from Trade Union disputes (he was a past President of his local National Union of Teachers chapter) to the anti-apartheid lobby. He was also a dedicated teacher, working with 'special needs' children at the Phoenix Special School in east London.

None of this counted for anything, however, as he was pursued down a side street by a gang of SPG officers, where, according to an inquest that took a full 13 months to reach a conclusion, he met with 'death by misadventure.' Or, as *Private Eye*'s legendary Dave Spart put it, he "was battered to death in front of hundreds of witnesses, none of whom were allowed to appear in the court."

Peach was not the first anti-Fascist to meet such a non-committal demise. Five years earlier, on June 5, 1975, Warwick University student Kevin Gateley lost his life during another anti-Front confrontation in Holborn's Red Lion Square. Despite both public and press misgivings, a subsequent investigation absolved the police of all responsibility.

On this occasion, too, the police would be found to have acted properly. No police officer was ever charged with Peach's death. Even the demands of 79 MPs could not force a public enquiry. Neither were the findings of an internal Metropolitan Police inquiry, headed by Commander John Cass, ever made public.

But still the killing of Blair Peach sent shockwaves through the country. In an age before complaints of simple 'police harassment' were routinely translated into accusations of 'police brutality', the notion that the law was simply doing a difficult job to the best of its ability had yet to lose currency, even among those people whose lives or lifestyles seemed most frequently to mark them out for attention.

Indeed, it was a sign of the almost overnight shift in public opinion that, long before the coroner delivered his opinion, it was widely believed that, as with Liddle Towers, Peach's killer – or killers – would get off scot free. And with that belief there arose the fear that, having got away with murder once, the police would indeed be committing it again.

Blair Peach was not the only name to be brought to the public's attention that dreadful day. Several other prominent figures were among the arrested or wounded, with one of them, Clarence Baker, having special significance in both the immediate Southall community and on the wider music scene.

As the manager of the locally-based Reggae band Misty In Roots, Baker was a familiar face at the multitude of RAR-and related shows that featured not only Misty, but also the clutch of other performers that worked beneath the banner of their own People Unite! artists and musicians collective. As a result of his encounter with the SPG, Baker received a fractured skull and a blood clot to the base of his brain at Southall. But neither his injuries nor his unconsciousness deterred the police from dragging him to the police station and holding him for eight hours before admitting him to a hospital.

"It is very difficult to convey what actually happened [at Southall]," Misty's Delbert Tyson later reflected. "We can't really tell you that, it's very difficult. Certain things you probably wouldn't even believe. Blair Peach was killed... Clarence was in a coma..."

Outrage over the events at Southall swiftly turned to action. Both Misty In Roots and dub poet Linton Kwesi Johnson were quick to issue musical commentaries on Peach's fate (Johnson's 'Reggae Fi Peach' remains one of his most powerful works), while Baker's beating became a key element in a new song by another local act that People Unite! had nurtured, the Ruts.

Politically aware, but rarely sloganeering, the Ruts stood at the crossroads of Punk, Reggae and Oi! and gave their heart to all three. The fact that they accomplished it all with just one album and a handful of singles, only emphasized their power. If the Ruts had survived into the 1980s, the 1980s as we know them would probably never have happened.

The quartet – vocalist Malcolm Owen, guitarist Paul Fox, drummer Dave Ruffy and bassist John "Seggs" Jennings – were west London schoolfriends before they were bandmates, and their initial musical efforts concentrated upon their immediate sphere of influence. Formed in August 1977, when Owen simply joined the rest at a rehearsal, without even knowing whether or not he could sing, the Ruts' first ever live show was at the Target in nearby Northolt. Another early gig found them supporting Wayne County's Electric Chairs at High Wycombe Town Hall. Their most regular appearance, however, was the White Hart in Acton. Just another local band playing local shows in local pubs.

It was Misty In Roots who first introduced the Ruts to Rock Against Racism. They already knew Owen "from the streets in Southall," as Wolford Tyson put it, and were only too happy to bring the band on board as their regular support act. Their first show together took place at Southall Community Centre – it was, said Owen, "a shambles, but it was fantastic. There were all these pogoing Pakistanis." He continued, "we gigged solidly in the RAR clubs with bands like Misty. We played gigs like that for a year with virtually nothing else. They were giving us gigs when no-one else was."

The union was not, however, simply a social convenience: it was a cultural master-stroke. Misty were full-fledged Rastas, the Ruts to all intents and purposes were Skinheads: they looked like Skins, they dressed like Skins and, when they played, their most compulsive anthems made them sound like Skins. For the two bands to appear on bills together was akin to detonating a bomb beneath a battalion of stereotypes.

The group was already building its own audience: one early admirer, Thin Lizzy's Phil Lynott, even gave the Ruts a song, 'Eat Your Heart Out' but it stood awkwardly amid the band's own fast-growing catalogue of originals and would never be recorded. In the meantime, Misty's plans for their own People Unite! Label were well-advanced: that autumn of 1978, the Ruts were asked to launch the label with their own first single, the anthemic 'In A Rut'. Misty, of course, advanced the recording costs, a grand total of £105.

An immediate independent hit, the single also brought the Ruts to the attention of John Peel. In January 1979, the band recorded their first BBC session, a five-track monster which climaxed with what would become the Ruts' signature song, 'Babylon's Burning'. (It was originally called 'London's Burning', but the Clash had already ignited that capitol.)

Blasting across the BBC airwaves, the Ruts' appeal was obvious from the outset. They carried the commitment and the energy of the early Clash, before that lot surrendered to the psychobabble of FM-oriented conscientious rabble-rousing. They mixed rock concerns with Reggae influences. And they were catchy as hell.

Occasionally, the political tag got too much. "My plan is for us all to leave the Ruts and reform under the name The Bag of Polos," Seggs told *Sounds*. "Then we won't get asked all this political stuff, and we'll just be able to enjoy ourselves. A political tag is a bit of a drag."

But it was also what the Ruts were good at. Maybe too good. Among the casualties of the Southall riot was the Ruts' plan to launch their own record label, under the aegis of People Unite! "[That was] the original idea," Owen said later. Their only concerns were "not enough money and too much hard work." They were already talking to Virgin Records about signing with them, but the self-sufficiency idea didn't truly perish until the riot police descended upon the People Unite! Headquarters, next door to Owen's own home, and proceeded to trash the premises. "The police smashed the place up, and nearly Clarence [as well]."

The Virgin deal would retain at least some of the ideals that the Ruts' own label would have upheld. "What we've tried to do is [keep] the idea of People Unite! in our heads, while releasing the records through Virgin," Owen explained. "With the album, we wanted lots of tracks, a cheap price and a good cover. That's what we've got. 'Don't pay more than £3.99'."

Of course, Virgin would wreak their revenge on the young idealists – if the Ruts' generosity was to cut into the label's profits, then the profits would cut into the band's royalty payments. "We really signed a dogshit of a record deal," Dave Ruffy smiled ruefully, years later.

Still, Virgin might not have realised precisely what they were letting themselves in for. Fiery rhetoric and political commentary were all well and good – and the bulk of the Ruts' canon certainly fit that bill – but Southall brought out a different side to the band, one that was capable not only of zeroing in on a specific incident, but also of grafting it to a musical soundscape that conveyed all the terror, rage and brutality of that infamous day.

Even more impressively, the song was debuted in the group's live set within weeks of the riot itself. It was called 'Jah War', close to seven minutes of earthquake dub, over which Owen detailed the damage done that day: "Clarence Baker, trouble-maker... the truncheon came down, knocked him to the ground."

'Jah War' was released in Britain that autumn, the follow-up to the two hits that the Ruts had already enjoyed since signing with Virgin, 'Babylon Burning' and 'Something That I Said'. More importantly, however, it was also timed to appear just as the first of the arrested Southall rioters were brought to court – a non-coincidence that, of course, rendered 'Jah War' all but unplayable by any London-area radio station.

The censorious cancer inevitably communicated itself elsewhere – no way was the single going to be a hit. But that was a victory in itself; in being so studiously ignored, the song drew attention to itself because of it. Besides, its presence on the Ruts' newly released, and defiantly Top 20-bound, debut album, *The Crack*, ensured that anyone who wanted to hear it was scarcely going to be thwarted by a handful of squeamish radio playlist-makers.

CHAPTER SEVEN

The tensions unleashed by the events at Southall were oozing fresh as the Specials took the Music Machine stage the evening after the riots, with the day's events – eye-witnessed and otherwise – still hanging on many lips.

Later, observers remarked that how surprised they were that the show itself passed off without incident. They noticed the apparently increased police presence that hung with only the pretence of unobtrusiveness around Mornington Crescent tube station; they saw the looks of obvious distrust that passed between fans who might otherwise have simply walked past one another. It was, they whispered later, miraculous that nothing actually happened. But, if there was any divie intervention that evening, it radiated out from the stage. The Specials were in blistering form, probably the best they'd played since arriving in the capital. The stage pulsed with manic energy, every player seemed a blur of movement, every song a raucous celebration.

Of course the Punks pogo'd into anyone who wasn't fast enough to get out of the way, of course the Skinheads moonstomped over whatever lay in their path. But they did so in a spirit, if not of outright unity, then at least of conjoined strength. Southall might have pitched right against left, and law against liberal. At the Music Machine, however, for the unaligned masses who far out-numbered the politicos among them, it also proved, at the end of the day, that it really was a matter of us against them. And the Specials now proclaimed themselves the soundtrack to the fight.

With just one week remaining before the General Election, a curious calm seemed to settle over the country. Among the major parties, of course, the battle for votes continued unabated. Labour trotted out the usual battery of homespun homilies that pledged things could only get better. The Liberals rolled up with the same vague equivocations that always seemed to replace concrete policies when election time came around. And the Conservatives launched in with a Saatchi & Saatchi-devised campaign that, quite frankly, made the other parties' efforts look pitiful – at the same time painting Mrs Thatcher in caring, sharing shades that her own shadow cabinet would surely have had difficulty recognising.

There were, of course, few surprises in the party's platform. Whatever Labour had done, the Conservatives would undo; whatever Labour had said, the Conservatives would drown out. Income tax would be cut, public expenditure would be reduced. They would curb the power of the unions, and make it easier for people to buy their own homes. Unemployment would be tackled, crime would be savaged. And, when they put it like that, it all sounded rather reasonable. The problem was all the things they didn't say, the actual nuts and bolts of the solutions that were so gamely being spouted.

Thatcher, after all, was no shrinking violet when it came to pushing through reforms. Many first-time voters in 1979 had still to forgive her for erasing the policy of free school milk during her tenure as Minister of Education under Edward Heath's early 1970s regime. Her three years as head of the party itself had seen her adopt an increasingly hard line on economics, law-and-order, defence and, as if to cast an even darker caste across the already formidable shadow of the Front, immigration.

Yet the alternatives (or, rather, *the* alternative: the country hadn't seen a Liberal government since 1922) really weren't much better. Against the short, sharp shock that the Conservatives would assuredly administer was placed the prospect of allowing Labour another five years in which to try and undo all the damage they'd done in the last five, during which they'd probably wind up doing even more. Projections and predictions for the election itself were everywhere in those last few days. But barely one of them anticipated May 3 as delivering anything less than a Conservative landslide.

As the day grew closer, at clubs and theatres across the country, bands

reminded their audiences to make their votes count – or, if that was not possible, to simply keep their heads down in the aftermath. In April, the Angelic Upstarts somehow landed a gig at Acklington Prison, running through a clutch of their most incendiary songs (plus a reworking of Sham's 'Borstal Breakout' retitled 'Acklington Breakout') before warning the 150-or-so convict crowd that, depending upon the outcome of the election, they'd probably be better off where they were.

The Specials were less inflammatory. Walking onstage at the start of the band's next Moonlight Club gig, the night before the polls opened, Terry Hall simply shrugged: "I haven't got much to say. It's the eve of the election and it's up to you" The following day, 76 percent of the electorate turned out to sweep the once-and-future Milk Snatcher into Number 10, with a majority of 43. (And, utterly unable to change her spots, within three weeks, her government raised the price of milk 10 percent.)

The National Front, on the other hand, was wiped out. The threatened 300 candidates did materialise – in fact, the party contested 303 elections, close to half the seats in the country. But they polled just 190,747 votes between them, one of the most pitiful performances ever registered by an even vaguely significant party, and sufficient to tear the party in half – within a year, long-time leader John Tyndall had been forced to resign as chairman, to be succeeded by the apparent (if only comparatively) moderate Andrew Brons.

It was a massive victory for everybody who had ever stood in opposition to the National Front. Even in the face of the Conservative victory, both the ANL and SWP were more than entitled to celebrate. The Front itself, however, was in no mood to acknowledge the existence of the organisations that had fought them every step of the electioneering way.

Their downfall, they insisted, was engineered elsewhere: by the association of the Front's policies with those of the Nazis; by a media smear campaign that culminated in the broadcast of the *Holocaust* television mini-series in the very week of the election; by the street-level emergence of such ultra-militant organisations as the British Movement and the League of St George, for whom even the Front's polcies were too lenient. But most of all, they were betrayed by the Conservative Party, after Margaret Thatcher threw her own lethal hat into the race debate. She "understood," she said, "the fears of the British people of being swamped by coloured immigrants." And she was going to do something about it – even if it only meant collecting the votes of everybody who had an axe to grind against Britain's blacks, but was leery of actively supporting the Front.

On May 3, with the election results still coming in, Madness squeezed themselves onto the tiny stage at the Hope & Anchor; the following evening, they were back at the Nashville, opening again for Sore Throat. The Specials, too, were active in the city, playing Dingwalls and the Hope & Anchor that same weekend, two more stops in a relentless stream of gigs that would ultimately keep them busy all summer. Behind the scenes, too, events were moving quickly. The first pressing of 'Gangsters' was sold out by the end of May, but Rough Trade's plans for a quick repressing were put on hold as every record company in the land descended upon the Specials.

Island, Virgin, Warners, A&M, Arista, EMI – all the majors were there, together with a battalion of smaller concerns: Stiff, Chiswick, Beggars Banquet. Even Rolling Stones Records, whose own profile had been raised immeasurably by the recent signing of Peter Tosh – the original Walt Jabasco! – showed an interest, with Mick Jagger personally turning up at the Fulham Greyhound to check the band out. Elvis Costello, himself pondering the formation of his own F-Beat label, was another 'name' admirer. Although it quickly became clear that many of the Specials' contract-waving courtiers simply wanted to take a look at the latest fuss, others were prepared to discuss a sizeable dowry.

Most, however, lost interest when they actually sat down with Jerry Dammers and Rick Rogers and learned the group's demands. The 2-Tone label had to remain sacrosanct. No matter what business structure lay behind any offered deal, the Specials' records, and those of any artists they chose to work with, would be released on 2-Tone.

In strictly financial terms, it was not an especially unreasonable request – and, of course, it was brilliant marketing. But, as the label-heads filtered through an unending series of meetings, the notion of creating a separate label identity simply to serve as the Specials' personal plaything proved too big a pill to swallow. One by one, the various labels dropped out of the running – or, at least, fell behind the one true front-runner. Chrysalis Records' A&R man Roy Eldridge was determined to sign the Specials, and was equally determined that nothing would stand in the way of that objective. By mid-June, a deal was in place.

The Specials themselves were signed directly to Chrysalis for five albums (with options up to eight). But they also had the right – and the budget – to record up to ten singles a year, with whichever bands they chose, all of whom would themselves be contracted to Chrysalis on a single-by-single basis. Of those ten, Chrysalis were obliged to release no less than six. It was not a perfect arrangement, but Dammers and Rogers had long ago realised that full autonomy and major label backing might never walk hand-in-hand. By the standards of the day, the group had secured an amazing arrangement.

The first consequence of the new deal, of course, was an immediate repressing of 'Gangsters', this time under Chrysalis' auspices. Any fears that its recent unavailability might have lessened demand for the single were quickly undercut. Long before its late June reissue date, advance orders for the record were guaranteeing a chart entry.

The Specials continued gigging constantly through May and June, including a pair of tumultuous shows, a fortnight apart, where they shared the Nashville stage with Madness. At the first, the demand for admission was so great that there were as many people standing outside while the groups played, as there were sweating their socks off in the pressure-cooker within; for the second, the Nashville took the almost unprecedented step of restricting admission to ticket-holders only – and still the North End Road seethed with several locked-out hundreds: black, white, Punk, Skin, Walt Jabasco Rude Boys and – turning out in ever-increasing numbers every time the Specials played – a peculiar new breed of parka-clad, scooter-riding youths who looked like nothing so much as a bunch of Mods. Which is exactly what they were.

CHAPTER EIGHT

For a couple of months now, it had become impossible to ignore the emergence of a clutch of combos who, without any self-conscious reference to the Specials or Madness or 2-Tone itself, were nevertheless sliding into the same stylistic arena, adopting similar clothes, espousing similar sentiments and pillaging similar pasts: the Purple Hearts, Secret Affair, Back To Zero, the Chords, the Scooters, Squire, the Small Hours, the Merton Parkas and, leading the way for all of them, the Acest Faces in the entire Modern Mod pack, the Jam.

The chronological alignment of a fully-formed Mod Renewal (briefly, it was considered exceedingly coarse to use the benighted term 'revival') and the incipient 2-Tone explosion is not one that can easily be explained.

True, the press had long been amusing itself by terming the Jam a Mod band – as far back as late 1976, while the trio still plyed the London pub scene, their love of old Motown, Who and Small Faces records nailed them ineffably to the old Modernist banner. But that, in itself, should not have made any difference. In the music press of the day, new movements were being championed on an almost weekly basis, usually by individual journalists who, encountering an unknown sound in some unbecoming basement, promptly declared them the rightful inheritors of some long-forgotten golden age... and themselves, of course, as its discoverer.

But, though the Jam themselves tried to play down the label, they knew that they were onto something and, when summer 1978 brought the news that the Who were about to begin filming their Quadrophenia concept album, suddenly Paul Weller and co's lonesome stance began to make a lot of sense. And, with a rumoured cast list that included Johnny Rotten, Jimmy Pursey and Billy Idol, it had a lot of credibility as well. (A lot more than they'd have had if they'd simply copped to Gary Holton, Toyah Wilcox and Sting, anyway.)

Still, a band and a film do not a lifestyle make, no matter how appealing they might be. No, what really fathered Mod was desperation, the real desperation of a life being scraped from the bottom of the barrel, as Labour's cauldron of hopelessness and failure hissed its last pathetic bubbles; and the even more real desperation of watching that life pass by without having anything to celebrate. For celebration was all that Mod stood for.

Even in its early 60s prime, Mod was a fashion out of time. Strangely ephemeral, delicate, neat and ferociously well-dressed, it was less a cult than it was a way of life, less a rebellion than a complete reassessment of the meaning of Youth.

If the Teds of the 1950s, with their studied Edwardian wardrobes updated to include the street-fighting accoutrements of the atomic age, were the past, Mods were the future. They were the first of the Baby Boomers, conceived in the bloodbath of frenzied post-war fucking, and coming of age just as the boundless possibilities of youth first started encroaching upon the privileges of age.

"It was the first movement that I have ever seen in the history of youth towards unity; towards unity of thought, unity of drive and unity of motive," the Who's Pete Townshend said later, although such thoughts were far from his mind when he first adopted Mod clothing in 1962. "Youth has always got some leader or other, some headman. The headman was Mr Mod. It could be anyone. Any kid, you know, however ugly or fucked up, if he had the right haircut and the right clothes and the right motorbike, he was a Mod. He *was* Mod!"

The Mod bible, if such godless, feckless cynicism as the Mods embodied could have such a thing, was a thin paperback called *Absolute Beginners*, written by a 55-year-old novelist named Colin MacInnes, and published at the dawn of the Age of Mods in 1959. Early in the tale, the unnamed protagonist (the book is written entirely in the first person) has a conversation with his father about the meaning of youth. 'Dad' was a product of the 1930s, embittered, angry and, most of all, jealous. 'It was a terrible time for the young,' he'd complain. 'Nobody would listen to you if you were less than 30, nobody gave you money whatever you did for it, nobody let you live like you kids can do today.'

Nobody let you live like you do today. For the first time, youth had money, influence, power. In a few years time, youth might even have the vote, and then they'd make the bastards run. It was a time of boundless opportunity and, in the eyes of the Old, the Tired and the Established, the Satanic antithesis of what Growing Up was meant to be.

"It was fashionable, it was clean, it was groovy," continued Townshend. "You could be a bank clerk, it was acceptable. You got them on your ground. They thought, 'Well, there's a smart young lad'." But it was a double-edged sword. "We made the establishment uptight, we made our parents uptight, and our employers uptight because, although they didn't like the way we dressed, they couldn't accuse us of not being smart. We had short hair and were clean and tidy."

Today, Mod can be described only in the most superficial terms, the hyperbolic phrases which the English media, always ready to turn incandescence into intransigence, slapped onto it the moment the first breath of action filtered down Fleet Street. Most of those remarks today revolve around the music, the sounds of the early Who, Kinks and Small Faces, the devotion to Northern Soul, the love of Ska. Prince Buster remembered how, the first time he flew to the UK in 1964, he arrived in London with newspaper and television reports of the 1958 Notting Hill riots still burning in his mind. Six long years may have passed since that time, but memories are longer: Buster hit Britain convinced that he was walking into a powderkeg of prejudice. He certainly didn't expect to see any white faces in his audience.

Instead, he was blown away by his reception. "There was this same bunch of kids at every show. White kids. I first saw them in London, then in Birmingham, Manchester, Nottingham." He visited the Ram Jam Club in Brixton, and received a hero's welcome. He went to the Marquee and the cheers drowned out the P.A. "Everywhere I went, [white kids] would go and make sure everything was alright, and would be around me like my bodyguards. They'd ride along all around my car on their scooters like I was royalty." Prince Buster had met the Mods.

Much of what Mod represented, the almost sexual explosion of liberty and equality, that were the bedrock of the movement, is so completely taken for granted today that entire generations have passed knowing nothing but the freedoms which, at the dawn of the Sixties, were still something to be secretively snatched and stashed away, to be celebrated only in the company of your fellows.

Mods spent their money, the limitless, boundless, sums of money which had suddenly dropped into the laps of the working class kid, on the things that money alone could buy. Looking good, looking sharp, a bottomless wardrobe of the latest street fashions. "They used to change their clothes maybe four times each day," laughed journalist Nik Cohn. "It was... dedicated stuff. If you got caught in last night's sweater, you were finished, you were dead."

Townshend continued, "To be a Mod, you had to have short hair, money enough to buy a real smart suit, good shoes, good shirts. You had to be able to dance like a madman. You had to be in possession of plenty of pills all the time, and always be pilled up. You had to have a scooter covered in lamps.

You had to have like an army anorak to wear on the scooter.

"It was an army, a powerful, aggressive army of teenagers with transport. Man, with these scooters and their way of dressing. A scooter was a big status symbol. [And] you could get all the equipment at the local store; you get the haircut at the barbers; there was nothing special. You just needed a job in order to get into the stuff and that was the only equipment you needed. It was an incredible youthful drive. It really affected me in an incredible way because it teases me all the time because whenever I think, 'Oh, you know, youth today is never gonna make it,' I just think of that fucking gesture that happened in England. It was the closest to patriotism that I've ever felt."

By 1979, of course, jobs and money weren't quite so plentiful. Neither was this generation's figurehead anywhere near as indulgent as Pete Townshend had been, when he reflected on all that he had wrought. "[The Mod revival] was a little saddening and cheapening for the kids involved," the Jam's Paul Weller sniffed. "It just seemed so desperate, these young working class kids trying their best to dress up and look the part while all around their environment was crumbling." But Weller – as one would expect from a man who, by his own admission, had yet to read *Absolute Beginners* – was wrong. The Mod Revival may not have been half as dedicated as its 60s forebear. But it was no less proud.

A going concern since 1974, the Jam had always drawn from the inspirations of the pop-art Who and same-period Motown. What made them unusual, as 1976-77 came around, was the energy with which they transfused those inspirations, a savagery that translated seamlessly into the prevalent mood of the early Pistols and Clash. Setting foot on their first London stages at the same time as the rest of the Punk crew, then, inevitably lumped the Woking three-piece into the entire explosion as it happened. Weller's refusal simply to bask in the New Wave spotlight, however, set the Jam up for a seemingly endless series of acrimonious incidents, ranging from a bad-tempered UK tour with the Clash through to the near-treasonous torching of the Punk zine *Sniffin' Glue*, after editor Mark Perry had the temerity to publish a bad review of the trio.

Weller waded into every controversy he could find. He talked of the importance of "the kids" and "the street" but, when questioned about his personal politics in 1977, announced that he'd be voting Conservative at the next election. While the Jam's audience turned out in Punk's *de rigueur* bondage strides and bin-liners, the Jam took the stage in Beatleboots and mohair suits.

The Jam looked good, but they were to blaze only briefly. Their first single, a musical and titular tribute to the Who's 'In The City', cracked the Top 40; an album of the same name went 20 places better. All-but note-for-note identical to its predecessor, their next single 'All Around The World' climbed to #13 in November 1977. But the group's second album *This Is The Modern World* faltered badly. When their label, Polydor, halted work on their proposed follow-up in early 1978, the Jam's 15 minutes seemed well-and-truly up.

Perhaps surprisingly, Polydor did not drop the trio; rather, they demanded a total rethink of the Jam's direction (or lack thereof); a criticism with which Weller found himself in full accord. So anxious had he been to maintain the Jam's first flush of success that he had allowed his own instincts and judgement to become wholly subverted by what he assumed were the audience's expectations, forgetting that there are few faster paths to oblivion than blind obedience to perceived fan loyalties. Drawing back from all that the abandoned third album had portended, Weller redirected the group's energies towards the third strand of his own personal iconography, the oh-so-English imagery of the mid-late-60s Kinks.

'David Watts', a cut from that act's 1967 *Something Else* album, served notice of his intentions, and restored the Jam to the upper echelons of the chart. 'Down In The Tube Station At Midnight', a foreboding epic littered with both real and imaginary Cockney-style slang (has anyone else *ever* described an Underground ticket as a "plum"?), confirmed their status. Finally, the Jam's third album *All Mod Cons* arrived in November 1978. Its punning title and stark cover showed group and audience alike a new direction – one that Weller himself would disavow as ferociously as he had denounced Punk, but in which he could not help but take secret pride. With a lightning enthusiasm that remains staggering, hundreds (maybe thousands: no one ever counted) of kids suddenly discarded whichever fashionable fancies they had previously marched around in and submerged themselves in Mod culture.

For some, it was enough simply to pick up a Parka and sew a Union Jack to it. For others, however, Mod was to become as fiery a fanaticism as any youth fad of the age. The same stores that the Specials and Madness had already picked over in search of their own gear were now descended upon and picked bare. Scooters, those most gleaming of all original Mod artefacts, were rescued from the mothballs of the past 13 years and diligently embellished in the image of their mid-60s forebears, a sea of aerials, mirrors and sharp angular symbols. Drop by the Barge Aground pub in Barking or the Bridgehouse in Canning Town any night of the week and you'd see them lined up in the car park, serried ranks of gleaming silver dream machines, polished to perfection and attracting admiring gasps and glances from every footsore Mod who passed.

There was an audience. There were venues. Inevitably, there had to be bands.

The Jam notwithstanding, the first and finest of all the Mod groups was the

Jolt, a punchy Glaswegian trio that had in existed in the Jam's stylistic shadow since their own 1977 debut single, 'All I Can Do'. Formed by drumming journalist Iain Shedden, guitarist Robert Collins and bassist Jim Doak, the Jolt (like the Jam) started life punching out hard-edged R&B covers, before the first shards of Punk provoked them, as Collins mused, "to move our ideas into the '70s."

With a local following so strong that even the London inkies described them as Scotland's #1 Punk combo (ahead of both the Rezillos and Johnny & the Self-Abusers), the Jolt headed south in summer 1977, little more than three months after making their live debut at the Burns' Howff in Glasgow. Now they were opening at the Marquee and the Nashville for every headliner that mattered. Although 'All I Can Do' didn't do much business, Polydor never lost faith, watching and applauding as the Jolt began delving into the same '60s Mod sources that *All Mod Cons* would soon be espousing, and getting there a shade quicker than the Jam, too; indeed, Weller himself was so enamoured with the group that he allowed them first crack at his own 'See Saw', for inclusion on the Jolt's *Maybe Tonight* EP in May 1979.

Romford's Purple Hearts followed the Jolt to Mod prominence. Once known as Jack Plug and the Sockets, in which form they occasionally supported the Buzzcocks among sundry Punk others, Simon Stebbing, Jess Shadbolt, Gary Sparks and Bob Manton renamed themselves for one of the the Mod amphetamines of choice, and were already gigging regularly by summer 1978.

Further bands flooded into prominence. The Chords had been playing choppy Motown covers around south-east London since early 1977; while the Wimbledon-area Merton Parkas had been together since 1974, albeit as a distinctly pub R&B flavoured combo called the Sneekers, before throwing themselves wholeheartedly into a world of windmilling guitar chords, 'Green Onion' keyboards and effervescent Stax and Motown covers.

And then there was Secret Affair, the band formed by vocalist Ian Page after catching his own first glimpse of the Jam when his last group, the power-popping New Hearts, opened some shows for them. Taking guitarist Dave Cairns with him, Page quit the New Hearts in spring 1978 soon after they were dropped by CBS and pieced together a new group from the small ads: bassist Dennis Smith arrived from power pop hopefuls Advertising, drummer Seb Shelton was from the Young Bucks.

Preparing to make their live debut at Reading University, opening for the Jam (who else?), Secret Affair had no concept at all of the burgeoning Mod movement when Page first sighted the tribe at the gig itself – and, he said, was elected their leader on the spot. "There were Mods there and they liked us. They said, 'Look, we're Mods, there's quite a lot of us and what we're really looking for – I mean, we love the Jam – but we're looking for a band of our own. Because they're famous already. What we want is a band that's part of us'."

Investigating this newfound phenomenon, Page made his way to the Barge Aground, "and there it was. A sea of suits and parkas and hairstyles. Fuckin' blew me out."

The feeling was, apparently, mutual. Over the next few months, every Secret Affair gig became a celebration of Mod as the singer, clocking the Jam's reluctance to don the crown for themselves, set about foisting his own new band to the peak of the pile on the strength of his verbiage alone. It worked as well. The Jolt, the Chords, the Purple Hearts, the Merton Parkas, all slipped back in the slipstream of Secret Affair's precipitous ascent and, maybe for a moment there, the group looked absolutely invulnerable. "The Secret Affair take it farther than the Jam," Page told *Melody Maker*. "They were a Mod band working in Punk, and their audience was Punk." Secret Affair, on the other hand, were a Mod band working in Mod, and their audience was... Glory Boys!

Fearful of the retro connotations of the Mod label, Page dreamed of renaming the entire movement. It never caught on; indeed, outside of the kernel of Mod itself, few outsiders viewed Secret Affair as much more than a smartly outfitted bandwagon-jumper – *if* they were lucky. Paul Weller certainly wasn't impressed. Page, he quipped, was "a prat, a once-failed Punk star who then tried his hand at Mod, told the lads that Punk was dead and had never lived up to its promises anyway, and the only way to win in the rat race was by joining the bastards in their own game! What? It was the complete antithesis of the original '60s Mod movement. *They* didn't want to join in anyone's fucking game, they played their own and made their own rules. If you didn't like it you could f-f-f-fade away!"

Such condemnations fell on deaf ears, however. Fuck the critics, fuck the oldies, fuck the world." If Punk was a question, then Mod is an answer," Page growled. "And some people don't like the answer." On the dancefloor at his pointy-shoed feet, the answering chant was as defiant as it was memorable: 'We are the Mods, we are the Mods, we are, we are, we are the Mods.' By April, 1979, the flood of other groups arising in the name of Mod was so pronounced that wily promoters were already lumping them together on the evening's bill, with an eye not only for a burgeoning scene, but also an awareness of the movement's iconography.

Historically the inspiration for seaside battles between rival gangs of Mods and Rockers, the first of the Bank Holidays that loomed so large in the calendar of the original Mod movement was just around the corner – the Monday following the General Election, in fact.

For the majority of young Mods, of course, a running ruck on Brighton prom probably wasn't practical, but both the Music Machine and, deep in Canning Town, landlord Terry Murphy's Bridgehouse pub served up the next best thing, multi-band Mayday festivals that between them brought together no less than 10 of the movement's finest. The only dilemma facing their audience was: which of the two shows to attend?

Not every participant was grateful for the attention that Mod brought, of course. Dexy's Midnight Runners, in particular, bucked furiously against every attempt to label them, and that despite there not seeming an uncalculated bone in their body. Their stage clothes and their own stated influences were pilfered directly from the Mod era; their finest number, 'Geno', was an unabashed tribute to 60s soul man and one-time Mod hero Geno Washington; even their name was a blatant reference back to the original heyday – Dexy's abbreviated another Mod speedball, Dexedrine. Dexy's was formed by the fiercely opinionated Kevin Rowland and a latter-day member of his Punk-era Killjoys, guitarist Al Archer, in July 1978. Rowland, by his own confession, was a disturbed young man. "I'd had a difficult childhood. I was bullied at school quite badly and I wasn't a tough kid. Then, a bit later, I started getting into trouble." By the time he left school, he'd been to court four times and "through my late teens and into my 20s, my life was fucking chaos. A lot of drinking and a lot of fighting. From time to time, I'd get a decent job. But I'd always fuck it up. I thought I was a loser, but I couldn't work out how to change. I was just charging through life, trying to hide the fact that I felt like shit inside. I know I would have ended up in jail if it wasn't for my music career. I was on a suspended sentence for violence by the time Dexys got big."

Distinctly second-rate in the scheme of all-things Punk, the Killjoys were coming to an end when Rowland first began scheming what became Dexy's – a soul mob that clashed the energies of Punk with the anger that he'd always detected in the best black music. It would be many years (and a spell in rehab) before he was prepared to admit that, while a lot of planning went into the band, there was a lot of accidental luck as well. "I'd told the rest of the band we were going to make it. But I didn't know for sure. When we did start to do well, I'd be asking myself, 'What the fuck do we do now?' Everyone thought I was this super confident bloke who knew exactly what he was doing. But it wasn't like that at all. I felt way out of my depth and I was afraid I was going to be found out and exposed as a fraud. That was the root cause of a lot of my bizarre behaviour in the music business."

Building around a nucleus of Pete Saunders (keyboards), Pete Williams (bass) and Bobby Junior (drums), plus a brass section comprising Jimmy Patterson, JB Blyte and Steve Spooner, Dexy's originally concentrated their attentions on their native Midlands. They shifted down to London in April 1979, embarking upon the same circuit of pubs and clubs as the rest of the crew – the night before the Specials headlined the Music Machine in late April, Dexy's trod the same boards, opening for Toyah.

Their path physically crossed with the Specials shortly after, although the musical and cultural connotations had already been drawn. As Dammers began piecing together the roster for what was inevitably being touted as the first-ever gathering of the 2-Tone tribes, a mini-festival to be staged at the re-opening of the Electric Ballroom in Camden Town at the end of July, Dexy's were second only to Madness on his shortlist of special guests.

Madness themselves were celebrating becoming the first-ever signing to 2-Tone. Produced by former Deaf School mainstay Clive Langer, their debut single 'The Prince' (the group's tribute to Buster, of course) was already scheduled for release in early August, just weeks after the 2-Tone festival; at the other end of the bill, meanwhle, Neol Davies' long-gestating The Selecter, were finally preparing to step out in their own magnificent right.

Response to 'The Selecter', the self-titled B-side to 'Gangsters', had been almost as strong as the reaction to 'Gangsters' itself – making it a hard act to follow, all the more so since John Bradbury's absorption into the Specials effectively removed him from consideration in any future plans that Davies might have had for his Transposed Men. Other members, too departed, as Steve Vaughan began rehearsing a new band, the Swinging Cats; as Kevin Harrison moved onto the Urge; and as Desmond Brown linked with Charley Bembridge, Compton Amanor, Charley Anderson and Arthur Henderson (themselves gigging regularly as the Reggae act Hardtop 22) to form a brand new group. But Davies wouldn't remain on the sidelines long.

A friend, Lawton Brown, had recently discovered a black female singer named Pauline Vickers, performing in a local folk club. With a presence that clashed the forcefulness of a young Mick Jagger with the sensitivity of Joan Armatrading, she astonished him – and continued to do so, after the pair began writing together.

One evening, the pair were rehearsing at the Wheatsheaf on Foleshill Road, when Lynval Golding turned up to listen. Vickers recalled, "he must have liked what he heard, because I was invited round to Charley Anderson's house in Hillfields, to meet Neol Davies." The Selecter – Anderson's entire band, plus Davies and Black – was formed that same summer evening.

A hospital radiographer and former biochemistry student at Lanchester Poly, Vickers – or Pauline Black as she soon started calling herself – was, indeed, a revelation. Born of a Nigerian father and a half-English mother, she was adopted by a white family and passed most of her childhood without a single friend of her own colour. "I didn't know any black people at all. Both my parents were white and all my brothers were. Everyone I ever related to was white."

Then, around the time she left school, she noticed people's attitudes towards her changing. "People stopped patting me on the head and saying 'What a nice little black girl with pink ribbons in her hair!' – because my mother liked pink ribbons, made me look a right prat." Suddenly, she told *Melody Maker*, people were seeing her "as a black mini-woman, who's supposed to have opinions of her own. Then all the prejudice comes flooding in, which people never show to black kids. Then the problems started."

So, however, did her liberation. Punk had shattered the pop mainstream's suspicion that female rockers as something somehow novelty-laden, all tits and tonsils, if you will. The days when *The Sun* could get away with publishing two-page guides to 'the saucy girl singers taking over the charts' or Chrysalis could advertise the latest Blondie single by asking 'wouldn't you like to rip her to shreds?' were over. But anybody searching for a sexual, racial and musical role model for Black would find themselves struggling. X-Ray Spex's Poly Styrene alone led the charge of young black girls into the enlightened world of post-Punk Britain, but her band's cacophonous mix of keening vocal, honking sax and an unhealthy obsession with healthy living was already nearing the end of its useful life. So Black wrote the blueprint herself.

Taking over a room at the Golden Cup pub, the seven-piece Selecter began working up a repertoire to blend, as Davies himself acknowledged, into the seamless vision that 2-Tone espoused. His own original material, songs like 'Missing Words', 'Too Much Pressure' and the prophetically caustic 'Three Minute Hero', was rearranged. Covers, ranging from Justin Hinds' 'Carry Go Bring Come' to John Barry's *James Bond* theme, were restructured. The Selecter finally made their live debut in Gloucester in early June.

It was dreadful. "We were all over the place," Black admits. "The sound system was appalling and we all needed some serious re-styling." Only her name-change would remain the same; by the time the Selecter were ready to appear in public again, the band had completely redesigned its appearance to match its music, sliding straight into heart of the Specials' own Rude Boy translation.

The Selecter made their live reappearance as the Specials' opening act at Leeds' f-club a few weeks later. Further low-key gigs followed, but steadfastly the band steered clear of the capital. The 2-Tone festival would mark the Selecter's London debut.

Dexy's, in the end, didn't play the Electric Ballroom, although they were prominently featured in the pre-show advertisements. But the gig went on without them and, afterwards, nobody even seemed to have noticed their absence. The converted cinema greeted each performer as a conquering hero – as though the Selecter were anything but a stageful of nervous provincials playing their first-ever capital show. Madness were far, far more than a bunch of local lads making good; as though the Specials… well, the Specials were special, and their performance proved that.

Looking out over the seething, sweating sardined bodies, the idea that three groups, with only one single between them, could enthral a packed, 3,000-capacity venue in the heart of London was more than Dammers had ever imagined. So, in fact, was the imminent fate of that single. Entering the UK chart at the end of July, 'Gangsters' commenced a three-month residency that peaked at #6 in September, with the Specials rubbing noses with the likes of Cliff Richard, Roxy Music and Earth Wind and Fire. But Terry Hall, at least, knew his feet were never going to leave the ground.

"I remember going on *Top Of The Pops* when I was about 19 and just shittin' myself. Try smiling when you're gonna fall over 'cos you don't know where you are… it was never my intention to be Sheena Easton."

CHAPTER NINE

The queues had formed, the tickets were bought, the popcorn was popping. On August 16 1979, the most hotly anticipated rock movie of the year was premiered in Leicester Square. Almost exactly one year to the day after the first casting call, *Quadrophenia* was about to hit the screen.

"The story is set," Roger Daltrey used to proclaim from the stage, "on a rock... in the middle of a stormy sea."

Quadrophenia was Pete Townshend's masterpiece. Other Who albums have better songs, some have stronger performances, a few pack more dynamic music. Indeed, of all the Who's albums – or, at least, those which any right-minded aficionado would consider their best – *Quadrophenia* remains the most misunderstood and, in a way, the most misrepresented. *Tommy* had its detractors, but it became such a monster that objections were lost. *The Who Sell Out* was barely conceived, but everyone loves it regardless. And *Who's Next* has become a law unto itself, a lumbering leviathan which almost single-handedly, and certainly unintentionally, rewrote the hard rock rules for the next half a decade.

Quadrophenia, though, never had it easy. Even at the time of its release, in late 1973, no album in the band's repertoire thus far had proven so divisive as Pete Townshend's manifesto for the disaffected youth of a decade past. Who biographer Dave Marsh hated it and never missed the opportunity to say why, while Townshend himself came close to clipping five minutes off the original double album to fit the whole thing onto its first CD reissue. Common sense ultimately prevailed, praise be, but the fact that he even willing to consider such desecration speaks volumes for his own uncertainty.

There again, one Mod's struggle to find some meaning to his life probably isn't the most appetizing synopsis of a rock'n'roll album and, of course, passing time has rendered pretty much everything Pete Townshend says into a load of old tosh. 'Coming soon, *Tommy,* the Toothbrush.'

But *Quadrophenia* never threatened to go the way of its deaf, dumb and so-bland predecessor because, concept album though it may be, the concept is the concept itself. Running the gamut of musical moods for which the Who became famous, from pounding semi-metal ('The Punk & The Godfather') to impassioned balladeering (the closing 'Love Reign O'er Me'), from 50s-style rock'n'roll ('5.15') to almost folky jig-a-jigging ('The Rock'), *Quadrophenia* was not only the last significant album of The Who's own career, it was conceivably also the first significant album of the late 1970s, and that despite being released a full three years before even the Sex Pistols had heard of Punk Rock.

Whether any of the young Punks (Paul Weller notwithstanding) even listened to it is immaterial: *Quadrophenia* tapped into the hearts of a youth movement which was still wearing short trousers when its own storyline first unfolded, but the quest for individuality at the same time as the search for acceptance was a story they could all understand. For a few long summer months, culture turned the clock back 15 years and *Quadrophenia* became reality.

Director Francis Roddam's movie version of *Quadrophenia* was originally conceived in 1977, when the Who's newly-appointed manager, Bill Curbishley, entered into negotiations with Polytel, the film wing of their UK label Polygram over financing. Roddam, the Who's own unanimous choice for director, had never made a feature film before but his BBC television play *Dummy* – the story of a deaf, teenage prostitute – had made a major impression on the Who, not least for its mischievous play on the title of their own sensorially impaired little whore.

Unlike Ken Russell's overloaded cinematic take on *Tommy*, the movie version of *Quadrophenia* was never conceived as a vehicle for the Who themselves; indeed, the principle roles in the movie were spread amongst a largely untried cast. Initial attempts to recruit Sex Pistol Johnny Rotten for the lead role of Jimmy having fallen through, Roddam turned instead to Phil Daniels, a cocky young Cockney actor who was scarcely out of drama school. Actress Lesley Ash played his (sometime) girlfriend. The only musical star in sight was Sting, leader of the then-still largely unknown Police, who took the role of the Ace Face. (The better known Billy Idol was originally considered for the role and, both on screen and in person, the peroxide blonde Sting could have been mistaken for a very bad, and considerably older, Billy impersonator. One wonders if he knew that?)

Although they were not to be involved in the movie itself, however, *Quadrophenia* dominated the Who's thoughts. In January 1979, when they finally announced the successor to the recently deceased Keith Moon, new boy Kenney Jones could scarcely have been more appropriate – in the mid-

1960s, his own band, the Small Faces, were the Who's greatest Mod rivals; a decade later, they remained among the new Mods' greatest heroes.

In the meantime, the Who worked on the movie's soundtrack, rerecording and/or remixing three songs that Townshend had dropped from the original 1973 album ('Get Out And Stay Out', 'Four Faces' and 'Joker James'), plus another ten tracks from the LP itself. The embellishments were seldom more than cursory, but still the result was a fabulous soundtrack to a marvellous movie, both as true to the album which spawned them as to the era which inspired it.

Dave Marsh, perhaps inevitably, would subsequently complain that Roddam "got much of the period detail wrong," and he was indeed correct. You know that tube train crossing over Shepherds Bush market? 1973 rolling stock. That Who album on the table at the party? Wasn't issued for another decade. That scene where Jimmy watches the Who on Ready Steady Go… they're still plugging their second single, but he's already got hold of their third. And so on.

But Quadrophenia is not a movie about period detail; it is about youth, it is about action, it is about excitement, it is about discovery; and even Marsh eventually had to concede that Quadrophenia "was exciting in just the way Tommy hadn't been – the script even made sense of the plot." Long-time Who associate and biographer Richard Barnes described it as "one of the most realistic and entertaining films about adolescence ever to come from the British film industry," while more recent commentators acknowledge that it would take 15 years before another British movie, *Trainspotting*, produced such a dramatic, and lifestyle-defining, impact as *Quadrophenia*.

It didn't do badly at the box office, either. Playing to packed theatres from the moment it opened, *Quadrophenia* became one of the year's biggest-grossing films. Even if (as cynics subsequently alleged) its audience largely comprised parka-clad serial viewers, its impact upon the musical landscape of summer 1979 was such that, by the end of the season, the storm of record company interest that had descended upon the Specials a mere three-or-four months earlier was little more than a squall by comparison. When the Specials were up for grabs, it was very much a case of winner gets all. But there was enough Mod bands for everyone.

Arista, one of the labels who had choked on the Specials' 2-Tone dream, now forgot their original hesitation and gifted Secret Affair with their own label imprint, I Spy. Squire quickly joined them there. The Merton Parkas went to Beggars Banquet, the Purple Hearts to Fiction – and what jolly labelmates for the Cure they made. Polydor snagged the Chords as company for the Jolt and the Jam, while Elton John's Rocket picked up the Lewes-based Lambrettas, who revealed their own enthusiasm for all things 2-Tone affair when their second single, a Ska-fied cover of the Coasters' 'Poison Ivy', was released on the 2-Stroke label, complete with a Parka-clad pastiche of Walt Jabasco.

There was no shortage of chart success, either. Two weeks before *Quadrophenia* opened, the Merton Parkas' anthemic 'You Need Wheels' was whizzing towards the Top 40; a month later, Secret Affair's 'Time For Action' – its coda a ferocious chant of "we are the Mods" – was rocketing towards #13, overtaking both Madness' 'The Prince' and, incredibly, the Jam's 'When You're Young.'

Sounds was sufficiently enthralled to devote four pages of newsprint to Gary Bushell's enthusiastic précis of the new Mods' 'story so far,' while the Bridgehouse pub's pre-eminence as the spiritual home of the entire Mod movement was already under serious threat from the Wellington in Waterloo, and the absolutely unequivocally-named Vespas Global Village, beneath Charing Cross station.

Indications that the Mod scene was very much running before it could walk were not, however, slow in making themselves felt. Again in August, Secret Affair, the Purple Hearts and Back To Zero launched the movement's first nationwide push, the sensibly-titled March Of The Mods tour. Unfortunately, neither they nor, it seemed, their audience and promoters, had even considered that, for every musical action, there is an equal and opposite reaction. To many people, the very mention of Mods was synonymous with just one thing: the Rockers, with whom the original 60s tribe had fought such tremendous battles on the seafronts of Bank Holiday Britain.

Rockers, of course, were long dead, but other groups had risen to take their place in the tangled lexicon of tribal loyalties – not least the Skinheads. No matter that any attempt to retell the twisted saga of British youth cults invariably traced the Skins' genesis back to a final transmutation of the original Mods, the notion that there was a new gang in town was not one that could be allowed to pass unremarked.

As the March of the Mods wound its way around the country, several shows were at least loosely disrupted by gangs of local Skins come to check out the competition – and express their disgust. It was when the tour returned to London on August 26, however, that the true time for action dawned.

For weeks beforehand, rumours had been circulating that an almighty row was about to go down in Brighton over the August Bank Holiday, with most antagonists intending to hit the beach on the Monday – the day, with exquisite bad timing on the Mod Marchers' part, following the tour's London climax. Neither was that the only mistake that hindsight would be able to draw out of the affair. In a gesture of genuine musical solidarity, both

Madness and The Selecter had been invited to appear at the London show – a certain draw, of course, for the Skinheads who had long since adopted the 2-Tone stride.

The best one could say about the ensuing confrontation was that it could have been worse. The worst thing was that it would be the following day – at the seaside, of course, as Brighton, Margate and Scarborough all suffered disturbances, but in London, too, where rival gangs clashed on the same Kings Road pavements that, just two years earlier, had seen the Punks and Teddy Boys letting off steam.

Apart from one of the era's all-time classic *NME* front covers (MODS! BANK HOLIDAY BATTLES!), the clashes made surprisingly few headlines. Indeed, that entire summer following the General Election was marked by an almost preternatural calm, as though the entire country, people and government alike, was simply marking time, waiting for the first great 'crisis' to emerge. Of course, the usual statistics continued to mount – petrol, bread, gas and electricity had all gone up, unemployment was still rising, and there was a bucketful of legislation pending that was certain to cause some future furore. For now, though, while summer – not a bad one, either – blazed into autumn, the party continued.

Brighton became the focus of attention again on October 19 although not, on this occasion, for the same wrong reasons. With an iconographical symbolism that one sincerely hopes was not accidental, Brighton was elected host for the opening night on what was already guaranteed to prove the sell-out tour of the season, the Specials' first full nationwide outing.

A close to two-month-long extravaganza that sought to replicate the frenzy of the Electric Ballroom festival on stages throughout the country, the tour even repeated the scheduled billing, as Madness and the Selecter both joined the Specials on the bill, and Dexy's Midnight Runners waited in the wings, to slip onto the itinerary when Madness slipped away for a low-key trip to America.

Surveying the line-up, the Selecter's Charlie Andrews could scarcely control his enthusiasm. "What we're aiming for is a family of music, the Coventry Stax if you like. That is what 2 Tone is all about. We're not aiming for competition. We're not going out to say that The Selecter are trying to run off the Specials, or that Madness aren't as good... It's a matter of trying to present each band at its best."

"[It was] was fantastic," Madness' Chas Smyth told the *Ska/Punk* webzine two decades later. "The Specials seemed to be a bit more Punky and harder, but I think really a lot of it was driven by Jerry Dammers. He was the political mind. His father was a Liberation Theologist priest, so I think he came from quite a radical background, in that sense. And Selecter was more of a good-time band, dance-wise, but they were pretty crazy in their own way, too. The keyboard player was a schizophrenic, tried to bite someone's ear off once. They had a fantastic start, but it was really something special, the Two Tone thing. It was great, the multicultural thing was a big deal for us, we felt we were part of a wave, you know. It was dance, it was good time, its ideals were honourable and progressive, pretty cool. Its camaraderie was strong, too, being on the coach, the three bands increased your chances of being played, the big boomers, a lot of fun."

It was not always easy, however, to remember that. "It was kinda heavy... a vibe in the air," Smyth continued. "It was like it was an antidote to Punk almost. Maybe the opposite to Punk at the time, and gigs were Punks, Skinheads, Teds. In hindsight, it was quite good, really, cause if you can get through that, you can get through anything. Three thousand skinheads baying for blood at a concert. It's like, wow! Difficult times in the sense of the audience being a bit over the top."

The Specials' sets were now almost habitually the cue for some form of stage invasion and, as Neville Staples laughs, "things just happened." A lot of what was described, at the time, as the Specials' personal chaotic charm was, in fact, the result of playing entire gigs on tenterhooks of one sort or another. Staples continues, "we never knew when we were going to have a stage invasion, we never knew when I was going to go mad and run across the stage, we never know when the whole stage is going to be full of people. Things just happened, and we worked with the vibe. If we had to stop a song and then start again we would... But the stage invasions were something else. It got to the stage where you just stood your ground while they came on, stay where you are and sing."

Neither could the musicians be certain that every kid who wanted to join them onstage was simply pursuing innocent fun. On October 12, the week before the 2-Tone tour kicked off, Madness headlined the Electric Ballroom in their own right, joined on the bill by the latest new entry into the 2-Tone stakes, Bad Manners. Sandwiched between the two was a new Liverpool quartet called Echo and the Bunnymen.

It was, of course, the mismatch of the month. The Skinhead hordes who turned out for Madness, but were delighted to find Bad Manners there as well, had absolutely no patience whatsoever for the Bunnymens' delicate mood-melding posturing, and made damned certain that the group knew it. Long before the end of their set, the Bunnymen had been howled, hooted and – and this was where Madness' following began to grow decidedly disquieting – 'Sieg Heil'-ed off the stage. Although the headliners at least tried to coax the crowd into giving the newcomers a chance, there was no way back.

No matter that the National Front itself was, if not dead, at least tearing itself to shreds in the aftermath of its election wipe-out. Even if there was only a handful of cropheads chanting Nazi-style slogans from the back of the hall (and many of them were only doing it because they knew it provoked an entertaining reaction), it did not take much imagination whatsoever to transform a bunch of yobs clustered round the bogs into a full-blown Nuremberg rally.

"Don't rock with the Sieg-Heilers!" bellowed London's *Evening News*, when its attention was drawn events at the Madness show (not to mention several other, less high-profile events). The article stopped just short of proposing a full-time boycott of the 2-Tone crew, but still anyone meeting the bands for the first time through that story would have had little alternative but to view them as an evil, fascist scourge. And even an accompanying photograph of the Selecter – six blacks, one white – struggled to contract that.

Neither were the musicians' own protests paid any heed. "If we wanted to talk about politics, we'd have formed a debating society," growled Suggs – perhaps a little naively, given the content of other bands' material at that time, but still he had a point. Of all the groups to tar with any kind of racist/Nazi brush, there were a lot more realistic targets around than two multi-racial line-ups and a bunch of Buster Keatons.

No matter. For, with the genie having finally left the bottle, other fangs were now being bared. Suddenly, Rock Against Racism was wondering aloud why the 2-Tone crowd were not a lot more active within their organization than they already were. Journalists who once viewed 2-Tone as the antidote to so many societal ills were now asking whether it was not, in fact, encouraging them. And, with the bands themselves continuing to maintain a stoic (or, more likely, bemused) silence on the subject, so sundry freelance vigilantes took to airing their own displeasure at this apparent acceptance of their audience's Nazi heritage .

Midway through the Hatfield Poly gig on October 27, some three dozen self-proclaimed members of either 'the Hatfield Anti-Nazi League' or 'the Hatfield Mafia' (their placards seemed divided on that point) burst into an adjoining room through one of the fire exits and proceeded to lash out with razors and Stanley Knives. 11 arrests, 10 hospital cases and £1,000 worth of damage later, they were finally ushered out of the building.

The assumption that they were on the prowl for National Front supporters – and figured a gig full of Skinheads was the best place to find them – was an easy one to make, and certainly seems to have been their own defence. Indeed, the Anti-Nazi League later trumpeted this same event as a major triumph – "the Hatfield comrades joined with other ANL supporters to attack the Nazis at the concert. The Nazi Skins were taken by complete surprise as they strutted around the hall. A vicious fight left many injured on both sides, but the Nazis took the worse of it. The Nazis never felt confident enough to turn up at any more 2-Tone concerts."

If only matters had been that simple.

Ugliness erupted elsewhere, and even when it didn't, controversy dogged the tour's footsteps. One hotel manager took one look at his establishment's latest guests and refused to check them in unless they could vouch that they were actually married to the young women accompanying them – fortunately, the first people he asked, Roddy Radiation and one of the Specials' roadies, were in fact with their wives, and that seemed sufficient. But it was not the end of the evening's entertainment. Members of the Madness party were clad in T-shirts pronouncing "Fuck Art, Let's Dance," outfits that simply could not be countenanced in such a swish establishment as this.

But would the offenders remove their shirts? Of course not, and it was a heated debate indeed that finally ended with a compromise that pleased no-one. As long as the group remained on the premises, the 'Fuck' would be concealed beneath a strip of gaffer-tape.

Such encounters were little more than light entertainment, of course, when compared to the true rigours of the tour, the stage invasions and fighting that so dominated the headlines that, as the scheduled date for Madness' departure loomed ever-closer, the rumour mill forgot that the switch with Dexy's had been booked (and announced) back in the summer and insisted that the Nutty Boys were being unceremoniously slung off the bus. Of course they weren't, but their unstinting support for their Skinhead followers, and the ease with which they found forgiveness for even the most violent transgressions amid their audience, was nevertheless garnering the band a most unsavoury reputation. It was an issue they were going to have to study very seriously once they returned from the United States.

Dexy's slid seamlessly into the 2-Tone tour madness, but did so, apparently, from the point of view of strict outsiders. They tolerated the insanity on stage, they studiously avoided the weirdness that blew up off it. Indeed, Jerry Dammers later admitted that his favourite – if not only – memory of Dexy's was, "travelling to a gig with them on the train and watching them go single file through a hedge because they wouldn't pay the fare on principle."

It was only later, after Dammers invited Dexy's to record a single for release on 2-Tone, that he discovered the true roots of their stand-offishness. The group might have been caught up in the Ska/Mod madness, but they had no intention whatsoever of remaining there for one moment longer than was necessary. Already they had scheduled their debut single, 'Dance Stance', for release through Bernie Rhodes' newly-formed independent, Oddball Records. Now Kevin Rowlands was informing all who would listen, "we don't want to become part of anyone else's movement. We'd rather be our own movement."

That moment would come. In April 1980, signed now to EMI's Parlophone imprint, Dexy's latest single, 'Geno', topped the UK chart and the band seemed set to dominate the headlines for ever. Instead they disintegrated. "From the start, I just couldn't handle it," Rowland admitted to *Dazed And Confused* in 1999. "I just freaked out at that point. And the more successful we got, the worse I felt, and I didn't have anyone to talk to. I just never felt comfortable with the pop star thing. I didn't feel good enough. I felt ugly. Also, I was busy acting the rebel, feeling that I was fighting other people's battles. Living out other people's fantasies. There was a part of me that wanted to sabotage the whole thing. So that's what I started to do. Just don't expect me to say I'm proud of the fact."

The legends surrounding Dexy's breakdown are legion. Angered by the music press, they announced that they would give no further interviews. Angered by their recording contract, they tried to kidnap the master tapes for their debut album, *Searching For the Young Soul Rebels* – when producer Pete Wingfield threatened to leap in front of their getaway van, Rowland was heard to ask the driver to accelerate. EMI did eventually double the group's royalty rate. But they also dropped the band and, less than twelve months after they were top of the pops, Dexy's Midnight Runners were at the end of their tether.

The 2-Tone tour was not, of course, conducted in a vacuum – it was timed to coincide with the most concerted blast of recorded music that the movement had yet mustered.

The Selecter finally released their own first single in early October. 'On My Radio' was a bare-faced assault on the anodyne radio programming of the day. Lyrically, of course, it was little more than a reiteration of the points Elvis Costello had made a year earlier with his own 'Radio Radio,' but that in itself was scarcely a topic that one ever tired of hearing. There is, after all, something deliciously satisfying about hearing a DJ play a record that dismisses his trade so brutally, while he seemingly remains oblivious to actual content... delicious, and faintly disturbing. If the DJs weren't actually capable of understanding the records they played, what hope was there of finding more intelligence among their listeners?

'On My Radio' scampered to #8, peaking in the same week as the Specials' second single, a cover of Dandy Livingstone's 'A Message To You (Rudy)' climaxed two places lower, and just seven days before a new Madness 45, 'One Step Beyond', made its debut in the Top 10. Simple chart statistics say little, of course, but there was one moment during this

remarkable run that truly indicated just how thoroughly the 2-Tone sound had taken off. On Thursday, November 8, the Specials, the Selecter and Madness were all among the guests on that evening's *Top Of The Pops.*

Although they would remain indelibly associated with 2-Tone for at least the next year, Madness had, in fact, departed the label while their first single, 'The Prince', was still on the chart. Their arrangement had only ever been for one single, a shop window for their wares that beat the pants off simply mailing out a demo. As it was, not every record label that came in search of their signature seems to have been paying that much attention to begin with – Suggs later complained that "Island Records didn't even know we had 'The Prince' out.... They'd just heard that everyone else was interested in us."

In the end, the competition for the group came down to a three-corner fight between Elton John's Rocket label, the Virgin subsidiary Dindisc, and Stiff Records – the granddaddy of British independent labels and still among the most courageous companies on the map. It was they who prevailed, and promptly proved their worth by rushing 'One Step Beyond' into the shops before 'The Prince' had even left the chart; with supreme timing, as one dropped out of the Top 75, the other moved straight in.

The Specials and Madness had albums imminent as well – an eponymous offering from the Specials, and *One Step Beyond* from the Nutty Boys.

Perfectly synchronized in every way – they even hit the stores in the same week – comparisons between the two LPs were inevitable; indeed, they still are. Both were, perhaps inevitably, little more than straightforward recountings of their makers' current live sets, captured in the studio to varying degrees of success by, respectively, Elvis Costello and Clive Langer. But both were also bold steps forward from acts whose ability to make the same sense in the recording studio as they did in concert had already been questioned more than once.

Today, of course, that is irrelevant. With only a smattering of period live and TV footage to even begin to recapture the sheer intensity (in the Specials' case) and mania (Madness) of the two group's respective shows, the two albums present a vivid snapshot of their makers at, arguably, the

The Tom Robinson Band (l-r Danny Kustow, Robinson, Dolphin Taylor) in full flight at the Nag's Head, High Wycombe, 1977.

The Ruts' Malcolm Owen and John Jennings Rocking Against Racism in 1979 – Stiff Little Fingers and the Leyton Buzzards shared the bill.

The Angelic Upstarts (and friend), backstage at the Marquee in 1979.

Dexy's Midnight Runners – did someone call for a plumber?

The Specials on The Old Grey Whistle Test.

The Specials' audience making as compelling a spectacle as the band.

Jerry Dammers, off duty in Coventry.

The American 12-inch "Ghost Town" label, Walt Jabasco present and correct.

Madness find a two-tone backdrop in Camden, 1979

The Nutty Boys on stage at the Lyceum in February 1980

"Let us grow up, not blow up" – CND marches on London in 1981.

Heading for Brockwell Park, the September 1978 Rock Against Racism carnival.

The Beat in London, 1980.

The Selecter – don't call them gangsters.

The Bodysnatchers at the 101 Club in Clapham, during the 2-Tone 2 tour.

UB40 at Milton Keynes, 1980.

peak of their powers, still excited by the first flush of success, still uncertain as to the directions in which that success might take them, and anxious only to cram in as much of their own exuberance and exhilaration as the grooves could possibly withstand.

The Specials is probably the better of the pair – even if its initial impact was deadened, somewhat, by the appearance of a bootleg recording from the Moonlight in May, that hit the streets just weeks ahead of the album itself. Surreptitiously recorded by simply running a line in from the recording studio next door to the club, a pristine live album could not have arrived at a worse time – as Roddy Radiation admits, "many of the fans felt that the bootleg was better as it contained the true Specials sound."

Nevertheless, the studio album does run it close, both in terms of energy and delivery. Wrapping up songs that dated back to the Automatics' first demos, but breezing through a wealth of more recent compositions as well, the presence of Rico Rodriguez and fellow horn player Dick Cuthel added an ambient authenticity to the proceedings that stilled any purist complaints that the band were messing with music that they didn't understand: Rico played on Dandy Livingstone's original 'A Message To You (Rudy)'. The sound of him reprising that part across the Specials' retake was an absolute thrill.

The choice of Elvis Costello as producer was more contentious. Although it, too, has been borne out by history, there's certainly some room for reservation over his occasionally stinted sound. It was Costello, after all, who famously informed the Specials that they didn't 'need that Punk Rock guitarist' – a clear indication that the group's true musical intent escaped him.

He was, however, perfectly in tune with the Specials' ambitions and ideals – indeed, as far back as his own Fascist-baiting debut single, 'Less Than Zero' ("calling Mr Oswald with his swastika tattoo"), Costello had maintained himself as a niggling thorn in the right wing's juiciest flank, all the more so for the apparent ambiguity of his finest jabs. His 'Goon Squad', 'Night Rally' and, most hysterically of all, the recent 'Oliver's Army' were each singled out by knee-jerk simpletons for lyrics that could (and, especially in the US, frequently were) misconstrued as racist rallying calls.

Costello's ability to withstand those attacks and keep coming back for more was one of the reasons that the Specials chose to work with him. Costello himself intuitively recognised the band as blood-brothers in the making and saw the confrontational even-handedness of Dammers' lyrical stance as a direct relation of his own. Staples explains, "Jobs were terrible, you couldn't get no jobs. Housing prices were shooting up, there was a load of... We were saying something, there was a sense of being. But we weren't trying to change things, we were just saying what we saw. We were in a position to do that. We could sing about it because it was what was happening in the place, and people would hear it and maybe understand it because it was happening to them at the same time."

The album's highlights literally spill out of the grooves: the lilting 'Doesn't Make It Alright', a song that would swiftly be snapped up by Stiff Little Fingers; the multiple choice poser 'It's Up To You'; and the caterwauling 'Nite Klub', with Chrissie Hynde howling among the backing vocals, all rank among the group's finest achievements.

Elsewhere, Neville Staples reprised his onstage toasting role by adopting the character of the draconian Judge Roughneck, for the unabashed Prince Buster tribute 'Stupid Marriage'. Back in '67-'68, Buster had entertained Jamaican record buyers with a series of 45s documenting the dramatic career of Judge Dread, a brutal authoritarian who thought nothing of slapping rude boys into jail for a thousand years at a time, then locking up their defense teams as well. Both musically and personally, Roughneck was a direct descendent of the draconian beak, but his transplant to late 1970s Britain had not phased him in the slightest. In fact, he probably rather enjoyed it.

Buster returns among the covers that illustrate the sheer energy of the group, providing a mini-history of 60s Jamaicana that extends from the Prince's 'Too Hot' to the Maytals' 'Monkey Man', then expands its brief into the heart of Mod territory by walking through Rufus Thomas' 'Do The Dog' (a successor, of course, to his hit 'Walking The Dog'). If history would prove that the Specials' debut album was almost all that they had to give the genre they had rejuvenated, maybe that was all they needed to deliver.

Madness, on the other hand, had still to hit their stride as songwriters, with their own worldview limited to their own pet Buster track, the title song. Of *One Step Beyond*'s other highlights, it is the visible gathering of the band's strengths that most impresses today, as opposed to actual delivery. Their studio attempts to ape their live act often fall embarrassingly flat: a Nuttified take on 'Swan Lake', for example, served no purpose beyond emphasising the slapstick approach that was still the key to Madness' persona.

Yet it was a classic album all the same, the sheer maniacal exuberance of the experience smacking the listener across the head time and again. Between the opening shout and the closing note, there is nothing less than unbridled mayhem, a musical roller coaster that clatters through a house of fun far funnier than any subsequent Madness chartbuster, while jamboree-bag gags, custard pies and itching powder trail out in the band's baggy-trousered wake.

Prince Buster slams into swan-clad ballerinas, while boats on the Nile call 'Chipmunks are Go!' and the sun never set on the 'Land of Hope and Glory'. Who could be so po-faced as not to want to join in? *One Step Beyond* has lost none of its goofy freshness in the years since its birth and for exactly the same reasons as Tommy Trinder and the music hall, the Kinks and the Village Green, the slinky side of swing and the silly side of *Dad's Army* have lost none of theirs. Without calculation or ambitious aforethought, without a thought for Nostalgia, or a pile of old *Beano*s, Madness conjured an idyllic world where the funfair never runs out of candy floss, the law never catches up with Mr Punch, and school is out forever. and, while both albums were successful, it was the happy, hopping, all mad-Madness that proved the *most* successful, climbing to #2 in the UK, while the darker, dourer, *The Specials* peaked at #4.

CHAPTER TEN

As 1979 prepared to meet its maker, Ska (whether expressly nailed to the 2-Tone banner or otherwise) was breaking out all over. Rumour was linking the label with every band or artist who even glanced in the direction of that old syncopated beat. Many – the vast majority, in fact – were doomed to rejection, as Dammers found himself swamped by more soundalike demos than he even had the time to listen to, let alone the patience to play.

Neither were his colleagues any more enamoured. Although Dammers inevitably had the final word on the acts that 2-Tone signed, the remainder of the Specials and all eight of the Selecter were equally involved in the process (as they were in the distribution of profits), and Pauline Black was very quick to complain that the majority of tapes sent into 2-Tone itself were simply clones.

Yet there were some intriguing talents out there. The Walkie Talkies were a Liverpool band whose first single, 'Rich And Nasty', was self-released shortly before Christmas. They were quickly followed into the racks by Diversion, offering up a cracking take on Prince Buster's 'Rough Rider', while the prosaically-named Gangsters even unleashed a Christmas skanker, 'Rudi The Red-Nosed Reindeer'.

But, if there was a growing crop of singles that seemed to be skanking on the 2-Tone bandwagon, the last months of 1979 also saw the release of one whose maker, had he only seen fit, could well have turned that accusation right around. Judge Dread's 'Lover's Rock' was heavy, honking and, naturally, horny. But flip it over and 'Ska Fever' was an electrifying jolt that didn't simply invoke every great rhythm that the Specials and Madness might have taken to heart, it also served as a reminder that, for seven years before the world had heard of Jerry Dammers, Pauline Black and Suggsy, Dread had kept Ska alive for all of them.

Far from the vibrant market that echoed through the end of the 1960s, early-1970s Britain had little time for Jamaican music. There was always a thriving underground, of course, out of which arose occasional hits from the likes of Nicky Thomas, Ken Boothe, John Holt and Susan Cadogan (whose timeless 'Hurts So Good' was first brought to Britain by the Specials' old friend, Pete Waterman). But still the days when any number of specialist labels could turn up any number of instant reggae classics were over and you could count on one finger the number of artists who remained true to the vision and the imagery of the now-receding explosion; who continued to speak to an audience that still wanted to crop its hair and do the moonstomp.

Tall and broad, a devout Ska fan, a Skinhead and a born performer, Alex "Judge Dread" Hughes first entered what one might euphemistically call the music industry at the very lowest end of the scale, as a nightclub bouncer. Ambitions to move into DJ-ing, however, saw him quickly graduate from throwing people out of clubs to making sure they stayed in.

A natural combination of music hall comedian and dancehall toaster, he named himself, of course, after Prince Buster's most legendary creations – a tribute that Hughes justified with a nonchalant shrug.

"Well, a man my size couldn't call himself the Magical Cabbage, could he?" He followed another of Buster's leads, too, by building much of his act around lewdly suggestively translations of innocent children's poems, chants and nursery rhymes, and reiterating rewrites that had been hanging out behind the bike shed for years: "The boy stood on the burning deck, playing a game of cricket; the ball rolled up his trouser leg and stumped his middle wicket."

At other times, he showed a genuine grasp of pointless bathroom humour: "two old ladies sitting in the bath; one blew off and the other one laughed, 'oh look, bubbles!'" But, though he was rude, often smutty and crude, he never overstepped the boundaries that separate simple poor taste from outright obscenity: "Mary had a little lamb, she could not stop it grunting; she took it up the garden path and kicked its little rump in."

Recited to the instrumental 'versions' which appeared on the B-sides of so many Jamaican 45s of the day, Dread's turns at the microphone quickly became as popular as the discs he played through without (much) interruption. By 1971, he was already a regular face at London's Gooseberry Studios, cutting acetates (at £8 a pop) of his most popular toasts for use in his roadshow.

One day early in 1972, Hughes was visiting a friend at Trojan Records, and playing his latest demo, toasted over the instrumental version of Verne and Son's 'Little Boy Blue'. Halfway through, label head Lee Gopthal walked in, listened for a moment, then pronounced, "That's great – is it one of ours?" And when Hughes said no, Gopthal replied, "It is now." 'Big Six', the numeric follow-up to Prince Buster's 'Big Five', was released just weeks later, the first in a sequence of increasingly impressive dimensions that included 'Big Seven', 'Big Eight' and even 'Big Nine' before Dread finally scrapped the tape measure and confessed, simply, to 'Big One'.

All followed the same formula and all were peremptorily banned by the BBC, a knee-jerk reaction that reached its climax (as Dread himself would doubtless smirk) when he released one single, 'Molly', which had nothing naughty in it at all, just to see what would happen. It was still banned. The Judge's name alone was sufficient to strike dread in the corridors of broadcasting power.

But a ban, of course, was like a red rag to the bullish British record-buying public. At the height of the age of Glam Rock, when the likes of Slade, David Bowie, T Rex and the Sweet were breaking records as fast as they could make them, 'Big Six' was a big hit, 'Big Seven' was bigger and, from thereon in, Dread was practically unstoppable. Ten Top 50 hits in under five years is a fabulous record under any circumstances. Ten Top 50 hits without an iota of radio or television support is little short of miraculous.

Beyond the sequence of ever-expanding big ones, the titles tell you all you need to know (or, perhaps, all you'd prefer not to know): a raucous rewrite of the 1975 chart-topper 'Y Viva Espana' found Dread celebrating 'Y Viva Suspenders'; Serge Gainsbourg and Jane Birken's super-seductive 'Je T'aime' was transferred from the bedroom to the chiropodist's office; 'Up With The Cock' celebrated the simple joys of life on a farm (of course!)' and 'Hokey Cokey' was all about putting things in and pulling them out, then shaking them all about. As it should be.

By the late 1970s, the hit-making machine had run out of steam (either that, or been eclipsed by a new wave of punning Punk inspired perverts, led by the legendary Ivor Biggun). But Dread never slowed down – indeed, he simply became even more prolific, turning out a string of often excellent (and generally smut-free) singles under a variety of pseudonyms, and gigging regularly around the country. Even before the Skinheads discovered the Specials, Dread was guaranteed a massive crop-topped turn-out, an audience that he had first celebrated as far back as 1976, with the anthemic 'Bring Back The Skins'. (Intriguingly, a lot of people thought that one was about circumcision when it first came out.) Now, his shows were pulling in the Rude Boy crew as well, while his musical children were everywhere – whether they admitted liking him or not.

Dread's greatest impact, after all, was not on the vocabularies, or even the sex lives, of his predominantly school-age audience. As the first artist to demonstrate to the British industry that Jamaican music, which had not hitherto produced a single artist of mainstream hit-making longevity, was

eminently capable of sustaining a successful career, Judge Dread was not only Britain's first Reggae superstar, he was the first Reggae artist to enjoy a lengthy run of hits anywhere outside of Jamaica. The fact that he was British to begin with remains irrelevant. The radio and television bans ensured that few of his fans had any idea what he looked like. (The confusion was not limited to home audiences. When Dread visited Jamaica in the wake of 'Big Six', fans were astonished to discover that he was white. "Most people thought I was my own bodyguard," he chuckled later.)

Even more importantly, Dread's elevation of Jamaican music from the cultural back streets of one-hit-wonderdom to something more lasting was a crucial ingredient in Reggae's own British breakthrough. Less than three years after 'Big Six', Bob Marley was elevated to stardom not on the back of a record company push, or the growing press support he was receiving, but from inside the pockets of a generation that had been spoon-fed the pleasures of his music – at the same time as the 'experts' were telling them that they shouldn't swallow a mouthful. Of course it is a very long way from 'She's A Big Girl Now' to 'No Woman No Cry' but you know that Dread could have found some way of shortening the journey.

Musically, Dread's impact echoed throughout the genesis of 2-Tone. It was Dread, in 1976, who first reawakened Prince Buster's 'Al Capone' from its decade-long slumber, for release under his Dreadnoughts alias; Dread who rejuvenated Dandy Livingstone's 'A Message To You (Rudy)'; and, of course, Dread who first resurrected forgotten 60s' skankers The Cats' flute-and-piano take on 'Swan Lake' for another Dreadnoughts 45.

Famously, Madness opted not to record a song that Dread wrote specifically for them, the distinctly Nutty-flecked 'One Eyed Lodger' (an ode, of course, to his television), but their own version of 'Swan Lake' acknowledges the debt to Dread regardless.

Similarly revelling in Dread's profound legacy were Bad Manners, the band whose appearance at the Electric Ballroom marked the dawn of Echo and the Bunnymens' nightmare. Even under his real name of Doug Trendle, the mega-kilo skinhead man mountain that called itself Buster Bloodvessel was always the world's most unlikely pop star. But Bad Manners were tailored for nothing less. Riotous, raucous, and remarkable even after you stopped pinching yourself in the hope that you'd wake up, the nine men/one noise Manners did indeed come crashing out of the musical undergrowth at exactly the same time as Madness and the Specials, with a similar musical agenda, and the same sense of dashing style. But all similarities ended right there.

If the Specials were 2-Tone, Bad Manners were 2-much. If Madness were the Nutty Boys, Bad Manners were certifiable. When they settled down and simply played, they were capable of creating some of the smoothest Ska sounds around, defiantly authentic, desperately beautiful. But settling down is what you do when you're old and grey with children and a mortgage, and who wants to spend an evening with their parents? Bad Manners kicked ass like kids kick cans, because they are there, because it is fun, and because they could.

Lunatic solos were played strictly for laughs, while Buster himself was the lasciviously chortling cheerleader who held the lunacy together. Like Judge Dread (to whom, in terms of sheer pin-up worthiness, Bloodvessel bore a distinct resemblance), it was impossible to take them seriously, and ridiculous to take offence. Of course people did, and that just made the joke even funnier.

From the outset, Bad Manners carved out their own corner. Formed in 1976 at Woodberry Down Comprehensive School in Stoke Newington, the original line-up comprised Bloodvessel, Louis 'Alphonso' Cook (guitar), David 'Reggie Mental' Farren (bass), Brian 'Chewitt' Tuitt (drums), Alan 'Winston Bazoomies' Sayagg (harmonicas) and Paul Hyman (trumpet) – although there was never a stable line-up for long; other members included such memorably named characters as guitarist Bolly Yusosevski and saxophonist Smelly Socks.

Neither could they settle on a name – or a musical identity – for long. As Stand Back, they tried their hand at sundry free festivals and hippy gatherings; as Stoop Solo and the Sheet Starchers, they blended tentative Punk with Judge Dread-style humour, while running through a set that ranged from 'Riot In Cell Block #9' to the theme for the 'Milky Bar Kid' commercial. TV and movie themes were a popular insertion in the set but, setting the stage for the group's later visual renown, the highlight had to be 'Cheese And Pickle Blues', performed by Bloodvessel with a plateful of food. Partial nudity, slapstick comedy and indecent exposure followed as a matter of course – and with it came a name. Bad Manners was just so self-explanatory.

By 1978, the group had swollen to include keyboardist Martin 'Mr Bogingong' Stewart and two sax players, Andrew 'Marcus Absent' Marson and Chris 'Krust' Kane, and their sound began to settle into a Reggae/Ska groove, shot through with glimpses of jump and jive jazz, children's songs ('Scruffy, the Huffy Chuffy Tugboat' would survive onto the band's first album), early rock'n'roll and blues.

Landing a regular gig at the Green Man pub, Bad Manners were never especially ambitious, Bloodvessel admitted, "we thought we were doing great by playing in our local pub." But word was spreading – particularly, it appeared, among railway and traffic workers, all of whom seemed to arrive at gigs bearing massive roles of the black and yellow tape with which roadworks are usually surrounded. Soon, Bad Manners gigs began to resemble a deranged construction site and it caused no end of amusement when, as 2-Tone took off and the Specials' chosen scheme of black-and-white chequers became a fashionable requisite, Bad Manners introduced their own variation, with black-and-yellow instead.

The excitement surrounding such horseplay shocked them, nevertheless. While other performers donned pork-pie hats and sharp Mod suits, Bad Manners wore T-shirts, boots and turned-up jeans. While others turned to the Jamaican greats for their earliest repertoire, Bad Manners followed Dread back to the nursery and the music hall, and led maddening mass singalongs of the tongue-twisting 'Ne Ne Na Na Na Na Nu Nu.' And, while other performers (Dexy's notwithstanding) might readily have jumped at the offer to join the good ship 2-Tone, Bad Manners thanked Dammers for his interest, then struck out for the same Magnet Records where Pete Waterman – again – cut his A&R-ing teeth. "There were a lot of problems with (2-Tone)," Bloodvessel shrugged. "So we signed onto an independent label, which helped the band get started."

Judge Dread, too, would swerve away from any offer 2-Tone may have made. But not every performer that Dammers cast an eye over dismissed his overtures. 2-Tone's final release of 1979 was to be the first to highlight a local scene that was quickly coming to rival even Coventry in terms of vibrancy and commitment, and which emanated from just down the road, in Birmingham.

Long a centre of British West Indian life, Birmingham had long since earned its reputation as a musical melting pot as well – as far back as 1965, the Spencer Davis Group slammed out of that city with a pair of UK chart-toppers composed by Jamaican singer-songwriter Jackie Edwards. A decade later, in 1975, it was Steel Pulse's turn to emerge, as David Hinds (lead vocals, guitar), Basil Gabbidon (lead guitar, vocals) and Ronnie McQueen (bass) arose from Handsworth Wood Boys School. (Selwyn 'Bumbo' Brown (keyboards), Steve 'Grizzly' Nesbitt (drums), Fonso Martin (vocals, percussion) and Michael Riley (vocals) completed the line-up.)

Their earliest concerts confirmed Steel Pulse's political awareness, as their attempts to slide into the traditional Caribbean-themed clubs and bars of the midlands were rebuffed by proprietors wary of the band members' Rastafarian beliefs.

Steel Pulse switched their attentions, then, to the rock-oriented circuit, apprenticing in pubs as they readied their debut single, the savage urban irony of 'Kibudu, Mansetta And Abuku,' for release on the local independent label Dip, there to discover that even the hardest bitten hard rock crowd could be won over if they could only be convinced that the music spoke to them. Steel Pulse, by addressing urban issues as profoundly as racial ones, spoke loudly.

Graduating to Anchor Records for a second single ('Nyah Love'), before finding a permanent home at Island, Steel Pulse were early recruits to the Rock Against Racism banner – hardly surprisingly, given their hometown's crucial role in fermenting the movement in the first place.

With its ferocious anti-racist tone, 'Ku Klux Klan,' the group's debut single, would become a RAR anthem following its release in March 1978, a status it lost only when the band followed through with the custom-built 'Jah Pickney/RAR,' a triumphant rocker whose chorus, "we're gonna hunt the National Front,"was picked up everywhere RAR supporters came together in protest: "Rock Against Racism – smash it! Rock against Fascism – smash it! Rock against Nazi-ism – smash it!"

Just as important as their political stand was Steel Pulse's decision to align themselves firmly alongside the Punk movement – a natural consequence, of course, of their early baptism in the rock circuit, but an acknowledgement, too, of their shared goals. When Steel Pulse took their first major touring trips out of the midlands, they frequently did so alongside a Punk band – XTC, the Stranglers and so on. The group featured alongside the Fall, the Buzzcocks, poet John Cooper Clark et al, aboard the Short Circuit: Last Night At The Electric Circus live album, documenting the October 1977 closure of Manchester' most legendary Punk venue, and were high on the bill at the Clash's Victoria Park event the following spring.

Steel Pulse's example readily percolated across the UK reggae scene of course, but their hometown was especially swift to respond. Indeed, no sooner had Steel Pulse released their debut album, the apocalyptic self-prophesy of Handsworth Revolution, than another Birmingham roots band was preparing its own politically supercharged assault on the city's rock citadels.

It was Alistair Campbell who first formulated UB40 in 1977, after receiving a Criminal Injuries Compensation payment for an attack he'd suffered on his 17th birthday, a year earlier. He spent the money on a drum kit and, while he quickly switched to guitar, he had already interested a few of his Mosely

School of Art friends... bassist Earl Falconer and saxophonist Brian Travers... in playing together. Bequeathing his kit to Jim Brown, adding Campbell's elder brother Robin to the brew, and plugging the entire band into a single 15 watt amp, UB40 spent most of their first months together simply learning to play their instruments.

By the summer of 1978, UB40's membership had swollen to seven, as Jimmy Lynn (keyboards) and Timi Tupe 'Yomi' Abayomi Babayemi (percussion) were brought on board. The group had their own regular rehearsal room in the cellar below Falconer's flat at 106 Trafalgar Road and, on February 9, 1979, UB40 ventured out in public for the first time, playing a friend's birthday party at The Hare & Hounds pub in Kings Heath.

Sharing the bill with fellow Brummies The Au Pairs, The Denizens and Pretty Faces, UB40's set was largely early 70s reggae covers, interspersed by a handful of their own instrumental compositions. It was, all agreed later, a less than auspicious debut but their efforts did not fall on deaf ears. In the audience that night, a former encyclopedia salesman named Simon Woods was so heartily impressed by the band that, within weeks, he was installed as their manager.

UB40 played their next show around the same time, a low-key slot at Birmingham University; it was to be Babayemi's final appearance, before he was deported back to his Nigerian homeland by the the immigration authorities. More gigs followed – UB 40 were regulars at the Fighting Cocks in Moseley and Mount Pleasant Community Centre; and, for the time being, they were happy to bathe in the inevitable comparisons with UB40.

It was during a show at the New Inn on Moseley Road that the group proved (and maybe even learned for themselves) that their musical destiny was to be very different to that enjoyed by Steel Pulse; echoing, in a way, Neville Staples' full-time recruitment to the Specials, UB40 found themselves joined onstage by DJ Terence 'Astro' Wilson, a magical Master of Ceremonies whose presence, though nobody realized it at the time, would finally transform UB40 from a competent reggae band, into something far more important.

Astro was not, in fact, the first DJ to have toasted along with UB40; in fact, 'Ranking' Roger Charlery, one of the star turns at Barbarellas, seemingly made a habit of cutting into the live sets of any visiting, even vaguely-reggaefied bands, and with such effectiveness that UB40 were not the only local group to seek out their own full-time DJ in Ranking's aftermath. So did the Beat, only they never found anyone who did it as well as Ranking Roger.... so that's who they recruited.

Like UB40, the Beat came together slowly during 1978, around a nucleus of vocalist Dave Wakeling, guitarist Andy Cox, bassist Dave Steele and St

Kitts-born drummer Everett Morton, a veteran of over a decade's worth of local Reggae acts. The group was initially uncertain of either a direction or a purpose; although, perhaps predictably, Wakeling himself credited his musical awakening to punk. 'The first gigs that I went to, I was so amazed by it that I didn't think that I could even be involved, but I knew that it was something that meant a great deal to me. My first gig was Black Sabbath when I was twelve. The next show was Led Zepellin, and then Hawkwind. But... it was going to Punk shows that made me say, "Hey, yeah, I want to do this." And probably if there was an epiphany for me it was a Wire show at Barbarella's (in Birmingham, England). They have like 500 great songs – none of them over a minute long – and I got to hear all of them. So that was terribly important for me and The Clash was terribly important for me. The first time I'd seen them that was like "well yes, I want some of this." Because, when I was a bit younger, at those big Sabbath and Zepellin shows, it was like a fantasy world...far above me. But by the time that Punk had gotten that kind of agit-prop "of the people, for the people, by the people" kind of vibe and, in many ways that seemed a reaction to what stadium rock had become. All of a sudden I was like – "Oh, I could do that. I want to do that. In fact, I'm not going to sleep until I do!"'

Despite such ambition, and despite the encouragement they received from their friendship with the smilarly-gestative UB40, for many months the band was most interested in throwing what Wakeling calls "terrific house parties," events that quickly became a magnet for a rash of local mini-celebrities. "Boy George used to live not far away; he used to come"; so did future Sigue Sigue Sputnikker Martin Degville, members of the Au Pairs, friends from local Reggae band UB40, "and the odd member of Dexy's Midnight Runners... but they'd always cause a fight."

Another feature of these events was the presence of two DJs, one specialising in Punk, the other in Reggae: "We found that if you alternated them, not absolutely, but alternated them and mixed it up, the dance floor always stayed full. If you played too many Punk songs in a row everyone would get burnt out and if you played too many Dubs all in a row then everybody was just leaning against a wall nodding their heads. [But] the combination was glorious. And it happened in an instant, me and Andy sitting on the floor, watching the crowd from the corner, saying 'what if you could get both of these elements going in the same three minute song? Then you'd have something going, wouldn't ya?' And we started The Beat on that basic premise."

The Beat took its name because, as Wakeling marvelled, nobody else had thought of it before. But it was appropriate. The first time the group met with Morton, the experienced sticks man sat through Wakeling and Steele's gentle acoustic ditties and asked, "it's a Reggae drummer you want? You're sure?" But, at the end of an hour's rehearsal, "five minutes music was *fabulous*. We were all looking at each other, wondering 'what have we created?'"

Roughly pursuing Morton's own past experience, the group made its first home at St Albans' mental hospital in Birmingham – Steele was a trainee nurse there, and regularly sneaked his bandmates in to rehearse in an empty part of the building. The subterfuge could not last – the inmates, apparently, complained and Steele came close to being dismissed.

The Beat relocated to a room above the local Yorkshire Grey pub, working out their own take on the Punky-Reggae mix. "It was never really meant to be Ska," Wakeling confessed. "It turned into Ska when we realized that what we were creating was about the same beat and tempo as some of our favourite Skinhead songs from about 5 years earlier. So we said, 'Oh, that's funny. We can do that 'Whine & Grind' [a Prince Buster oldie] like this."

Little more than a month after UB40 took their own first steps into the public arena, the Beat made their live debut at the local Matador Club on March 31, 1979, opening for the Dum Dum Boyz; and it was within that group's ranks that the Beat met Ranking Roger for the first time.

Ranking adopted the Beat on the spot. While they made a point of attending his already semi-legendary DJ spots at Barbarellas, he became a regular at the Beat's gigs, jumping up on stage for a wicked toast through another Prince Buster song, 'Rough Rider', and spreading the band's name as far as he was able. Wakeling recalled, 'After a few shows Roger said "Do you think I could be in the group then?" And I said "You see that over there?" – pointing to a Bass amplifier – "Yup" – "You see that over there?" – pointing to the van – "Yup." "Well, you put that in there and you're in the group." And he did, and he was.'

UB40 were especially taken with the Beat, and frequently invited them along as support at their own shows – though a mere six weeks separated the two groups in terms of actual public visibility, UB40 were already headline material around the midlands and were looking to advance their cause even further. But, as that spring merged into summer, two outfits that already shared common goals and a common audience found they also nursed a common disappointment. The Specials and Madness were exploding dramatically, Dexy's and the Mod mob were whaling in behind them. How come those groups were all taking off, and they weren't?

The Beat had been gigging for around three months, said Wakeling, before they first learned about all that was taking place in London. "David Steele walked in with the *Melody Maker* or *NME* and said, 'Look!' – throwing the paper down – and we said, 'The Specials!!! Oh God, they beat us to the punch.' It wasn't quite the same, they had elements of Rockabilly and all other kinds of stuff going on... but a lot of it ended up with a similar kind of vibe [to our music.]"

It was disc jockey John Peel, that early champion of the Specials, who came to the rescue, for both bands. That summer, UB40 hooked up with local producer Bob Lamb to record a clutch of demos at Lamb's own eight-track studio in Moseley. Circulated around the local media, the demos came to the attention of BRMB DJ Robin Valk, who both broadcast the tapes on his show, and alerted Peel to the group's existence. By mid-December, UB40 were in London, recording their maiden session for the Peel show, versions of 'Food For Thought,' '25 Per Cent' and the anthem-in-waiting, 'King.'

The Beat, meanwhile, came to the DJ's attention when they performed at a Radio One roadshow concert he was hosting at Aston University. Describing them as "the best band in the universe after the Undertones," Peel promptly offered the Beat a live session on his show in October. He was still enthusing wildly about the group when he returned to London to broadcast his nightly radio show.

His enthusiasm was contagious. Just weeks later, Jerry Dammers turned up at one of the Beat's Birmingham shows and invited them to open for the Selecter at the Cascade Club in Shrewsbury. The headliners, in turn, were sufficiently impressed to invite them back for another clutch of shows, including one in London, at the Nashville on September 23.

If the 2-Tone hierarchy liked the Beat, audiences were less enamoured. The group's sound may have been built around the same basics as the Specials and co, but stylistically they were several steps removed from the sheer manic exuberance of their contemporaries. Songs like 'Mirror In The Bathroom' and 'Ranking Full Stop,' premiered on the Peel show, were catchy enough, but the band also packed its fair share of mere Skank Lite ballads, a difference which everybody who encountered them seemed to sense instinctively. Indeed, their pessimistically subdued response to the Nashville audience – the largest concentration of Skinheads that the Beat had ever encountered – brought harsh words down from on-high. "Don't you ever fucking do that again," Desmond Brown chided. "You can just forget about being in a group or anything, if you let that happen again."

The Beat persevered, training themselves not to panic at the first sign of trouble; convincing themselves that the stomping, roaring, swearing mob that clustered around the stage was simply out to enjoy itself; and working to convince that mob, as Wakeling put it, that "bubblegum pop... can be subversive." They succeeded as well – less than three weeks after the Nashville show, following an Electric Ballroom gig on October 13, Jerry Dammers invited the Beat to record a single for 2-Tone. They jumped at the chance.

The Beat's choice for their debut was a song that had already done service in Madness' early live show, Smokey Robinson's 'Tears Of A Clown', infected with a gently lilting Ska rhythm and haunted by a beautiful sax line from Jamaican veteran Saxa. It was a simple performance, driven by Wakeling's sweet-as-sugar vocal, and struck even cynics as a sure-fire hit.

Jerry Dammers, however, was less enamoured. His own choice for the group's debut was their own 'Mirror In The Bathroom' and the Beat were initially ready to follow his advice. "But then we read the contract," says Wakeling. "[It] was a simple one-page contract, but it included the awful phrase that Chrysalis Records will own the rights to that song for 5 years. We were like 'Get out of here. We're not giving you that one. People tell us it's a good-un. We'll make a single, but we don't know these people, they're not keeping our song for 5 years.' We went backwards and forwards, and then I said, 'Why don't we insist on recording "Tears of a Clown"? They can try to get the rights to that as much as they'd like, it's not ours to give away'."

So, that is precisely what they did; and, whatever reservations may have accompanied the decision, 'Tears Of A Clown' not only made #6, it also, perhaps, did more than either the Specials, the Selecter or Madness to prove that the Ska sound had a life to live far from the 2-Tone circus itself. The other bands' hardcore fans would never take the Beat to its heart – and how ironic is it that it was precisely that rejection which proved the key to the Beat's eventual longevity.

If the musical edge that stoked 2-Tone was somehow alien to the Beat, of course, the ideology that fired the label was not. Even as 'Tears Of A Clown' was climbing the chart, Arista swooped for the Beat's long-term signature, and found them in belligerent mood. "We decided that if anyone offered us a deal, we'd go for the same sort of thing as 2-Tone," Dave Wakeling explained. "2-Tone did us a lot of good, so it would be nice to pass it on and do the same for other bands."

And so it was that the same old handful of labels trotted out to hear the same old request for the band's own record label. And so it was, too, that less than a year after Arista baulked at the Specials' demand for a personal identity, the impressively-named A&R man Tarquin Gotch found himself negotiating the creation of the company's second successive subsidiary, as Secret Affair's I-Spy concern was joined on the books by the Beat's Go-Feet imprint.

With 'Tears Of A Clown' making it five hit singles out of five releases, 2-Tone bade farewell to 1979 on a high that nobody could ever have imagined just nine months before. The Specials themselves wrapped up the year with solidly sold-out appearances at the London Lyceum and the Lewisham Odeon, before lining up alongside the Who, Queen, Paul McCartney, the Clash, Elvis Costello, Ian Dury, Rockpile and the Pretenders, at the pre-Live Aid charity event of the age, the People's Concert for Kampuchea.

The sprawling billing represented the biggest names of the year gone by, but it escaped nobody's notice that, even among the relative chart newcomers on the bill, only one of the participants represented anything that had actually happened to distinguish 1979 from any other year you could mention. And only one seemed likely to have any say in the events of the New Year to come. The Specials were granted just one track on the souvenir *Concerts For The People Of Kampuchea* live album, compared to the side long contributions of the Who and McCartney. But nobody who heard the triumphant rendering of 'Monkey Man', then compared it to the bloated meanderings of 'Theme From Rockestra' or a tiresome 'Sister Disco', could be left in any doubt that the Specials were the best thing in sight.

CHAPTER ELEVEN

1980 began with 2-Tone embroiled within a quite remarkable legal snare. Towards the end of the previous year, Elvis Costello found himself in limbo as Radar, the label he had been with for the past two years, collapsed – but in such a way that WEA, the company's majority shareholder, assumed that its greatest assets, at least, remained viable.

In fact, they didn't. No written contracts existed between the label's founders, Andrew Lauder and Martin Davis, and such performers as Costello and Nick Lowe; record releases were negotiated by handshake alone, on a disc-by-disc basis. Indeed, Lauder and Costello's manager, Jake Riviera, were already planning to launch their own label, through which Costello's recordings would now be handled. As of December 1979, their greatest dilemma seemed to be whether to call it Off-beat or Fuck-beat. Finally they split the difference – F-Beat: 'The Stax to 2-Tone's Motown,' as Costello described the label's aims.

Costello already had a new single ready to go, a distinctive cover of Sam & Dave's old soul chestnut 'I Can't Stand Up For Falling Down'. With F-Beat still some weeks away from full operation, however, it was suggested that he maintain his alignment with the Specials, and release it through 2-Tone. With a release date of January 11, 1980, the pressing plants swung into action and acetate advances were dispatched to both the press and the radio. Almost a week before the record's actual release, the *NME* had already run a laudatory review ("guaranteed to spin some heads") and London's Capital Radio had playlisted the song.

WEA lunged. Still unable to accept that they had bought into a record label, Radar, whose biggest (honestly? *Only*) stars weren't even signed to the company, the mega-corp launched injunctions against the BBC, to prevent them from joining Capital in playing the record; against 2-Tone, to prevent them from releasing it; and against F-Beat, for even presuming to exist outside of WEA's loving embrace.

Two of the three, of course, were readily cured once F-Beat agreed to resume Radar's own alliance with WEA: 'I Can't Stand Up For Falling Down' was rescheduled for February on F-Beat itself, and would quickly climb to #4. 2-Tone, on the other hand, were left with 13,000 copies of a single that they couldn't actually market. (The entire run was ultimately handed over to Costello, who distributed them to fans on his next UK tour; later in the year, a few thousand more were manufactured for sale when Costello played New York.)

Already granted the catalogue number TT 7, the non-appearance of 'I Can't Stand Up For Falling Down' threatened to blow a gaping hole in 2-Tone's hitherto unblemished hits-to-releases ratio. To the bemusement of future collectors, then, but to the satisfaction of more down-to-earth statisticians, the number was re-used for the Specials' own next single, a four-song live EP recorded at gigs back in November.

With the band still smarting from the criticisms that greeted *The Specials*, the decision to release a live recording was easily taken. The Moonlight Club bootleg was selling strongly and had, in fact, already been joined by another, recorded at the Lyceum in early December and readily available from at least one stall in Soho market the week before Christmas. The EP was obviously shorter than that particular treat. But still it made an adequate substitute.

The lead track 'Too Much Too Young' was revamped from the group's debut album – and rendered vastly superior in the process. It was the remainder of the EP that really made it worthwhile, though, a punchy run through 'The Guns Of Navarone' and the revealingly titled *Skinhead Symphony* that stormed through 'Long Shot Kick The Bucket', 'The Liquidator' and 'Skinhead Moonstomp' to portray the Specials at their stomping, skanking finest.

The Specials themselves would not be around to support the release. Just as the record hit the streets, the band were jetting off for their first visit to America, just weeks after Madness returned from their maiden voyage, but with an itinerary that made the Nutties' look like a day trip.

No flying visit this, the Specials were scheduled for no less than six weeks' worth of gigs, with more than a handful placed so far off the beaten track that even Punk Rock was still considered a force from outer space.

Although Madness had played a smattering of low-key gigs in the US during their pre-Christmas visit, spending more of their time at less arduous promotional shindigs, they reported back on an American scene that was gagging for some fresh excitement, and which had already been primed for 2-Tone by imported singles and the British music papers.

Of course, nobody imagined that the country was going to be anything less than a tough nut to crack. Even leaving aside Roddy Radiation's belief that the American heartland was never going to take to songs of despair set in the English midlands, the idea that a bunch of English provincial kids could succeed where countless Jamaican superstars had failed, and set the United States a-skanking, was preposterous.

Millie's 'My Boy Lollipop' and the occasional Jimmy Cliff single aside, Jamaican music made very little impact on the US. Even Bob Marley – who, for most Americans, *was* Reggae music – boasted little more than an illogically chequered career: *Rastaman Vibration*, in 1976, was a massive hit; *Exodus*, the following year, an only marginally smaller one. But subsequent LPs scarcely registered, and the feeling was, if the best known Jamaican in the world couldn't break his native music, what chance did a bunch of kids from Coventry have?

About as much of one as Eric Clapton, who topped the American chart with 'I Shot The Sheriff'. About as much as Hall and Oates, whose first Top 20 album included a U-Roy song. And about as much as the Police, two Top 30 albums into a career that had scarcely even got off the starting blocks in Britain. Most Americans, it was true, wouldn't know an island rhythm if it was wrapped in apple pie. But they sure liked to dance to it, given half the chance. And the Specials intended giving them that chance. At their first US press conference, just hours after they arrived in the country, a journalist asked, "Now you're in the States, are you going to continue playing Jamaican music?"

Jerry Dammers just laughed. "We don't play Jamaican music." Even after it became apparent that many of the people queuing up to see the Specials make their Stateside debut at New York's Hurrah had little idea of what to expect, the band could take solace from the fact that at least they cared enough to try to find out.

Chrysalis, whose American wing would be handling the release of *The Specials*, pulled out all the promotional stops. Just two days after the Hurrah gig on January 24, *The Specials* entered the US chart. The gig itself shattered the venue's own attendance record, with an already wound-up audience retaining its wild enthusiasm even when the show kicked off two hours later than scheduled. "This is our first-ever gig in America," Hall was finally able to tell the waiting hordes. "And we just can't say how pleased you must be to have us here."

At the same time, however, Dammers was adamant that the Specials would not be party to any attempt to hype them up, for either the media's benefit or their own. Disgusted to find his merry men booked into some rather plush hotels when they first reached America, Dammers took to sending the tour manager on ahead to make sure that the accommodations were not too good. No matter that such sensibilities meant absolutely nothing to the band's American following; no matter that, to his colleagues, a few nights in such establishments made a glorious respite from the cheesy English hostelries they traditionally stayed in at home. Dammers' own sense of class righteousness (and, perhaps, the knowledge that even the most benevolent record company largesse wound up being deducted from the band's accounts at some point) refused to compromise an iota.

As they bounced around the major cities on the East Coast, the band found audiences to be gleefully receptive. As the bus edged into the interior, however, the Specials quickly discovered the true nature of an American tour. "Even though Punk rock had changed things a bit in the UK, America was still hippie land," laughs Roddy Radiation. "Everybody seemed to be into coke, something we hadn't really come across. We were mainly weed and beer boys, with a bit of mod whiz."

The huge distances that the group was expected to travel between shows took their toll – certainly nothing that the Specials had experienced bouncing around Britain and the continent could have prepared them for the mind-numbing voids that stretched out before them. The tour was barely half over, and Sir Horace was already comparing the tour bus to a mobile funeral home. When the *Los Angeles Times* asked Dammers how he was enjoying his first visit to America, the organist simply snarled, "I had more fun on a school trip to Russia."

Everything seemed to be falling apart. The individual members of the Specials had never been the tightest of friends – all eight were far more likely to separate completely, or at least break off into twos or threes, than socialise together once a show was over. But the bus did not allow for that. Most evenings, the band would come offstage and barely have time to change before they were being shepherded back on board for another drive through an endless prairie night. When they did get a break and a chance to get out on their own, it was no surprise that the first thought in their minds should be to try and re-establish their own personal identities.

Dammers insisted the musicians wear their suits at all time. They refused. Radiation continues, "Jerry said I'd come back [from shopping trips] looking like Marlon Brando circa *The Wild One*. I'd suddenly discovered that I could get all the gear I ever wanted in American thrift shops – leathers, cowboy shirts, hats and motorbike boots, Marlon Brando, James Dean.

"I also started getting into rockabilly in a big way. I'd always liked the music, but now it became my religion. The music being played on the tour bus would usually be heavy Reggae or jazz... which, after several weeks, would fail to excite me. So I started putting my own records on." Soon everyone else was following suit, and usually settling on something that none of the rest of the passengers wanted to hear.

Fighting about clothes, fighting about music... by the time the Specials reached the West Coast, they were fighting about everything. Tempers routinely flared. In San Francisco, Radiation was talking with a local journalist when he became aware of Hall standing behind him, pulling faces and entertaining on-lookers with his own Roddy Radiation impersonations. The guitarist turned around and punched him on the nose; Hall retaliated by throwing his drink in the guitarist's face. Then they went onstage and played what Radiation describes as one of the greatest gigs of their lives.

Matters worsened when the Specials arrived to open their three-night/six-show residency at Hollywood's Whiskey A-Go-Go, to find the entire venue redecorated in black and white chequers. Dammers was furious – again, he'd insisted that Chrysalis refrain from hype. Instead, they'd gone in the other direction entirely. When a party of label execs turned up between sets at one of the shows, to demand the musicians pose for photos with them, Dammers snapped.

Radiation shudders, "We were shattered, partly due to non-stop partying but mainly exhaustion. The Chrysalis USA guys came in wearing suits and ties, smoking cigars... and Jerry just told them to fuck off. Most of the band joined in." The guitarist smiles ruefully, "They stopped pushing the record after that. But, I must say, it felt good."

Back in Britain, meanwhile, the Specials' absence was scarcely even noticed, as the party continued unabashed. A new Madness single, 'My Girl', was knocking on the Top 3 – a fair return, indeed, for a song that had been around since the Invaders days. The Selecter's 'Three Minute Hero' was pushing towards the Top 20; a bandwagoneering reissue of Booker T & the MGs' R&B honker 'Green Onions' was bound for the Top 10. The Specials' own 'Too Much, Too Young', the lead track on the live EP, was simply hurtling skywards. Crashing into the chart at #15 on January 26, a week later it was #1, gazing down on everything from the Boomtown Rats to Captain Beaky, and remaining there for two weeks, until Kenny Rogers finally knocked it off.

The Specials were in Oklahoma, supporting the Police, when they heard the news; and they kept up with the rest of the chart action too. By the time they finally got back to the UK in March (shortly after Madness launched their own first full tour of the United States), however, it was to discover that much, much more had happened in their absence.

Simaryp's decade-old 'Skinhead Moonstomp', already revived as part of the *Skinhead Symphony* medley on the Specials' live EP, started clomping its own way to #54 in February, even as the 2-Tone cover clung to the #1 slot. Spreading the largesse even further, the Beat's old compatriots UB40, burst into view when the tiny independent Graduate label muscled the double A-side 'King'/'Food For Thought' into view, as the band itself toured the UK with the then fast-rising Pretenders. Soaring to #4, on sales of 400,000+, 'King' became the first ever single ever to reach the National Top Ten without the backing of a major record company.

Secret Affair's I-Spy label, too, seemed to have hit the ground running, looking beyond the frontiers of the group's own Mod circuit to recruit veteran Jamaican vocalist Laurel Aitken to its roster – then looking past the Ska market by teaming him up with the Ruts.

That band's own love of Ska had itself already flowered with the arrival in their live set of the anthemic 'Staring At The Rude Boys', a tribute to all-things 2-Tone. Bassist Vince Seggs recalls, "Malcolm [singer Owen], in particular, really got into the Ska look, the hats and clothes. It was a real crossover point. Malcolm, in his inimitable way, started to wear a pork-pie hat and a mauve 2-Tone suit. It was a bit of a fashion thing, but it was kinda normal as well, because I came out of Ska and Motown, that's what I listened to as a kid. With cross-fertilization and all that, blah blah, gigs with Misty In Roots, all the Reggae bands in London, it was kind of inevitable that [something like] 2-Tone would come out of that. And, as the 2-Tone thing picked up, we were getting some of that crowd come along to see us."

The union with Aitken, however, was not quite as inspiring as it ought to have been. Seggs continued, "It was [actually] an awful period. It was a good time at the time, but when I listen to the stuff we'd done, it was fucking horrible. We did a tour supporting Secret Affair; it was a good laugh, but then we made this awful single called 'Rudie Got Married' with Laurel, and it was horrible. Laurel couldn't even sing the last verse on the single, so [Ruts guitarist] Paul Fox did it. He went in and did the harmony on the last verse, because Laurel couldn't hit the notes."

Aitken himself felt nothing but admiration for the new generation of Rudies. "Lots of people said that they were ripping off the original sound of Ska, but I wouldn't say that, because lots of black people don't want to play Ska. So it was great for me to see Jerry Dammers and his posse doing what they were doing, because a lot of black people weren't interested in it. I don't know why."

Rico Rodriguez, now an active member of the Specials' own line-up, agreed with Aitken. Speaking enthusiastically of relaunching his career with Island Records and cutting yet another remake of 'The Guns Of Navarone' with the Specials, he remarked, "Some writers... they say that the Specials is stealing Reggae and Ska from the black man. But this is just pure foolishness, just pure fuckery, the things they say. For when I lived in Jamaica... I was playing this music and was a most loved and respected musician in Jamaica. So would I be playing with the Specials if the things these people say are true?"

Other veterans followed. Jimmy Cliff, Toots & the Maytals, the Heptones and Prince Buster all announced British tours, while Desmond Dekker – the first Jamaican artist ever to score a UK #1 when his 'Israelites' went all the way back in 1969 – relocated full-time to London, where he signed with Stiff Records and set about recording 1980's amusingly-titled *Black and Dekker* album with Graham Parker's backing group, the Rumour.

A flood of new aspirants was emerging, too. In the few weeks that the Specials were abroad, a storm of new releases appeared: Cairo's 'I Like Bluebeat', the Akrylykz's 'Spyderman', the Charlie Parka's 'Ballad Of Robin Hood' (featuring another 2-Tone knock-off sleeve, with a befeathered Walt Jabasco lying felled by an arrow), Graduate's 'Elvis Should Play Ska', the Ska City Rockers' take on 'Time Is Tight' and T & The Unknowns' Ska'd-up 'My Generation'.

Ray Fenwick, guitarist in the early 1960s with one of Britain's first ever homegrown Ska bands, Rupert and the Red Devils, re-emerged as producer of the Teenbeats, and came close to launching a major hit when they scored a Canadian smash with the old Troggs number 'I Can't Control Myself'. He masterminded the *Uppers On The South Downs* compilation of Brighton area Ska and Mod bands, and pulled off one of the era's greatest novelties with the South Coast Ska Stars: "A bunch of guys I put together to do all instrumentals. We put together a whole load of stuff, all set to a Ska beat – 'Hall Of The Mountain King', the old Duane Eddy guitar stuff... it was just a piece of fun, but it was good stuff."

Tongues similarly ever-so-slightly in cheek, the Ska-Dows emerged with a cover of 'Apache', an astonishing collision between the Jamaican originators, the Skatalites, and Britain's own guitar twanging Shadows. It was the first in a chain of unforgettable singles that included the Tornados' 'Telstar', the Animals' 'We Gotta Get Out Of This Place' (that band's bassist Chas Chandler was head of the Ska-dows' own label, Cheapskate) and 'Ska's On 45', a dramatic entry into the *Stars On 45*-style medley records then in vogue.

The list goes on. The Rent Boys, Mix Blood, Mobster, Boff (who signed to RAK, then changed their name to Boss when it was pointed out that their original choice was a not-so-obscure colloquialism for 'fuck'), the Equators: all flickered into life during the first months of 1980. Although not one of them would even threaten to enjoy the success that 2-Tone to confer, not everyone involved was doomed to obscurity.

Akrylyx vocalist Roland Gift would later re-emerge, alongside the Beat's Andy Cox and David Steele, in the Fine Young Cannibals, and prove that his apprenticeship was not wasted with the exquisitely Motowny Mod flavoured 'Good Thing'. West Country natives Graduate morphed into Tears For Fears;

the Walkie Talkies' Wayne Hussey would one day front the Gothic kingpins The Mission; and Paul Sampson, who enjoyed a handful of mid-80s hits with a new group, King, was first sighted fronting the Reluctant Stereotypes (whose quartet of singles during 1980-81 justified at least one-half of their name).

Yet, as Jerry Dammers never tired of pointing out, commercial success was simply an occasional by-product of musical success, and not necessarily a pleasant one. Remembering the Oklahoma morning when he was awakened from a sound sleep with the news that 'Too Much Too Young' was Britain's top-selling single, he reflected, "I just went back to sleep. I could not face it." He had created the monster he always dreamed of. What he wasn't expecting was the burden of responsibility with which that monster would present him.

CHAPTER TWELVE

Into this morass of aspirant talent, 2-Tone had their own new name to deliver, with the March, 1980, debut of the Bodysnatchers. Like the majority of the bands appearing elsewhere, the all-girl septet represented – *so soon!* – the second generation of 2-Tone, the groups that formed only after the Specials and co had shown them the way to go.

Bassist Nicky Summers saw some of the Specials' first London pub gigs and, originally looking only to join a band, auditioned for the similarly unisex Mo-dettes. They passed her by, so legend insists she then, somewhat ill-advisedly, ran a classified ad in the music press, demanding 'rude girls.' Overlooking the inevitable punchline – "three months of dirty phone calls later…" – by September 1979, she had pieced together a group: the unrelated Jane Summers (drums), Pennie Leyton (keyboards), Sarah Jane Owens (guitar), Miranda Joyce (sax) and Stella Barker (guitar), plus Rhoda Dakar, a distinctively beehived vocalist whom Summers met at a Selecter gig and invited along without even knowing whether her discovery could sing.

She could, but musical ability was not necessarily at the top of the Bodysnatchers' agenda. Joyce confessed, "We were all joining to learn as we went along. I don't think [any of us] would have joined a group… I know I certainly wouldn't have… if there'd been men involved. Boys usually start playing an instrument at 14 or 15… it would have made us look ridiculous!"

Nor would they allow their lack of proficiency to hold them back. Taking more than a leaf from the text book of early Punk, the Bodysnatchers rehearsed just enough to ascertain that they had the rudiments of a set together, then made their live debut at one of Madness' old stomping grounds, the Windsor Castle pub, on November 24, 1979. The audience initially didn't know what had hit it but, once they learned to live with the false starts, misplaced tempos and all-round faltering, a fair-sized crowd relaxed into an enthusiastic evening of some of Ska's greatest hits – the group hadn't yet worked up any original material.

Chaotic but compelling, word of the Bodysnatchers' debut performance spread fast. At their very next show, the Selecter were in the audience, offering up a berth on their own next tour, to be launched in conjunction with their debut album, *Too Much Pressure*, and titled, as successor to the Specials' last British outing, 2-Tone-2.

The Bodysnatchers accepted, but the tour itself looked less than stable. The outing was scheduled to kick off on St Valentine's Day, 1980, with the Beat completing the three-act bill. However, with their Go Feet label debut, 'Hands Off She's Mine', set for release at the end of that same month, wiser heads counselled that the group might be better off promoting it in a more hospitable environment – memories of the early reception by the Selecter's audience were still fresh. The Beat pulled out, followed, amazingly, by the Bodysnatchers.

It had been taken for granted that, despite the record company interest bubbling up around them, the Bodysnatchers would make their recorded debut under the auspices of 2-Tone. The Specials' Horace Gentleman, however, was not necessarily convinced that it was the wisest decision – "I'm not sure if it's too early," he mused in a period interview. "If we sign the Bodysnatchers, what are we letting them in for?"

Dave Wakeling of the Beat questioned the wisdom not only of signing the group to 2-Tone, but of offering such a young and inexperienced band any exposure at all. "Every record company's going mad over this 2-Tone thing... look what's happening to the Bodysnatchers. They're going to get killed, because they're not ready for it."

The Bodysnatchers raised their own doubts, not necessarily over their ability to cope with the situation, but over 2-Tone's commitment to their future. Were they going to release the band's record or not? Were they going to promote the group or not? The first date of the tour was already drawing dangerously close before the matter was finally resolved, and the group was restored to the bill at the same time as they went into the studio to cut their first single.

Roger Lomas, producer of the Selecter's recordings, accompanied them into the studio to cut a cover of Dandy Livingstone's 'Let's Do Rocksteady'. But anyone who expected it to recapture the caterwauling glory of their live set was in for a surprise.

Punching up Livingstone's laconic original around a riff-heavy romp and some stomping beats, the group avoided the song's lightweight lyric by using it to showcase the band members' talents, as Rhoda Dakar, all rolling 'r's, introduced the musicians one by one – a live routine that, amazingly, worked perfectly on record. The B-side, 'Ruder Than You', was even more resonant, a celebration of rude-girl-dom that was swiftly adopted as an anthem.

Released a month into the tour, the single quickly climbed into the Top 30, its peak of #22 belied by the impressive nine weeks that it spent on the listing.

The tour itself, however, didn't turn out so well. In an ambitious attempt to broaden their own appeal at the expense of the die-hard Ska community, the Selecter replaced the Beat with Holly and the Italians, an Anglo-American pop-Punk act whose keening 'Tell That Girl To Shut Up' was on the edge of the hit parade. But hopes that a less partisan audience might be drawn to the shows were dashed when it became obvious that the 2-Tone crowd's reputation was enough to keep all but the most dedicated (or oblivious) outsider away. While the handful of skirmishes that did erupt might not have deserved a second glance, still the only girl being told to shut up was Holly herself.

The Italians withdrew from the tour and immediately launched their own outing, the pointedly Right To Be Italian tour. Their place was taken by the Swinging Cats, and pressure on the Bodysnatchers ratcheted up another notch when they were elevated to second-on-the-bill.

Unfortunately, the Swinging Cats were no more inclined to cater to the Skinheads than the Italians had been – their presence on the bill amounted to nothing more than an accident of geography, and friends in high places. Guitarist Steve Vaughan had known Neol Davies since they played in the Transposed Men together, but the Cats themselves could scarcely have been further from the 2-Tone ideal; rather, they were an unashamedly kitsch-flavoured dance act, capable of turning their hand to everything from Latin-tinged calypso to oddly idiosyncratic TV themes: the sort of music, they explained, that you'd encounter in an ice cream parlour. Or a trendy dentist's waiting room. The hope that it might also be accepted as a logical variation on the 2-Tone theme, however, was doomed to disappointment. Though, for the most part, the Swinging Cats dodged the bullet of full-on audience opprobrium, still here were some hairy moments, and the Cats used up at least a few of their nine lives as the outing progressed.

From the Selecter's own point of view, the tour was a stunning success. Few venues were less than packed, while *Too Much Pressure*, the album they'd been working towards for close to nine months, came within a breath of out-performing the Specials' own – it peaked at #5, one place lower than *The Specials*.

Musically, the Selecter displayed a dexterity that many other bands on the circuit simply couldn't match. 'Missing Words', released as the group's third single in March, 1980, was an absolute gem, a delicate ballad whose lightly Ska-flavoured accompaniment was neither the most noticeable, nor the most important part of the song. Only its disappointing chart performance (it fell one place behind the Bodysnatchers' debut) clouded the horizon. The 2-Tone audience was as loyal as could be. But only to what they perceived as '2-Tone'. Step out of that envelope for a moment, and all bets were off.

For now, however, there was little time for recriminations. No sooner were the Selecter off the road in the UK, than it was their turn to cross the Atlantic for an American tour of their own, an affair that echoed the Specials' outing not only via its highs and lows, but also with some remarkable insights into some of the less savoury corners of the American psyche. 2-Tone historian George Marshall relates how the group was entrusted to an openly racist tour-bus driver who simply couldn't understand why he was having to drive half a dozen Negroes around, and seemed almost spitefully pleased when he dumped the musicians outside another venue, to find themselves sandwiched between two heavy metal acts, and a Wet T-Shirt competition.

Like the Specials, the Selecter found their political message – universal sentiments, of course, but forged within the closeted parochialism of the British Isles – frequently fell on deaf ears. But they had no intention of changing for America's benefit, and Pauline Black remains unapologetic about the Selecter's lyrical stance: "We sang about things that mattered, about things that make a difference in people's lives. We wrote songs about society and politics, we took stands on important issues of the day."

The Specials themselves made a flying visit to the US to record a seething 'Gangsters' for television's *Saturday Night Live* on April 19. Back home again, mid-May then brought the release of their new single, Roddy Radiation's seething 'Rat Race.'

Radiation wrote 'Rat Race' "after a night in the local college bar. While sittin', suppin', I chanced to hear several well-to-do student's in conversation. They were discussing the jobs their parents had lined up for them when they finished college. It struck me that their places in college would be better used by students of a less wealthy background, but not everybody understood the song's sentiments. In fact, I was told I was anti-education."

The video surely reinforced that perception. With the entire group dragged out in fierce (albeit decidedly *Please Sir*-ish) school-teacher drag, Dammers a terrifying schoolma'am and Staples a ruthless head master, the promo's one screening on *Top Of The Pops* brought down a hail of complaints – principally, it transpired, from parents who claimed it had frightened their children. The BBC promptly locked a ban on the video, and while that wasn't enough to stop the single quickstepping to #5, Chrysalis' plans to release a second Radiation song, an old Wild Boys-era rocker called 'Concrete Jungle'. as the follow-up single were scotched by Terry Hall.

As 'Rat Race' fought one battle, the Specials were girding their loins to take on another, as they announced their next UK tour, a unique outing in that all but two of the scheduled dates took the band to the seaside – or, at least, the coast. Kicking off in Great Yarmouth on June 4 and taking in Skegness, Bridlington, Barrow, Blackpool, Colwyn Bay, Worthing, Bournemouth, Hastings, Margate, Southend and Portsmouth, only Leeds University (June 8) and Aylesbury Friars (June 12) gave the lie to the title, *The Specials Seaside Tour*.

Once again, the Bodysnatchers were on board the bus, joined by the Go-Gos, the all-girl Californian quintet who had shared a few LA-area bills with the Specials in January and were now undertaking their first ever British tour. It was, the five agreed, a hair-raising experience.

Vocalist Belinda Carlisle told *Zig Zag*, "some of those gigs were really terrible for us." Drummer Gina Shock quickly added, "At first we were really upset, but then we just started to laugh about it all, and we wound up having a good time amongst ourselves." She admitted, too, that the experiences of Holly and the Italians earlier in the year had at least prepared the Americans for a less-than-patient reception. "We did expect it. But when it's happening, it gets pretty hard to take."

The Bodysnatchers, on the other hand, were rejoicing in the limelight of what might have been the smartest decision they ever made. Back in May, they joined the Mo-dettes in boycotting the Hastings Mod Convention in protest at the organisers' decision to ban both Skinheads and Punks from the event. Like Madness the year before, the Bodysnatchers justified their decision by explaining that there was good and bad in every sector of society, and that cropped hair and DMs did not make someone an exception to that rule. Lke Madness, they were rewarded with the undying loyalty of the fans they took a stand for. No matter what fate awaited the Go-Gos as the tour wound on, the Bodysnatchers would be feted as conquering heroines.

It was a short outing, but it was exhausting. The Specials had been on the road for 15 months without a break, a period whose pressures were exacerbated by the need to supervise not only their own career, but also those of the other acts who called 2-Tone home. Relations with the Selecter were strained, as that band complained that 2-Tone's attentions were so frequently focussed on the Specials that their own career was suffering. The (now long-forgotten) dispute with the Bodysnatchers proved just how tenuous things could become without anybody even realising.

The Specials were aware, too, that with the year already half-gone, 2-Tone's promise of unearthing and nurturing new talent had fallen completely by the wayside. Tapes were still pouring into the offices but nobody listened to them anymore. There was always something else that needed to be dealt with first.

Money was another worry. With seven silver discs on the 2-Tone office wall, the assumption was that both group and label were rolling in it. But the musicians themselves were still on no more than £75-a-week apiece, while the nature of 2-Tone's deal with Chysalis entitled the label to a mere 2 percent royalty from every record that sold. Each of those silver discs, therefore, represented less than £700 for the company coffers – coffers that were, in any case, then split 16 ways, to every member of the Specials and the Selecter, plus the two band's respective managers.

"I'll tell you where the money went," offers Neville Staples. "One thing we used to do – in those days, bands used to have to pay to go and support other groups. We never charged bands to come on our tours, you never had to pay to support us, and we were providing most of the stuff, the equipment, the travel, the hotels. People ask: 'How come you guys haven't got any money?' That's why. Nobody else did it – half the bands who came out with us, they didn't do it when they toured. But we did."

For Dammers himself, the entire dream had turned sour. At the beginning of the year, he'd sincerely believed there'd be a new Specials album in the stores before summer. Now summer was here and, not only was the album far from complete, most of it hadn't even been started yet, as the band members quarrelled not only over the record's content, but its very direction. Everybody agreed that they wanted to take the band's music somewhere new. But precisely where that somewhere was… that was something they might never agree on.

Yet when Dammers suggested that the band cancel the seaside tour altogether, and concentrate on the studio, he was out-voted seven-to-one. The tour would go ahead – but relations within the band itself would never recover from the mutiny.

It was Dammers' relationship with Radiation that suffered the most. Old friends long before the guitarist joined the band, for a long time theirs had been the most stable relationship within the group. While the other players went off on their own, it was Dammers and Radiation who stuck together, sharing hotel rooms, sharing a pint, whatever. Now, the pair seemed worlds apart, with the Specials' visit to Blackpool finally turning their world upside down for good..

Radiation recalls: "After the sound check, a photo session had been arranged for the music press. Jerry looked uncomfortable, the band looked wrong! Jerry picked on Horace, who was less likely to bite back, and said we would all have to go back to the hotel to get changed. We all came out of the hotel slightly more appropriately dressed.

"A little later Jerry appeared, dressed in a red tartan suit with matching hat. We stood sullenly by the sea wall, Jerry climbed on the top and began to clown... I pretended to push him. Jerry screamed, 'You all witnessed, he tried to kill me!'

"It was that kinda tour."

Just as wearing, as the tour wound around the resorts, was the constant threat of violence now spilling out of the audience from the moment the theatre doors opened – accompanied every step of the way by a media spotlight forever zigzagging in search of trouble. And trouble was what they found, even when the incident itself had little to do with any fighting. A stage invasion at Skegness brought so many people onto the stage that the old wooden boards collapsed. 'Mindless hooligans!' screamed the tabloids. 'Skinhead riot!' grumbled the broadsheets. "Really good kids [who] just want to be part of it," responded Jerry Dammers, and he was right. But sometimes, being right isn't enough. You need to be listened to as well and the sad fact is, few people were doing that.

The end of the tour didn't provide respite. In July, the Greater London Council slapped an outright ban on a proposed 2-Tone festival, to be staged on Clapham Common, to celebrate the label's first birthday. Sets by the Specials, Madness, the Beat, the Selecter and the Bodysnatchers were promised but, in the face of 'local opposition,' which was easily translated into a fear of filling the field with fiercesome Skinheads, the GLC refused to grant a license for the event.

Shortly after, Lynval Golding was viciously attacked by three men as he left the Moonlight Club following a Mo-dettes gig. The beating, however, had nothing to do with who he was – he doubted that his assailants even recognised him – but for what he was. Racial attacks were on the rise all summer, and Golding, the recipient of 31 stitches, had just become another statistic. (He later relived the attack in the haunting 'Why?')

And, when the Specials flew to Japan for their first tour of that country, the opening night in Osaka simply served up a repetition of everything the Specials hoped they'd left behind in Britain. Thrilled by local press coverage of the group, confident that they knew *precisely* how to behave when the 2-Tone army hit the stage, the audience rose as one to join them onstage, and sent the local police into paroxysms of fury. By the end of the evening, both the show's promoter and the band's own manager, Rick Rogers, were cooling their heels in a jail cell, while the Specials themselves were confined to their hotel.

The following night's gig was cancelled as a matter of course.

CHAPTER THIRTEEN

While the Specials were tearing – or being torn – apart, Madness were going from strength-to-strength. The success of 'My Girl', despite the relative failure of the Selecter's similarly mould-breaking 'Missing Words', had shown that it was possible to shake off the shackles of the 2-Tone menagerie. The group's efforts to dispel the undercurrents of violence and politicking that had dogged them through 1979 were finally beginning to pay off as well.

Echoing Sham 69's similarly desperate pleas for calm, threats to abandon live work, or even break up completely, had made little difference to Madness' so-called following. There would always be another mob to follow. The group tried another tack, then, working not to distance themselves from one audience, but to lose it within another. Without quite turning their back on the Ska sound of old, Madness were nevertheless broadening their musical horizons with the express intent of widening their appeal. Everybody talked about making music for 'the kids' – that was precisely what Madness were going to do.

Their next major London show, at Hammersmith Odeon on February 16, 1980, wasn't simply closed to anybody over the age of 16, it was given a mid-morning start time as well, as a treat for all the weenies and teenies who'd only ever seen the group on childrens' TV. It was a phenomenal success, one of the most joyous concerts Madness had ever played, and the first shot in a campaign that would, the next time Madness toured, see even the toughest Skins squeezed out of the queue for tickets by an equally ferocious army of tiny tots and teenyboppers.

America, too, treated Madness somewhat better than it did the Specials, recognizing in the Nutty Boys a twisted streak of Pythonesque English comedy with which the Specials' drier (if not deadpan) humour simply could not compete. It was one thing for Terry Hall to announce a song as "the last dance before the Third World War" or to lead his fellows through a funereal recounting of the music hall staple 'Enjoy Yourself'; it was quite another for

Madness to relive every great Keystone Kops film you've ever wanted to see, then round it out with the musical soundtrack to a hail of flying cream pies.

Madness always appeared more approachable, as well. Dicky Barrett, the future frontman of the Mighty Mighty Bosstones, encountered the group in 1983, following their characteristically riotous performance on *Saturday Night Live*, and still remembers how profound an influence the group would have on his own embryonic ambition.

"The first band I met was Madness in New York City. Me and my friend Patrick got on a bus late at night, got into New York early in the morning, had to stand in line all day for tickets, drank in an Irish pub somewhere really close to the NBC Studios and ended up hanging out with guys who became members of the Toasters – and Django, who went onto the Stubborn All Stars. That was a realization we had years later: 'I saw Madness on *Saturday Night Live*', 'Oh, I was there', 'You were the guys we hung out with all day!'

"Anyway, after the show, we hung around outside waiting for Madness and they spotted us, took us in their limo, let us hang out with them. Suggs was introducing me as his American cousin. That, to me, has given me a lot of the way I treat people who come and see our band. I was thrilled; if I hadn't been in the Bosstones afterwards, meeting Madness would have been the biggest musical thrill of my life. It's just as easy to say, 'Hey, come on hang out' or 'Yeah, I'll sign that' as it is to say 'Get the fuck out of here!'" – which is, apparently, how another of Barrett's idols, J Giels Band frontman Peter Wolf, greeted him.

'Night Boat To Cairo', the lead track from the *Work, Rest And Play* EP, brought Madness their fourth successive hit in April 1980. It was followed that summer by the infantile knockabout of 'Baggy Trousers', and the group's transformation was complete. Cartoon capers of the highest degree leeched out of the grooves. The accompanying videos – shot when the medium was still in its commercial infancy – were nothing short of a riot. Had the proposed 2-Tone birthday bash taken place on Clapham Common that July, Madness would have been among the performers. But it would also have marked their farewell to the movement they had helped to establish.

As the summer wore on, it began to look as though several other groups might have been wise to pack their bags, as well. Having supported 2-Tone throughout the past year, the music press was showing signs of becoming bored.

Nobody had ever claimed 2-Tone was the only game in town, even at the height of the excitement. Bands like Public Image, the Gang of Four and the Pop Group, with their dark, angular experiments on the edge of funk, continued to lodge themselves in the heart of the less excitable journalists. The Psychedelic Furs, a sextet that sounded exactly like its name suggested it should, had risen to Next Big Thingdom almost hand-in-hand with the Specials. Joy Division spearheaded a brutally cerebral movement that did not lose speed even after the May 1980 suicide of singer Ian Curtis. An explosion of new talent from Liverpool, led by the Teardrop Explodes and the Skinhead-scattered Echo and the Bunnymen, was already sending sales of dark raincoats through the roof. How could 2-Tone compare with any of that?

The Selecter sensed the way the wind was blowing and, at a time when they should have been planning their next single, they were instead wondering how to break the news to Jerry Dammers that they were leaving 2-Tone.

They did not intend travelling far – just an office or two down the hall, to the parent Chrysalis label. But the break with 2-Tone wasn't intended to be either physical or personal. It was symbolic, the Selecter's one chance to prove, like Madness and the Beat, that they could stand on their own many feet. There was, however, one major difference. Whether by virtue of the brevity of their tenures or because of their subsequent success, those bands had never been truly seen as 2-Tone groups. The Selecter, on the other hand, had more than a history with the company, they had a stake in it. Had their first record not backed the label's own debut? Had they not fermented from the same sea of musicians as the Specials? Weren't they the only other group to actually have a say in the running of the label? The Selecter weren't simply *a* 2-Tone group. Alongside the Specials, they *were* 2-Tone. And, outside of the Specials, there were no other stars.

As it turned out, that was part of the problem. The Selecter's farewell statement made it plain. Pauline Black complained, "Every 2-Tone single has reached the charts… a situation which the Selecter feel is ultimately stifling new talent, leading bands to feel they need to stereotype themselves to what they believe to be the 2-Tone sound. 2-Tone was intended to be an alternative to the music industry, a label that took risks and, we hope, injected some energy into what had become a stale music scene. The time has come when we want to take risks again."

They were certainly doing that. The 2-Tone tag didn't guarantee chart success, as the label's own next few releases would prove. But it did induce a level of interest that other companies could not always ensure – including Chrysalis. The Selecter would enjoy just one further hit, a minor chart entry for 'The Whisper' in August 1980, and that, as Black subsequently acknowledged, was "the beginning of the end for us."

In-fighting savaged the group. Despite, as Black put it, "the themes of harmony and unity that filled our songs, we found it difficult to live that reality in the band." Attempts to record a new album at Horizon Studios in Coventry were scuppered when Desmond Brown and Charley Anderson quit to form a new group with Silverton Hutchinson, the People. Although they were quickly replaced by James Mackie (keyboards) and Adam Williams (bass), the Selecter *as a band* was finished. When their sophomore album, March 1981's *Celebrate The Bullet*, misfired, it was all over.

"'Celebrate the Bullet' [itself] is still my favourite [Selecter] song,' says Black. Its release as the title track to an album, however, was horrifically mistimed. In the previous three months, John Lennon had been murdered, while American President Ronald Reagan had only narrowly escaped an assassination attempt. Mentioning the LP's title on air was frowned upon by the BBC, a fate which ensured that airplay for even its most innocently themed songs was discouraged. Barely was the album on the shelves than Black announced her intention to quit – wrapping up their American tour, the Selecter played their final show at Bonds in New York on June 17, 1981. Davies folded the entire group soon after.

The Selecter's relationship with 2-Tone, however, was not the only casualty as the summer of 1980 wore on, and the 2-Tone backlash got underway with a vengeance. Last in, first out, the Bodysnatchers were the first to feel the fury, as their second single, 'Easy Life', took a quick look around from a chart peak of #50, then sank like a stone – the least successful 2-Tone single ever. It was not, however, to be alone for long. The Swinging Cats made their debut with the pumping 'Away' and, even before they became the first 2-Tone act ever to serve up a flop, the *New Musical Express* was casting a disgruntled ear over their offering and asking, "Is the 2-Tone quality control on holiday or what?'" The unspoken suggestion was that the vacation would soon become a vocation.

Rico followed the Cats into the litterbox. Dropped by Island Records earlier in the year, he made the inevitable switch to 2-Tone and, with sundry Specials in his backing crew, released an excellent coupling of 'Sea Cruise' and 'Oh Carolina'. It bombed. Even partisan observers began wondering: if 2-Tone was no longer able to sell, what hope did the rest of the Ska-Mod equation have?

Suddenly, bands forged in the white heat of the previous summer's explosion were falling by the wayside weekly, most unnoticed, almost all unmourned. One day you'd see them in the gig guide, the next day you wouldn't. It might be months before you wondered again where they'd gone, as Arthur Kay, whose 'Ska Wars' so memorably pipped 'Gangsters' to the pioneering post, testifies.

Kay had already resurfaced with a second single, the quaintly imploring 'Play My Record', when he decided to move out of the studio and onto the live circuit. With accompaniment from a local soul combo, Life And Soul (whose guitarist, Bob Coltart, and saxophonist, Paul Mylnarz, both appeared on 'Play My Record'), Arthur Kay and the Originals played their first gig at the Cabin in Herne Bay – "and went down a storm," according to Kay. However, Life and Soul's own commitments were a constant bugbear. When Kay had to turn down the chance to support the Bodysnatchers at Folkestone's Leas Cliff Hall because his bandmates were already booked to play some place else, it became clear that the arrangement was not working out.

As luck would have it, another new Ska band was forming in Herne Bay at the time, and were in search of a bassist and a vocalist. Kay, who was both, got in touch and the Originator, as he called the new group, were quickly embarking on a diaryful of sold-out shows around the Kentish countryside. Attempts to broaden their appeal, however, simply weren't working, as the market for any but the biggest Ska names first began to contract, then to calcify. Calls to London promoters were greeted with less and less enthusiasm every time. 'Another Ska band?' they'd sniff disinterestedly. 'Sorry, that was last year's thing.' Or words to that effect.

"All too soon," Kay reflects, "the band started drifting apart." By the end of the summer, Kay decided it was time to call time on his great Ska adventure, and returned to London. There he fell in with the Balham Alligators, destined to become one of the most popular pub performers of the 1980s. It would be another decade – and a whole new revival – before he returned to the music which history can be written to insist he helped kickstart.

There was one casualty that summer, however, who would never be making a comeback. On July 15, 1980, the world awoke to discover that Ruts vocalist Malcolm Owen was dead. No matter how much the band's music meant to everyone else, the only song that truly resonated with him was the first one the Ruts ever recorded, the anti-heroin anthem 'H Eyes'. "It's gonna screw up your head," he counselled. "You're gonna wind up dead." Just two years later, he did.

Heroin was scarcely the drug of choice at the time. It haunted Johnny Thunders and Sid Vicious, of course. But there were so many other options on the street, so many that fired precisely the energies that the street wanted to hear, that smack itself was a draggy sideline that few outsiders ever imagined would enter the equation.

Owens' colleagues were scarcely aware of the moment when the singer shifted from small-time dealing to big-time using. "He was a very well connected young man," marvels Dave Ruffy, "very handsome, he had this fantastic woman named Rocky who he married." He had everything going for him and, as the Ruts took off, he had even more. But, it turned out that even that wasn't enough.

"He wanted to be a rock star," bassist Vince Seggs continued. "Malcolm wanted to be a pop star. He wanted a lamé jacket for a laugh, to earn money, and take taxis. And he was hanging out with Phil Lynott, who was a lovely man, but was maybe not the best kind of influence for someone like Malcolm to be around."

For a time, through 1979 and the succession of ever-more incredible triumphs that seemed to be the Ruts' for the taking, Owen kept his demons at bay. "There were a lot of other different things around," Ruffy reflects. "We were big on drinking, we were big on spliff, like most young men given the chance; and, somewhere along the line, it all started going off for us." Unfortunately, that's also when smack came into their world.

"When we first started playing," Seggs continues, "Malcolm used to be late sometimes because he'd have 15 whiskeys down the road – but that was the way he performed. In a similar way, that's what the smack did, only it took over. And, in the end, he wasn't that dynamic person I first knew. He was a grey, struggling person in the end."

Seggs detailed the next stage. "You tell someone to get themselves together, and they can't. And what happens is, they lie. Malcolm and I used to share a hotel room and, when the little bag came out, I'd tell him, 'You're not doing that in my room.' So he'd go 'okay' and, a while later, he'd off into the toilet and do it. Then I caught onto that, so he'd go off and do it somewhere else, and it just became seedier and seedier.

"We'd get to a gig and just before the soundcheck, he'd disappear. He always said he'd never do it before a gig, but then sometimes we'd be waiting 20, 25 minutes to go on stage, and he'd come out of the bathroom, his eyes pinned and say, 'Ah, I couldn't get me laces undone.' We'd just be: 'Oh, fuck.' Or in the studio, he'd disappear for the toilet with his bag: 'Just going for a piss before this take.' He'd come back 25 minutes later, out of it. You'd go in there, there'd be blood in the toilet and the little cigarette filter. It was so sad."

When the Ruts first came together, Owen's pride and joy was a massive, and massively expensive, stereo system, with a vast and eclectic record collection to go with it. Early band meetings would be held at his house, simply listening to music which nobody else but Owen could have owned. He sold it all for smack. The rest of his possessions followed. So, early in 1980, did Rocky, his wife, driven away by Owen's heartless quest for the only thing he now cared about.

"The band was really suffering badly," Ruffy regrets. "Even getting Malcolm to rehearsals was difficult. He'd turn up five hours late, or not turn up at all and make some bullshit excuse, or other times he'd come in with his face smashed up, because he hadn't paid someone."

That spring, with the mood-melding 'Staring At The Rude Boys' behind them, the Ruts went into the studio to begin work on their second album. It was a disaster from the start, but they persevered, according to Ruffy, "because this was a bloke that we loved, there was the four of us, we were like a family, we'd been together about two years. But it just wasn't working."

One song gave them a glimmer of hope, 'Love In Vain', an earthquake dub B-side that documented both Owen's addiction and the break-up of his marriage. Ruffy remembered: "When we did 'Love In Vain', that line 'I don't want you in my arms'! Smack was taking its toll, and Malcolm didn't really want to be into it any more. The song was romance and the heroin at the same time. He said, 'yeah, it's really, really bad, I'm going to clean up.' And we believed him."

But it wasn't as easy as that, as Ruffy soon discovered. "Like a lot of junkies, he just gave us a complete load of bollocks. It was well meant but we'd go on tour, we'd be at gigs, and he had a fucking secret compartment in his shoe! We'd be: 'Malcolm, come on, we're going on!' And he'd be in the toilet."

"The only way we dealt with it," admitted Seggs, "was... we couldn't. We tried to help him, and it didn't work." By the time the Ruts' spring tour reached the south coast town of Bournemouth, the singer was in such a bad way that the only way they could keep him going was make sure there was a constant supply of coke on hand. "Someone had to keep giving him lines of coke so he could go back onstage, just to keep him going. He'd become like an old man. All his hands were withered and everything. He lost it. He got a nodule on his throat, and in the end he just collapsed."

The Ruts were in Plymouth, facing a sell-out crowd, and Owen was completely out for the count. "He couldn't get up for the gig." The show was cancelled; so was the next one, and the one after that. Almost overnight, the remainder of the tour was wiped out.

"You wanna know if I'm a heroin addict, right?" In an interview with *Sounds* in May 1980, Owen denied the rumours which had finally escaped the Ruts' own circle and were now swarming around the media. "I'll tell you the truth, the same as I told my mum when she rang up, scared to death. I've dabbled a bit in anything you could name. But everything's alright now, so don't worry."

Behind the brave words, however, it was crisis time. Ruffy bemoans: "His voice was shot, but as far as he was concerned, everything apart from smack was irrelevant. It was really sad, this remarkable man, who was really loved and respected by everybody, was just becoming an asshole, basically. All he cared about was smack. Nothing else mattered, all the stuff we did together didn't matter.

"So we thought the only way we can confront this is to say: 'Fuck you, we're not gonna do this anymore, we're not gonna be the Ruts, you can fuck off!' Because he kept saying he'd stop, then you'd see him and he'd be all pinned out, and it was still going on. So we said: 'OK, we'll knock it on the head'."

It was the most brutal shock treatment they could imagine. Virgin Records, the Ruts' label, had already given their blessing to the Owen-less team continuing as a trio, and studio time was booked. Whether they remained the Ruts or not, the group would go on. "And it really did Malcolm in," declared Ruffy. "Suddenly he went into rehab for a couple of weeks." From there, he retired to his parents' house to convalesce.

"I went round me mum's, and she locked me in for a week," Owen told *Sounds*. "Literally. I stayed in bed shivering and moaning, but it worked. I'm totally free of the filthy stuff now." He celebrated his recovery by going into hospital for another reason entirely, for the removal of the nodules at the back of his throat. Without them, he was confident, he'd be singing like a bird. On Friday, July 11, he arranged a meeting with his estranged colleagues.

"He'd done a clean out and said: 'Look, lads, I'm okay now,'" Seggs reflects. "He had the old sparkle back in his eyes, he was the old Malcolm, and he said: 'Look, how about one last farewell gig?' And we were: 'Shit, okay!' He'd been off the smack for three weeks, he was clapping his hands: 'I'll get the band back together.' And we said: 'You know, maybe he will. Maybe splitting the band was the best thing we could have done'."

Owen spent that night at the house Ruffy and Seggs shared in south London. The following morning, his father came over to drive him home. At some point over the next day or so, while his bandmates were in the studio recording the demos which they now desperately hoped they would not ever need, Owen borrowed £700 from his father to pay off his drug dealer and close the book on his habit.

What happened next was anybody's guess. According to Andy Damon, the Ruts' manager, "He was feeling so great when he paid the dealer, he must have thought, 'Aw, it won't hurt to have another hit'." Returning home with his booty, Owen sat on it for one night, maybe two. But that Monday morning, July 14 1980, he ran a bath, got out his works, and he fixed what had been his usual dosage.

Ruffy documented the inevitable conclusion. "Someone had gone round to meet Malcolm for a lunchtime pint, turned up and waited in the front room, because Malcolm was having a bath. His dad's looking all sheepish. The friend says, 'What's going on?' and his dad says, 'I can't get any answer from Malcolm.' So he got a ladder and went up the side of the house." Owen's body lay submerged in the bath.

"They kicked the door down, but by then it was too late." The sudden massive infusion of smack into Owen's detoxed body knocked him unconscious, and slowly, the singer slipped beneath the cooling water. The actual cause of death was drowning.

The following morning's tabloids simply reported the death of another rock star. The next week's music press gave him every headline he had ever craved, but all Seggs could see was hypocrisy. The Ruts were never critical favourites, "and I got very, very annoyed afterwards, because they were always slagging him off in the press while he was alive, then he died and suddenly our new single ['West One'] got Record of the Week. Everybody was saying he was great, and how he died for his art and all that. And he didn't. He didn't die for his art, because we weren't doing fucking art. We were a noisy Punk band. He died because he couldn't handle the heroin."

CHAPTER FOURTEEN

It would be satisfying to remember Owen's death that summer as a watershed of some sort, as the moment when *this* changed and *that* altered, when nothing was ever the same again. In fact, nothing happened. There was no terrific outpouring of grief, no tributary chart entry for the Ruts' final single. Virgin Records *did* cobble together a compilation-of-sorts, reviving the band's biggest hits and best bits, but Owen himself simply faded from the mind. 'The Ruts? Ah yes, they used to be good.'

Something did change, though, as Owen was laid to rest. Whether his passing hastened or confirmed or had nothing whatsoever to do with it, its consequences would impact on his corner of the British music scene for at least the next year.

The Ruts never fit into any single stylistic bag. Musically, their closest relatives were the Clash – the guileless slide from Punk to Reggae confirms that. But the Punk they played was itself out on a limb, sharing more with the terrace stomp of Sham 69, Cock Sparrer and the Angelic Upstarts than it did the melodic blast of the movement's other forebears.

But they were willing to learn, to take from other styles. More than any other group of the time, the Ruts straddled the musical and stylistic divides between Punk and Skinhead, Mod and 2-Tone, a feat which established them as the single place where every one of those tribes could gather in unity. Without them, the entire prism shattered.

Madness had long since distanced themselves from their Skinhead following; Sham, by summer 1980, existed in name and reputation alone. On July 27, less than a fortnight after Owen's death, Jimmy Pursey announced "I've just sacked my backing musicians" and made good on his oft-repeated threat to retire. Only the Upstarts, two albums into their major label career, kept faith with the fans who'd brought them this far – and they were going off the boil. So the fans did the only thing they could – they started forming their own groups. The fallout from that decision would form the third of the great musical movements of the era: Oi! The first of its offspring was also the greatest – the Cockney Rejects.

Fronted by a pair of east London boxing champs, Micky Geggus and Jefferson 'Stinky' Turner, the Cockney Rejects played their first live shows in early 1979. Their initial audience was drawn from the West Ham United football crowd within whose ranks the musicians themselves rose – early Rejects gigs were little short of an after-hours supporters' club meeting, with Hammers anthems drowning out all other chants.

Football, oddly, had remained largely untouched by the cultural wars being fought elsewhere on the youth circuit – oddly because, more than musical gatherings, the terraces were a natural recruiting ground for the Fascists. Across the League, racism had been on the rise since the first black player was greeted with monkey noises, and West Ham was one of the most notorious hotspots. It was there, according to former West Brom manager Ron Atkinson in his autobiography *Big Ron*, that "we had to endure the usual banana-chucking episodes." Atkinson recalls how the black players on his team – the so-called Three Degrees, Cyrille Regis, Laurie Cunningham and Brendan Batson – dealt with the abuse. "Cyrille... would grab the freely tossed fruit, ram it down his shorts and give further evidence that what they say about black men is quite possibly true. Brendan, on the other hand, simply peeled his banana and ate it, which brought a roar of applause from the Hammers fans and instantly defused a potentially nasty situation." It was that humour, as opposed to the ugliness that birthed it, that the Cockney Rejects aimed to capture.

Musically built around the same foot-stomping, fist-waving anthems as the early Upstarts and Sham, the same riff-heavy approximation of an 'oggie oggie' chant tidal-waving through a packed football stadium, the same bellow of working class discontent, the Rejects' attitude was pure no-nonsense to the point of echoing the original Punk crew's complaints about the stagnation of the then-contemporary music scene ('Oh goody, a new ELP double-album to look forward to') by pointing out that the new wave itself had become as bloated as its predecessors: 'Oh goody, a new Clash triple album to look forward to.'

"Betrayed?" snarled Micky Geggus. "Yeah, course I feel betrayed. It's like everything's gone back to what it was like in '74 and '75." Only as the Rejects' own stock began to climb did he sense any kind of salvation. "I honestly think it's started again. The feeling's come back again."

With former Sham roadie Vince Riordan on bass and a revolving procession of drummers, the Rejects were 'discovered' by *Sounds* journalist Gary Bushell in May 1979. He became their manager and immediately introduced them to Jimmy Pursey, who produced the group's first single,

2-TONE, THE SPECIALS AND A WORLD IN FLAME

'Flares And Slippers', for release (by the Walthamstow indie Small Wonder) that August.

Bushell insists that the Rejects were absolutely apolitical – their songs concerned nothing more controversial than "East End life, boozers, battles, police harassment and football." Gigging with the Angelic Upstarts, however, swiftly taught the band that it isn't what you say that matters – indeed, what you say is often the last thing anybody listens to. When their first major London show, opening for the Upstarts (and the hideously mis-billed Mods, The Low Numbers, turned nasty within seconds of the show beginning, the group knew exactly what to do.

Road-manager H told *Rising Free* fanzine, "I used to follow Sham 69 and the difference was, when trouble started at Sham gigs, they used to run off stage crying. But at Rejects gigs we sorted it out ourselves. We don't wanna be known as a violent band 'cos basically they're just normal geezers like you or I and, if you get upset, you don't take shit from anyone, right? At the Electric Ballroom… we vowed beforehand if there was any trouble we'd sort it out ourselves. There was trouble, but we sorted it out in five minutes. It might have seem a bit drastic to the onlooker, steaming in and giving them a good pasting… it was nothing to be proud of, but [it] needed doing. Afterwards the kids responsible came up to us and said 'Where are you playing next?' We had gained the crowd's respect."

Determined to avoid an audience whose methods of showing appreciation made old-time Punkers' love of gobbing seem polite, the Rejects turned their attention away from the high-profile Skinhead shows, and became regulars at the Mod hang-out, the Bridgehouse (it was the Geggus' local). There, a near-residency allowed them to merge a Glory Boys following with their own, and there, they fermented what *Sounds* quicly labelled a new musical movement – even if they did have problems finding a name for it. In the space of just a few months, confused readers were introduced to 'Real Punk', 'New Punk', 'Street Punk' and, finally, Oi!

In fall, 1979, Bushell stepped aside as the Rejects' manager in favour of Tony Gordon, who already handled Pursey's affairs. Pursey himself remained at the production helm as EMI swooped for the group and set them to work on their debut album, 1980's *Greatest Hits Volume One*, together with the first in a year-long stream of (minor, for the most part) hit singles, 'I'm Not A Fool'.

As their own profile rose, the Rejects answered the inevitable questions about their political affiliations by ferociously dismissing the National Front and the British Movement ("we're not gonna take no bollocks"). Nor were they shy about admitting that their most fervent delights included punching Nazi noses. But, of course, they could not control the politics of those who followed them. The imagery of a Union Jack banner was akin to a red (white and blue) rag to a bullish minority, regardless of whether or not it was tied in with West Ham United's own crossed hammers logo.

Not that that was less likely to rouse passions. In April, the Rejects celebrated West Ham's arrival in the FA Cup Final by recording a pulsating rendition of the team's own anthem, 'I'm Forever Blowing Bubbles' – and set themselves up as a target for every Hammers-hater in the land. The band's next Electric Ballroom show was ambushed by an army of belligerent Arsenal supporters, while their appearance at Birmingham's Cedars on June 6, 1980, brought out a couple of hundred Skinheads blues to challenge the Cockney Rejects' allegiances. From the moment the group appeared, the stage was bombarded with abuse and the occasional bottle – a shower that became a veritable hailstorm after Stinky Turner suggested that the troublemakers might want to meet him outside. With everything movable (and breakable) now flying stagewards, Micky Geggus leaped into the audience and flattened one of the locals, before himself being struck with such force by a missile that he wound up in hospital, receiving nine stitches.

But the Brummies had not finished with the Rejects. While one gang converged on the hospital (Geggus escaped by leaping 20 feet from a window), another remained behind at the venue and cleared out all the band's gear.

While the rest of the party drove off to the next gig in Huddersfield, Geggus and Grant Fleming, vocalist with the supporting Kidz Next Door, remained behind in Birmingham to search for the stolen equipment. They didn't find it, but the search itself soon ran into further trouble as an iron-bar-toting Geggus was taken into police custody on a charge of malicious wounding. (He received a suspended sentence when the case came to court the following year.)

Although the tour continued, the Cockney Rejects were now marked men, with every show an excuse for some local firm to descend to test what they were made of. It was a bloody period that climaxed in Liverpool with some of the most violent scenes ever seen at a concert… up to that point, anyway. With blades and other weapons being flashed in every direction and the Rejects' road manager being threatened at knifepoint, the group was forced to cancel the gig. Their days as an active touring unit were over.

And so, it seemed, was the Oi! movement. Sham had shattered and the individual members were planning musical existences far from the rallying row of old, a solo career for Pursey, a liaison with Stiv Bators for his bandmates. Dropped by Warners, the Upstarts, too, had come off the road while they considered their options. That summer, as Gary Bushell set about compiling a long-planned compilation album of the best of Oi!'s brief burning,

Strength Through Oi!, even he must have wondered whether he was writing its epitaph.

From the moment that the cry went out for unsigned bands to submit their demos, however, it became clear that the legacy of Sham, the Rejects and Upstarts was stronger than anyone had suspected. Bushell was astonished by the number of new groups answering his call, stunned by their geographical spread. Infa-Riot from Plymouth, Criminal Class from Coventry, Sunderland's Red Alert, Edinburgh's Exploited, and many more testified to a nationwide need for all that Oi! represented. The musical force that had recently been deemed deceased was revealed as more vibrant than ever.

And more potent – at least so far as readers of the *Daily Mail* were concerned. In an age in which a full-scale race war remained the biggest bogey on the British political scene, the Oi! movement's glorification of the Skinhead cult played into society's greatest fears. And the album's cover photo, a stomping Skin with his face contorted by aggression, was scarcely going to pacify the music's foes.

Maybe the *Mail*'s condemnation of *Strength Through Oi!* as "a Nazi record" was a shade over the top, but the rest of Britain's tabloids fell into line regardless, without even bothering to listen to such anthems as Splodge's 'We're Pathetique', Barney Rubble's 'Beans' and the Toy Dolls' 'Deirdre's A Slag' – a song commenting upon the romantic life of a character (Dierdre Barlow) from TV's *Coronation Street*! They also overlooked the presence of RAR stalwarts Criminal Class, whose 'Blood On The Streets' fired a dramatically unequivocal warning shot over the Fascist bow.

But why let reality get in the way of a good scare story?

Of all the incoming missiles, the most potent were the 4-Skins, a London-based quartet which joined the Bridgehouse scene during 1979 (Micky Geggus filled in on drums at their first-ever show, opening for the Damned), and rapidly filled the void left by the Cockney Rejects. There was one major difference... they didn't like football – or, rather, they did, but not enough to martyr themselves to its mobs.

Neither did they intend to get drawn into the political arena, instead adhering to what they themselves considered an even-handed refusal to align themselves with any organisation whatsoever. But, of course, their determination was doomed to failure, as they promptly fell foul of Rock Against Racism's own decidedly illiberal insistence that, 'if you're not with us, then you must be against us.'

The 4-Skins shrugged off RAR's condemnation, insisting that the race issue had nothing to do with them. It wasn't 4-Skins shows which were routinely interrupted by gangs of Sieg Heiling thugs; it wasn't their gigs that were descended upon by swastika-garbed right-wingers. Let the bands facing these problems confront them. For the 4-Skins, there were other issues – unemployment, class, Thatcher – that demanded just as much attention. When *Sounds* convened an Oi! debate early in New Year 1981, bringing together musicians from across the Oi! spectrum (Infa-Riot, the UK Subs, the Cockney Rejects, Max Splodge, the Business, the Last Resort and the Angelic Upstarts all took part), the 4-Skins remained resolute on that point.

Unfortunately, it was a stance that would very quickly backfire upon them.

CHAPTER FIFTEEN

Autumn 1980 was when the heavyweights came out to play. The Specials' second album, the plaintively-titled *More Specials*; Madness' much-anticipated *Absolutely* sophomore; and, delayed more than many might have expected, but imminent at last, the debut set from UB40, *Signing Off*. And it was indicative of just how much steam the Brummies had built up over the past year that, while both the Specials and Madness would find themselves having to defend their offspring against all manner of challenges, *Signing Off* emerged one of the year's toughest, tautest declarations of intent.

The group's political stance, like their music, had already been noted over the past few months, the nightmares flourishing around them unquestionably impacting upon the group's own view of the world. But whereas other bands aimed their responses straight into the soul of the beast, UB40 dove instead into comparative allegory, opening the album with 'Tyler,' a song that focussed not on some local injustice, but on one that was rapidly becoming an international *cause celebre*.

The story of 'Tyler' began in 1975, when a racial disturbance broke out at a High School in Louisiana, as a massive mob of whites gathered and attacked the black students. Within minutes, a 13 year old white student, Timothy Weber, lay dead from a single gunshot – fired, insisted the authorities, by 16 year old black Gary Tyler. Incriminated by a single witness, and with the alleged murder weapon only located during a third search of his school bus, the teen was swiftly convicted by an all white jury and sentenced to death.

But problems arose almost immediately, as the student witness promptly recanted, complaining of police coercion. Further investigation revealed serious problems in regards to the discovery of the gun. But Tyler remained on death row and, when the Supreme Court struck down Louisiana's capital punishment law, still Tyler's sentence was merely commuted to life imprisonment.

A series of appeals were dismissed; Tyler's applications for a pardon were turned down. Amnesty International became involved in the struggle against what an increasing number of people now regarded as a major injustice, but to no avail. UB40's championing of the cause, then, could be regarded as little more than an irrelevance in the face of the uproar as a whole, but still 'Tyler' remains as significant a milestone in the fight for racial awareness as, earlier in the year, Peter Gabriel's lament for the murdered South African activist, Stephen Biko.

Oppressive, emotive and stark, the song lays out the facts with the minimum of fuss, chanted down by an almost sardonic chorus, and almost mockingly melodic, the prettiness of the tune both belying, and amplifying, the strength of the message. With the haunting exception of 'Burden Of Shame,' a delicious rewrite of Van Morrison's 'Moondance' drawn through the perceived stigma of black British citizenry, nothing else on *Signing Off* matched 'Tyler' for impact, but nothing else needed to – even the tastiest cake can be over-egged, after all.

But still the album emerged a virtual iconoclasm, and one that left both the Specials' and Madness' own efforts looking patchy (if not pasty) by comparison.

That said, there was much to celebrate as *More Specials* played through, not least of all the almost unimaginable broadening of the band's actual horizons. Guest appearances from Rhoda Dakar ('Pearl's Café'), Madness' Lee Thompson ('Hey, Little Rich Girl') and the Go-Gos ('Enjoy Yourself') all fleshed out the Specials' own sound, but anybody hoping for a second helping of the hopping adrenalin that marked out their debut was in for a serious shock, as Roddy Radiation recalls:

"Jerry wanted a concept album of muzak, which he referred to as 'lounge music'. Unfortunately, not everyone was into this idea and there was considerable disagreement."

Neville Staples continues. "The second album – it reflected a lot of the travelling we were doing, and the kind of music we were surrounded with while we were travelling, which was muzak. That's all we used to hear: hotel music, elevator music, fucking airport music, that's all we'd hear, and things reflected onto that album." But he, too, was less than enamoured with allowing such shallow strains to overtake all that the Specials had represented in the past – all the more so since the Swinging Cats had already been chasing similar demons to no avail all year. "Trouble," Radiation concludes, "was brewing."

Everyone agreed, as Sir Horace pointed out, that "you can't keep churning out the same old music, as, say, Yes have for the last five years ... there's so many bands playing similar stuff... that's more reason to change." But

Brad leaned towards a more soulful direction, Radiation wanted to push forward a fascinating fusion of Ska and Rockabilly: Skabilly! Staples favoured a heavier Reggae sound; Hall was looking towards plaintive pop... "Our musical tastes had taken on many different styles," says Radiation. "Everyone had songs ready to record. But Jerry wanted total control of the album, image everything!"

One of Radiation's own numbers, 'Why Argue With Fate?' was even transformed into the instrumental 'Holiday Fortnight' after Dammers read the lyrics and concluded that they were about him – which, Radiation now concedes, they may well have been. For another, 'Hey Little Rich Girl', only Radiation's utmost stubbornness prevented Dammers layering the track with a drum machine.

Even in the teeth of this opposition, Dammers remained unbowed. "There was quite a bit of disagreement in the band when we first started doing it [but]... I had the idea in my mind and I could see and hear it as finished product." In the end, the rest of the group were allowed to stretch the concept a little: the free single issued with the first 10,000 copies of the album, 'Braggin' and Tryin' Not To Lie' backed with Staples' Judge Roughneck recreation 'Rude Boys Outa Jail', was absolutely in keeping with the group's original sensibilities. Some of the tracks on the LP proper were not too far removed.

The overall feel of the album was a retreat from the full frontal frenzied Ska-Punk hybrid that characterised *The Specials*, a retreat that in other circumstances might have been seen as a step forward. Radiation now acknowledges: "[Although] many of our original fans became confused by our new sound, we gained new fans from the student population who liked the new direction."

Neville Staples, too, puts a brave face on the turnaround. "People were expecting something similar to the first album, because that's how people are. But we'd moved on. We'd already done the first album, so what was the point of doing it again? We saw it that way. People just wanted us to stick with what they wanted us to play..." *More Specials* wouldn't do that.

Lyrically, the group remained

firmly on course. The first single from the album, the brooding lament of 'Stereotypes', traced the misadventures of the kind of character who, in mid-1990s parlance, would be described a 'lad': he drinks his age in pints, he gets all the girls and he fancies himself something rotten. Then he wraps himself around a lamp post while driving home drunk after a night of carousing.

It was a powerful, haunted song, with exactly the kind of message that the last few years' worth of 'Don't drink and drive' adverts had been trying to hammer home with their own use of pop music – and it was rewarded with a far more receptive audience than any of those well-meaning homilies.

Radio One, however, seemed less than certain that the message would get through – either that, or they objected to the word 'pissed' in the penultimate verse. Without going so far as to slap an absolute ban on the record, 'Stereotypes' didn't get the regular rotation that the Specials had come to take for granted. Thankfully, *Top Of The Pops* was a little less uptight – the single stood at #25 when the Specials turned out to perform on the show. The following week, it was #6.

The eternal horror of racism, of course, fuelled several more of the album's lyrics. But there was another terror sweeping into view that summer, too, as Thatcher announced that, in accordance with NATO's latest battle plans, she had given the US government permission to begin stationing nuclear Cruise missiles at Greenham Common airbase in Berkshire (the first 16 were due to arrive in 1983). Already unnerved by the sabre-rattling response to the Soviet invasion of Afghanistan in late 1979, Britain now found herself firmly in the front line of whatever boys-with-big-toys exchange the Americans and their Cold War adversaries might trigger.

The shadows cast by Greenham Common were to overhang much of the UK music scene that autumn. Former Adverts frontman TV Smith's Explorers debuted with the premonitory 'Tomahawk Cruise' – armageddon seen from the Bomb's point of view. Liverpudlian synthipoppers Orchestral Maneuvres In The Dark launched 'Enola Gay,' recounting that fateful day in August 1945 when the US bomber of the same name flew to Hiroshima, Japan, to usher in the nuclear age. And *More Specials* positively luxuriated in the fear and paranoia of waking up one day to find the entire country thrust into the muddy trenches of the Cold War, with Terry Hall and Jerry Dammers' 'Man At C&A' emerging so powerful an anti-nuclear lament that it was quickly adopted as an anthem-of-sorts by the Campaign for Nuclear Disarmament (CND), as it, too, emerged from a decade in mothballs to spearhead opposition to nuclear proliferation.

CND is one of the oldest organised protest bodies in British politics, formed in late 1957 in response to an article published that November by the *New Statesman* magazine, JB Priestley's *Russia, The Atom and the West*. Targeting the Labour party's decision to abandon its long-held policy of unilateral nuclear disarmament, the article prompted a massive wave of protest against party head Aneurin Bevin – a wave that the *New Statesman*'s own editor, Kingsley Martin, coalesced via a meeting of Priestley's most storied supporters, which led in turn to the inauguration of CND.

With its membership drawn from the cream of British left-wing intelligentsia (aside from Priestley, early members included authors Bertrand Russell, Vera Brittain and EP Thompson, publisher, Victor Gollancz, historian AJP Taylor and politician Michael Foot), CND first made its presence felt on the British landscape via a succession of annual, Eastertide marches from Aldermaston to Trafalgar Square – the birthplace not only of great swathes of British political thought during the late 1950s/early 1960s, but also of the British folk boom of the same period. Such protest classics as 'The Sun Is Burning,' 'The Crow on the Cradle' and 'Can't You Hear The H Bomb Thunder' all date from this tense period, while there was also a massive movement towards CND-oriented folk clubs.

At a time when the Cold War paranoia of successive British and American administrations scarred an entire generation with the fear of imminent nuclear disintegration, membership of CND was seen by many as their only hope of convincing their rulers to back down from the increasingly crazy crash course upon which West and East appeared to be bent. In the event, the entire nuclear debate seemingly fizzled out the moment the Americans got their teeth into a somewhat warmer conflict, and the "conventional" war that they came to wage in Vietnam for the next ten years.

From its peak during 1962-63, and the so-called Cuban Missile Crisis, CND's profile and, indeed, membership had declined considerably – by the late 1970s, in fact, were aware that the organisation even existed any longer. Now that era of quiesence was at an end, and the hawks were again scouring the sky for new prey. The nuclear stockpiles began growing once more, and with them, an entire new generation of weaponry.

In the past, nuclear missiles had simply lurked in vast concrete silos. Now, however, they were mobile, requiring nothing more than a trailer to manoeuvre them into position. Greenham Common was to be just one of several sites across western Europe where these terrifying new missiles would be placed, as a horrifying doomsday scenario suddenly flickered into the realms of possibility. Once, Europe had seen itself simply as the no-man's-land over which the bombs would fly, should the US and the Soviets ever come to blows. Now, however, it looked likely that Europe itself would be the battlefield.

Of all the bands within the Specials' immediate circle, it was the Beat and

UB40 who were the most closely aligned with CND, with the latter voicing a country's fears in late 1980, with the truly terrifying imagery of 'The Earth Dies Screaming' – still one of the most effective visions of the apocalypse yet set to music. When that same season brought a theatrical reissue for director Peter Watkins' 1965 drama-documentary *The War Game*, depicting the effects of a nuclear attack on southern England, 'The Earth Dies Screaming' played out as an unofficial soundtrack for every sleepless night that the film inflicted upon its audience.

The Beat's contributions to the debate, while less immediately eviscerating, were no less effective, as the recently written 'A Dreamhouse In New Zealand' took Neville Shute's *On The Beach* post-armageddon escapology even further away from the action. Incoming pianist Blockhead was a veteran of the organisation's 1950s heyday, while Dave Wakeling admitted that further impetus for the band's concerns arose from within their audience itself. "We ran a drawing competition [among fans]," he told the *NME*, "and there were kids of 14 drawing pictures of the world blowing up, with Margaret Thatcher leering... 59 percent of young people think there'll be a nuclear war. That's enough to make it happen."

His fears were echoed elsewhere. Folk songwriter Steve Ashley speaks for many observers when he recalls, "I got fired up after watching a *Panorama* programme focussing on Nato's decision to station short-range nuclear Cruise Missiles in Europe. It also reported on rich people building shelters all over the place, while the public was being encouraged to stock up with tinned food, and tape up their windows. It was quite a shock, and from that moment, I went 'critical'. I started reading up and writing songs about the whole issue. In the end I put on a gig called Moles And Skylarks, inspired by an article I'd read in the *Guardian*, which identified two types of response to the growing crisis – people either buried their heads or indulged themselves in a manic lifestyle."

The ironically gleeful rendition of 'Enjoy Yourself' (originally a hit for Doris Day in 1950) that opened and closed *More Specials* could have been drawn from the same inspiration. As the lyric insisted, it was looking a lot "later than you think" and, when the song was reprised as a doomladen dirge at the far end of the album, it imbued the entire album with a prophetic darkness that was difficult to dispel. And useless even to try.

So far as the government was concerned, the only official word on the nuclear issue so far had been a rather daft civil defense pamphlet titled, with undue optimism, *Protect And Survive*. Drawing just a little short of suggesting we all paint ourselves white (gloss paint deflects the blast better) and hide under the table, *Protect And Survive* was nevertheless a masterpiece of obfuscation, highlighted, perhaps, by its apparent insistence that there was no reason at all why anybody should actually die in a nuclear explosion. So long as you follow these simple directions...

As early as September 1980, however, the government had isolated CND as a potential threat to its own insistence that we remain calm in the face of instant vapourisation. When Steve Ashley followed the Moles and Skylarks show with a public meeting at a local club, even he was astonished when a local Tory councillor agreed to appear, alongside the Chair of CND, a Liberal counsellor and a solicitor member of the Green Party. "This was unheard of, since all members of the Tory party were disallowed from debating with CND at that time."

It was a policy that savagely cut both ways. If Tories refused to discuss the nuclear issue, there was no danger of them tripping up either themselves, or their party's policies. But remaining mute left them unable to defend themselves against the accusations that were piling up against those policies, an imperious silence that was all the more damaging for its very arrogance.

For the nuclear issue, although it focussed people's fears, remained only one of the myriad blades that threatened to cut the last remaining threads of national sanity.

The country – or, at least, the way of life that people had accepted was the best that the country could hope for – was now visibly decaying. The Health Service was still crumbling, prices were still rising and, despite the Conservatives' attacks on Labour's unemployment record, the dole queues continued to grow. Official figures for 1980 saw the jobless totals soar to over 1.6 million. Thatcher herself admitted: "I am profoundly concerned about unemployment. Human dignity and self-respect are undermined when men and women are condemned to idleness."

Her concern did not affect her policies. "The lady's not for turning," she famously announced when her party held its annual conference in Brighton that October, as the streets outside choked with the roar of several hundred 'Right to Work' protestors. Thatcher allowed rumour to float the possibility of reintroducing National Service – rounding up all the young unemployed and sticking them in the army for a couple of years and, while that particular idea was dropped, the headlines that attended the conference and the indifference with which the government seemed to regard the plight of the country's disenfranchised youth, were not going to go away. The opposition began to speed up.

Lynval Golding's aching paean to ennui, 'Do Nothing', had been chosen as the Specials' next single. Now it was decided to couple it with a reworking of Bob Dylan's 'Maggie's Farm', a song from his 1965 *Bringing It All Back Home* album which took on an entirely new meaning 15 years on.

The Beat had already declared their feelings about the Prime Minister with 'Stand Down Margaret', an in-concert spectacular that was transformed into a chilling dub on the B-side of their latest (fourth) single, 'Best Friend'. Previous releases, the hits 'Hands Off… She's Mine' and 'Mirror In The Bathroom', had seen the band blithely pursuing the melodic breeziness of their earliest performances. 'Best Friend' didn't deviate from the winning formula. Its b-side, however, was something else.

With all its proceeds – a substantial £15,000 (minus £4,000 in taxes) – destined to raise further funds for CND, 'Stand Down Margaret' caught the group entering musical and political territories that previous 45s had never hinted at. Even the group's detractors found satisfaction in learning that *some* things could disturb Dave Wakeling's impermeable cool, just as Wakeling was thrilled to find the soul of the song adapted as a veritable anthem at CND rallies the countryside over. From the smallest local gatherings, to the 250,000 strong demonstration that flooded London in 1983, the war chant of "Stand Down Margaret" that would rise spontaneously from the marchers was more potent, and more poignant, than any considered offering that the events' scheduled performers could muster.

'Maggie's Farm' was more than a response to the Beat's challenge to their militant image, however. Even before the single's release in December, 1980 (when it rose to #4), live performances of the song were among the highlights of the Specials' latest British tour, drowning out the clamour for the old favourites. Neville Staples: "People were genuinely not happy with Thatcher, and that song said it all."

The reception which greeted 'Maggie's Farm' was, in fact, one of the few lasting highlights of the entire tour – an outing which was ill-starred from the outset.

The original schedule had been delayed by the problems attending the completion of *More Specials*. Although the band had planned two weeks' rehearsal before the tour, Dammers remained largely absent from proceedings, suffering from a barrage of health problems that apparently defied every medical man who inspected him.

For Dammers, the uncertainty surrounding his ailments was compounded not by fear, but by a peculiar hope: the affliction which had laid him low might be serious enough to justify cancellation of the tour. The Specials' mood had still to recover from the traumas of the studio. Press reaction to *More Specials* left him reeling. Like the most vociferous fans, the critics seemed outraged that the Specials should have stepped so far out of character – even as previews of the tour wearily predicted another evening of the same old Ska. It was a no-win situation. The idea of complicating that dichotomy with an audience that regarded a Specials gig as nothing more than an excuse to kick each other to pieces left Dammers dreading the month-long outing.

There was to be no escape, no comfortable hospital bed. Though serious enough in its way, the diagnosis delivered just hours before the first gig, in St Austell on September 13, pegged Dammers with nothing more debilitating than mental and physical exhaustion – nothing that couldn't be endured while the Specials went on the road.

Still the problems piled up. For support on the tour, the Specials originally planned to make a clean break by recruiting a group that was as far from the 2-Tone family as they could manage, an American rockabilly crew that Roddy Radiation (of course) had discovered playing in a Soho club.

Formed in suburban New Jersey, the Stray Cats had arrived in London the previous summer. A chance meeting with ex-pat Englishman Tony Bidwell had convinced frontman Brian Setzer that Britain represented opportunity: an audience, a country, an entire generation, for whom the Americans' Cochran-with-attitude twang would sound as fresh as tomorrow.

Of course, London initially failed to live up to the Stray Cats' expectations. When Radiation caught up with the band in early 1979, they'd spent six months clawing their way into whichever gigs they could find, sleeping between-times on publicist Keith Altham's office floor. But they had a dynamic repertoire. No messing around with scratchy old 45s rehearsed as close to the original as was humanly possible, the Stray Cats wrote their own material, defying the listener to spot the joins. Anthemic long before they were recorded, songs like 'Runaway Boys', 'Rock This Town' and 'Stray Cat Strut' were already in the group's set, and would soon be joined by 'Rumble In Brighton', Setzer's commentary on the march of Mod-ness that was awaiting them when they landed.

After so much hardship and disappointment, the offer of a berth on the Specials' tour looked like the Stray Cats' biggest break yet. However, not everyone within the group's orbit was convinced that it was the best career move they could make and, the closer they came to the tour's kick-off, the more uncertain they became.

Those doubts were finally crystallised in September, when the Stray Cats played their biggest show yet, opening for Elvis Costello. It was an incongruous pairing, but a triumphant one. Costello professed himself as enthusiastic about this new band as he'd been about the Specials. His words translated directly to the record-buying public. 'Runaway Boys', the band's debut single, suddenly started picking up speed. Although posters and T-shirts for the Specials' tour were already in production, a support slot in front of a notoriously awkward audience no longer seemed so inviting.

With just weeks to spare, the Stray Cats made their excuses and left the tour schedule. They were replaced, perhaps inevitably, by the *Swinging* Cats, but even that simple decision brought its own tensions to bear. Not a soul on the tour believed audiences would allow the group to perform unmolested, and so it proved. Nightly, the Cats would scamper through their set and vacate the stage as fast as they could – not simply to make way for the headliners, but to give way to the stage invaders as well. The Specials' position on that form of idolatry was well known: "Who am I to say they can't come up onstage?" Terry Hall once asked. "They've paid their three pounds. They can do what they like." In the past, however, the dam had not broken until the show reached its final leg. This time around, there were nights when the first waves hit the stage before the first song was over.

There was no end to the fighting, either. At Edinburgh Playhouse on September 20, just three nights into the tour, only quick thinking by the venue's management prevented a full scale riot when the power failed. For 20 minutes, free drink and records kept the crowd happy while electricians worked to restore the system.

Shows in Newcastle and Cardiff did not fare so well: major fighting broke out during the Specials' performance. The London Hammersmith Palais gigs on October 6 and 7 passed off peacefully enough inside the venue, but were scarred by the glowering presence of a massive British Movement contingent on the streets outside. It was in the Specials' Coventry hometown on October 9, however, that the entire outing exploded into the full-blown riot that previous incidents merely presaged.

The gig was taking place within a massive tent pitched on Midsummer Common but the carnival atmosphere the big top promised was soon shattered. Facing an audience already torn between footballing rivalries and racial conflicts, the Swinging Cats were still early in their set when a gang of apparently ticketless Skins (Manchester United supporters, it was later alleged) shoved in, demanding "Where are you, Coventry?"

Coventry, of course, rose to the challenge – as did the Swinging Cats' Chris Long, inviting the rowdies to address their grievances to him. One of them promptly tried. The Cats beat a hasty retreat, hoping that an extended intermission might calm the crowd down. But, the moment the Specials appeared on the stage, the fighting broke out anew.

Twice, the musicians left the stage to wait for the can-throwing and fist-fighting to subside; twice, the trouble simply picked up where it left off upon their return. Finally, the band announced that they'd had enough and walked off. This time the crowd didn't care. By the time the group was coaxed into finishing the show – the alternative would have been too ghastly to contemplate – the tent was swarming with police, bouncers were lashing out at anyone who came close and the promoter was totting up the damage that the Specials would be held accountable for.

Neither were the police so caught up in the fighting that they failed to pay attention to the Specials themselves: after the show, Dammers and Hall were both charged with using threatening words and inciting behaviour. In court, three policemen and two bouncers were happy to give evidence against them. A local councillor publicly insisted that the group itself had planted the troublemakers. They were given £1,000 fines.

The Swinging Cats left the tour days later and replaced by the soulful Team 23; they had simply had enough, not just of the road but of being a band. The group split on the spot and, as the tour finally wound down, it was looking like the Specials might follow suit.

The Specials' second American tour was the first casualty of the band's need to sit back, take stock, and make some final decisions on what was left of their career. Scheduled for January 1981, it was pushed back until the summer – ostensibly to give Dammers the chance to recover from his still-nagging ailments, but also (and more pertinently) to buy time for the players to figure out their next move.

Their reputation was ruined. Plans for the Specials to headline CND's first major rally at Trafalgar Square on Saturday, October 26, were abandoned when the Department of the Environment refused to allow the organisers to mount a PA big enough for the anticipated crowd of 100,000. While other, smaller groups were given permission to play from makeshift stages erected on the backs of lorries, the Specials were withdrawn from the event.

Organised out of CND's tiny offices at the top of a house in Great James Street, London, the Trafalgar Square event was itself the culmination of a series of smaller, independently organised rallies and protests throughout the summer, aimed not only at awakening people's awreness of the issues but, in some cases, awakening people full stop. Steve Ashley's gigs, for example, were intended simply to challenge the apathy that still swirled around much of the British populace, although he now confesses, "looking back, I can see that my approach may have been a little heavy-handed.

"When people arrived, they were given different coloured paper badges to wear. I think they were red, yellow and black. The songs were interspersed with political sketches and, at the end of the show we announced that there had been a hypothetical nuclear explosion 50 miles away and the coloured badges randomly defined the distance of each individual from the blast. Then the various effects upon people and buildings at the three distances were read out in scarifying detail. There was no encore."

CND staged an early portest at Greenham Common on September 21, well in advance of the arrival of the Peace Camp – there, around 2,000 people listened as Joan Ruddock and others railed against the incoming missiles. The following day, Bristol University staged a concert to raise funds for a group of anti-nuke demonstrators from Stroud, who'd erected scaffolding to stop a train carrying nuclear waste from Berkeley Power Station to Sharpness. An exclusively folk-oriented bill included Ashley, Martin Carthy, The Watersons, Fred Wedlock, Hedgehog Pie and The Old Swan Band – scarcely the kind of fare that other politically active groups were then arranging, but enough, still, for Karl Dallas' *Melody Maker* review of the gig to insist that Monday night "might well be noted as the day the [folk] revival regained its conscience."

All of this activity, of course, was simply the run-up to the major event. "Trafalgar Square was filled with marchers and fabulously ornate banners waving in the sunshine," Steve Ashley remembers. "The sound of speeches echoed against the buildings all around and every now and then a huge cheer would rise up among us. Helicopters clattered overhead and there was a large police presence, but the march was orderly and peaceful. The word was that we were 150,000 people – although I think the police put it at 100,000.

"This was probably the largest peace rally in that place since the old Aldermaston days. It was a great day for anyone concerned about the arms build-up and good to see so many other like-minded people prepared to stand together." There was an especially powerful atmosphere as EP Thompson [author of the official CND riposte to *Protect And Survive*, the suitably retitled *Protest and Survive*] addressed the crowd. Ashley continues, "I think it was at this rally that he said 'Feel your own strength'" – a slogan that became one of CND's most vital pieces of advice to its followers. His encouragement seemed to work, as well. The next demo pulled in some quarter-of-a-million people, the one after that topped the 300,000 mark.

Had the Specials appeared at that first rally, their own future might well have taken on a very different timbre, so prominently and publicly aligning them, as it would have, with concerns that rose far above those concerns that had hitherto dominate their agenda. What, after all, did it matter what one person thought of another's skin colour, when we were all about to become identical piles of dust? We are all one in the glare of the nuclear flash.

Instead, the Specials remained silent – the group would play just two more concerts that year, the final nights of a fortnight's worth of benefit shows at the Hope & Anchor at the end of October. The event was being staged in aid of Blanket Coverage, a charity focussed on providing bedding and winter clothing for London's homeless and elderly, although for the Specials, the venue itself was as much of an attraction as the charity. It was within the subterranean glory of the Hope that the entire 2-Tone ride had begun 18 months earlier and, if this was to be the Specials' last stand (as many predicted), what better place could there be for them to strike the flag? And what better company could they hope to have as they did it?

Madness, Bad Manners, the Selecter, Ian Dury, the Damned, the Only Ones, the Skids, former Penetration vocalist Pauline Murray and Tom Robinson's new group, Sector 27, were all likewise committed to shows that season.For each of them, the gig offered a welcome opportunity to return to the kind of club setting where they all started out, but which they had long since left behind. Bad Manners had just scored a #3 hit with their third single, 'Special Brew', while Madness were preparing to one-step beyond even that, as they confirmed the brilliance of their just-released second album, with a few hints as to the make-up of their third,. For the Specials, however, the two shows represented more than a nostalgic rush. They reminded the musicians of just how much joy had slipped by them unnoticed, in the frenzy of simply keeping up with their own career's demands.

"Everything just went past so fast," Staples lamented 20 years later. "You're not actually able to think about what's happening to you, because TV, travelling, train rides, recording, gigs.... For a young kid it's like... wow! Because I always wanted to do music. When that started to happen, it was just out of this world. But they had us doing two shows a day, one in the afternoon, one in the evening. We never ever got a chance to sit down and look around at what was actually happening."

Now they would. Even before the first of the Hope & Anchor shows, the Specials had resolved to put their activities on hold for the next six months. Then they would decide whether they wanted to continue.

With admission to the Hope & Anchor restricted to just 200 people a night, the £3 tickets were at a wild premium. More people were turned away, disappointed, than were able to cram down the narrow steps to the dance floor. The lucky ones were treated to a performance they might never forget, the Specials showcasing their entire career with a delight that shrugged off the problems that assailed them elsewhere. And for those that didn't get in, an equally historic event was taking place just a couple of miles down the road at the Music Machine, as the Bodysnatchers prepared to play their last ever show, and a thousand-or-so of the faithful turned out to do the rock-steady one last time.

Defying almost every prediction about their future, the Bodysnatchers had continued going from strength to strength throughout the summer of 1980. The departure of drummer Jane Summers in June 1980, to continue her education, was managed with surprising ease: Judy Gray Parsons simply stepped into her place. The failure of the group's second single, 'Easy Life',and the glowering malcontents in the media were shrugged off. The band started planning their debut album (for release on 2-Tone), all the while

159

maintaining a hectic live schedule.

When Toots and the Maytals visited London at the end of September for the Hammersmith Palais show that secured their place in the *Guinness Book of Records* (the resultant *Toots Live* album was mastered, pressed, packaged and in the stores within 24 hours), the Bodysnatchers opened proceedings with a tumultuous set of their own – even though it was their third concert in 24 hours. The evening before, the Bodysnatchers both opened for Split Enz at the nearby Odeon, then staged their own show at Chelsea College.

From there, the Bodysnatchers headlined their own tour of the clubs. But the frenetic workload disguised a serious gulf that was opening up within the band. Of all the stalls that had dogged the album sessions, the greatest was a serious division of opinion: Nicky Summers and Rhoda Dakar agitated for the Bodysnatchers to take a more political stance, while their bandmates leaned towards a purer pop base. Neither was either side willing to give in – finally, in October, Summers and Dakar announced their departure. They would play out the remainder of the band's tour, to its Music Machine conclusion on Halloween, and that was it.

They were true to their word – as were the remaining five. Renamed the Belle Stars and completely redesigned, the new group made its live debut in January 1981 with a set that didn't even glance in any direction other than a rollicking sense of fun fun fun. And, although they didn't completely distance themselves from their bodysnatching past – the group's debut single, for Stiff in June, was a reworking of the old band's 'Hiawatha' – the emphasis was firmly on the word 'reworking.'

CHAPTER SIXTEEN

Of all the proposals and recommendations made by the Cass inquiry into the death of Blair Peach, the suggestion that the Special Patrol Group be somewhat better supervised was the one that received the most coverage. And it was the one most loudly ignored.

The unspoken suggestion that the SPG was, at best, an undisciplined vigilante group and, at worst, modern successors to the Black And Tans, seemed to vindicate every accusation and complaint that had ever been thrown their way.

Yet the force remained at large and unfettered, ignoring even the pretence of 'civil rights' with their increasing use of the so-called 'SUS' law, a 19th century social control legislation (section 4 of The Vagrancy Act 1824) which gave the police the right to stop and search anybody they suspected of having been involved in a crime – whether or not an actual crime had been brought to their attention.

The majority of the law's victims were either black or young, and its use had been of increasing concern for a couple of years now. The London punk band Reacta cut the seething 'Sus' for the indie Battery Operated label during 1978, around the same time as Linton Kwesi Johnson's 'Sonny's Lettah', unequivocally subtitled 'Anti-SUS Poem', detailed and dramatised Johnson's "own experiences of being arrested and beaten up by the police." The Ruts' first-album favourite 'SUS', meanwhile examined the law's application from the other end of the truncheon. With a lyric supplied by their black roadie Mannah, it detailed the glee with which the police added one more statistic to their quota: "We got you on SUS, you look too obvious, you'd better come with us."

On April 2, 1980, just three weeks before the Cass inquiry was published – and at the same time as the government's own Commission for Racial Equality purged five of its most "outspoken" (as *Private Eye* put it) commissioners – the SPG turned their attentions, and their powers, to the

Black and White cafe in Grosvenor Road, in Bristol's largely West Indian St Paul's district. Although the café was a well-known centre for drug distribution (a reputation which it has apparently retained: there was another high profile raid in January 2003), it was better established as one of the social hubs of the local community, a sanctuary where entire families could converge. Officially, the mid-afternoon raid was an enforcement issue. Clearly, it was also a racial one. The disturbing thing is, there seems to have been little attempt to disguise that fact.

As the café's owner was arrested and led away, officers began loading alcohol into their vans. A crowd gathered to watch and cajole until, an hour or so later, the first bricks were thrown. The police promptly retreated into the cafe and called for reinforcements – by which time the crowd had swollen to several thousand. By the time the embattled lawmen were finally able to leave the area, deep into the night, the streets were littered with the wreckage of burned-out squad cars. The tally of arrests and injuries confirmed the incident as the worst civil disturbance in Britain in years.

In the days that followed, the media tried hard to portray the St Paul's riot as wholly racially motivated, blacks against whites. It wasn't. Nor was it a random orgy of destruction. As Linton Kwesi Johnson (again) predicted in 1978's 'All Wi Doin Is Defendin' and researcher Steve Reicher proved in a 1984 study, the action was purely one community – St Paul's – repelling an invader – the police.

"It was definitely against the police," explained one of Reicher's interviewees, "because nothing or nobody else got hurt, except a bus got a window smashed. That could have been deliberate but I think it was probably not. Everyone went 'Ugh, idiots'." In fact, elements of the crowd moved to prevent any repetition of that attack, reminding the offenders who the real enemy was.

That same injunction – know the real enemy – would be repeated tirelessly over the next few months, as an apparently open policy of police harassment, targeted almost exclusively at blacks, kept tempers simmering until finally, a government promise to look into the application of the SUS laws did a little to calm the mood. Indeed, when the law was repealed in late 1980, many people believed the worst was over.

It wasn't. Early in the New Year, the police unveiled what many people regarded as an even more oppressive power, Stop And Search, the 'son of SUS' which was, if anything, better suited to intimidation than its predecessor.

The notion that the police had no interest in the black community beyond its ability to bump up their arrest quotas was not new. Crimes reported in such neighbourhoods routinely went uninvestigated, emergency calls frequently went unanswered. Such criticisms, however, saw little circulation beyond the immediate circles of their victims; tended to be ignored by society at large – until something happened that brought the entire situation into hideous, and unavoidable focus.

Early in the morning of January 17, 1981, fire swept through a home in New Cross Road, Deptford, South London, killing 13 young blacks attending a birthday party. Worse yet, survivors of the blaze seemed united in one observation: a white Austin Princess was seen driving away at speed at the precise moment that the fire broke out.

The suggestion that the house had been purposefully set ablaze, presumably by a fire bomb, was difficult to avoid. The last year or so had seen a growing number of such attacks take place all around the country, albeit with less tragic consequences. The New Cross Massacre, as it quickly became known, bore all the hallmarks of another.

A murder inquiry was launched, with the 'seriousness and magnitude' of the tragedy prompting Commander Graham Stockwell, head of the south London CID, to take charge of the investigation himself. Beyond off-handedly ruling out the racial motive, however, there seemed an appalling lack of urgency to the police investigation and, by the time the police concluded that the inferno had, in fact, started within the house, those suspicions had hardened into rage. At the beginning of March, two months after the fire, disquiet over the lack of progress prompted upwards of 15,000 people – mainly black, but swollen by a number of whites – to make a 10-mile protest march from Deptford into central London. The placards they carried said it all: "13 dead, nothing said."

Twenty years on, former Deptford community worker Ros Howells described for *The Guardian* the sense of disbelief that swept through the local community as their worst fears about the police and the media were seemingly realised: "There was an assumption that something illegal had been going on at the party. [The newspapers] didn't believe it could just be a group of children enjoying themselves. It was at that point that the black community started to believe that the lives of their children were worthless. We felt the view was 'What's 13 dead? Let's have a few more'."

It was into this volatile situation – and into the heart of the same smouldering community – that the police dropped Stop and Search, a key component in the newly instituted Operation Swamp 81 campaign against mugging and street crime.

Though touted as a London-wide affair, Operation Swamp 81 was, in fact, launched and almost wholly localised in the largely black neighbourhood of Brixton. Was it coincidental that the campaign itself was named after a speech given by Margaret Thatcher three years earlier, in which she warned, "people are really rather afraid that this country might be rather swamped by people with a different culture"?

At the time, the people who seemed most disturbed by the remark were the National Front, who feared (rightly, as it happened) that their own electoral prospects might be damaged by the Conservatives leaping aboard their racist bandwagon. Now, however, they undoubtedly felt proud to have played even a small role in such a successful enterprise. According to the local CID, there was no other way of looking at Operation Swamp 81. In the course of just six days from the end of March into early April, 120 plain-clothes officers had investigated no less than 943 potential criminals and arrested 118 of them – including, oddly, three members of the Lambeth Community Relations Council.

In numerical terms, Operation Swamp 81 might have been a resounding success. But it did little to improve community relations – a fact that Enoch Powell MP, the ferociously anti-immigration politician whose energies had long ago influenced Margaret Thatcher, was quick to point out. In 1968, Powell had raised anti-racist hackles when he warned that, unless the tide of incoming blacks was halted, the streets would one day become rivers of blood. Thirteen years later, on March 28 1981, the MP for South Down, Ulster, rose again to announce that racial "civil war" was imminent. A mere two weeks later, his prediction finally appeared on the eve of coming to pass.

On April 10, 1981, police were called to the scene of a stabbing on Railton Road, Brixton. Two black youths had been involved in an altercation: one, 19-year-old Michael Bailey, now lay bleeding on the street. Rather than calling for assistance, however, the police appeared more intent on interrogating him – just another Stop and Search. Suddenly, the 50-or-so youths gathered at the scene pushed their way through the police, scooped the wounded teen into a taxi and rushed him to the hospital – apparently, the last place that the lawmen had in mind for him.

More police arrived on the scene – and more angry onlookers. The stand-off faded after a few hours, but the tensions did not. When another black was arrested outside a minicab office in Atlantic Road the next afternoon, following some kind of disagreement with a plain-clothes police officer, the powder-keg detonated. By 5pm, the first police car was burning brightly; by 6.30, the first petrol bombs were flying.

Gathering at one end of Atlantic Road, 200 police in full riot gear charged towards what they believed to be the heart of the rock- and bomb-throwing crowd. Minutes later, they were charging back again, as windows on both sides of the street opened to disgorge their own hail of missiles.

Burnt-out police vans – 61 were destroyed before the night was out – were transformed into makeshift barricades. One group of rioters hijacked a double-decker bus and drove it at the police. Scarlet Macguire, a journalist for the IRN news agency, reported, "There was organisation. All the people I spoke to were politically aware. They hated the way they were treated, the way the police have provoked and harassed them for years. This wasn't a race riot. It was really cut-and-dried. It was the community against the police"

The *Socialist Worker* newspaper, meanwhile, reported positively heart-warming scenes: the Skinhead standing in a looted off-licence window, "handing out six packs to a group of Rastas"; the middle-aged white woman who was knocked off balance by a young Rasta as he ran down the road. "He picked her up, dusted her down and apologised. Both went on their way smiling."

This time, the rioters *were* destroying property, but their targets were well-chosen. The Windsor Castle pub, long despised for its racist door policy, was well ablaze. When the fire brigade arrived to fight the flames, neither the mob nor the police gave way – in fact, another fire engine was set alight on Railton Road. By the time calm returned to the streets, 14 buildings, including a school and another pub had been burned out.

The peace lasted less than 12 hours. On April 12, the Home Secretary William Whitelaw arrived in Brixton to see the damage for himself, while crowds gathered to greet him with scarcely ironic taunts of *'Seig heil!'* By nightfall, the streets were ablaze again. The police, while insisting that Brixton would never be permitted to become a 'no go area,' later revealed that it required no less than 7,300 officers to restore order to the neighbourhood.

The Observer newspaper was swift to condemn the rioting – but in a manner that gave no succour to the establishment. "We cannot afford to let British citizens conclude that riots are the only hope of improving their lives," the newspaper concluded before setting out the lamentable state of relations between local black communities and the police, the legacy of SUS and Operation Swamp 81 as well as years of abuse and harassment.

"If only a fraction of the allegations [of harassment and mistreatment] are true, some police officers in Brixton have recklessly jeopardised good relations with the local community by abusing the powers entrusted to them. The allegations range from impoliteness in everyday dealings with black people, to breaking down the door of private homes in unauthorised searches, physical violence against suspects, and disregard of [judicial rulings] when dealing with young suspects, especially minors. These charges may be exaggerated, but it must be obvious to anyone who cared to listen that the people of Brixton, black and white, believe them to be true."

The government was no less bullish. While Whitelaw promptly announced a public enquiry into the riots to be headed by Lord Scarman, Thatcher was swift to dismiss any suggestions that either police racism or the area's massive levels of unemployment could be blamed for the unrest. "Nothing, but nothing, justifies what happened," she shrieked. When reminded of the government's own admission, days earlier, that jobless totals had risen by a full million, to 2.5 million, in the last twelve months – with black unemployment up by a staggering 82 percent – she remained defiant. Unemployment had nothing to do with it. "Money cannot buy either trust or racial harmony."

Nor was she impressed when local council leader Ted Knight condemned the police for behaving like "an army of occupation." "What absolute nonsense and what an appalling remark," she snapped. "No-one should condone violence. No one should condone the events. They were criminal, criminal." Only Enoch Powell seemed unphased. Britain, he said, "[had] seen nothing yet."

CHAPTER SEVENTEEN

On February 15, 1981, the Specials unveiled either a tribute to, or a memorial for, the rollercoaster ride that was 2-Tone. *Dance Craze* was the work of American Joe Massot, a writer and film director who first came to prominence in 1968, when his *Wonderwall* tale of psychedelic London was released with a specially-scored soundtrack by Beatle George Harrison. Two years later, Massot was involved in writing the underground oddity *Zachariah*, a self-styled 'electric western' that roped the likes of the James Gang and Country Joe and the Fish into the action. His greatest moment, however, came as director of *The Song Remains The Same*, the 1976 fantasy-documentary built around Led Zeppelin's 1973 Madison Square Garden concerts, still widely (and wisely) regarded among the best-*made* rock films of all time.

Selective in his subjects, Massot originally intended making a movie about Madness alone – he caught them live in LA towards the end of their first full American tour in early 1980 and was instantly impressed. It was his son, apparently, who introduced Massot to the wider 2-Tone picture. Soon after, the director was in the UK, witnessing the movement as it screamed towards its spring-summer climax.

He began filming almost immediately, setting up his cameras in the heart of the dance floor, and simply letting them roll – a document, he pointed out, not only of the music, but of the mayhem that the music was capable of inspiring.

Jerry Dammers had himself already considered the possibilities of a 2-Tone movie; it was an easy collaboration as their ideas overlapped. 2-Tone would release the ensuing soundtrack album, with the vast majority of the featured performers being drawn from the label's own roster: the Specials, the Selecter, the Bodysnatchers, Madness and the Beat would all be included, with Bad Manners providing the only outside influence.

The possibility of investing the movie with a documentary slant was quickly passed up. Even in its early days, Dammers was aware that any attempt to document the rise of 2-Tone would also have to account for its fall. Any investigation of the movement's so-called 'philosophies' would only muddy the waters. *Dance Craze* was to be nothing more than a non-stop concert, the stream of music interrupted only by the insertion, exactly amidships, of a short sequence of vintage newsreel footage depicting past dance crazes. The suggestion that 2-Tone was simply the logical successor to such past fads as the Twist and the Locomotion may not have been intended to be dismissive but it certainly put some of the movement's apologists in their place.

Also unmentioned was the casualty rate. By the time *Dance Craze* received its world premiere at the Midem music industry conference at the end of January 1981, the Bodysnatchers had already shattered. Selecter would be gone within a couple of months of the film's UK debut, at screenings at the Manchester, Leeds and Sheffield Odeons on February 15. And recent releases by the Beat and Madness had readily consigned their portions of the movie to the realms of archaeology.

For the Beat, the six months since 'Stand Down Margaret' had seen them step away from the cosy pastures of the Lovers' skank they'd long since perfected, with a second album *Wha'ppen?* which exploded their reputation as the safe face of Reggae-based rock. Broaching jingoism, paranoia, unemployment and electioneering, 'I Am Your Flag', 'All Out To Get You', 'Get A Job' and 'Cheated' bespoke a political awareness that lay far removed from the songs the Beat were best known for, with 'Monkey Murders' addressing the climate of racial attacks with chilling precision. Compared to 'Too Nice To Talk Too,' the Beat's last big hit, in late 1980, even the Police had sounded slyly subversive (and would soon prove as much when their

'Invisible Sun' took a well-worded swipe at Britain's Northern Ireland policy). Compared to the biting best of *Wha'ppen*, however, even Crass sounded unconcerned.

Madness, too, had changed beyond all recognition, as they had completed their transformation into everyone's favourite madcaps, a giant grinning space-hopper whose greatest *faux pas* in the past twelve months was getting themselves banned from *Tiswas*, the anarchic Saturday morning TV show hosted by Sally James and Chris Tarrant. It was not Suggs' fault that he poked James in the eye while trying to wipe some cream off her face; it probably wasn't Lee Thompson's fault that he didn't appreciate being bitten by passing toddlers. But the show forbade Madness to darken its doorstep again. The next time they turned up on kids' TV, it was in the less glamorous surroundings of Mike 'Frank Butcher' Reid's *Runaround*. Which was staged, to celebrate Christmas, on ice. Of course.

The visual arts intrigued Madness. Taking the utmost advantage of the infancy of video, the group threw itself into the genre, pumping out a stream of absolutely irresistible shorts that effortlessly captured the imagination of the major outlet at that time, the American 24-hour music video channel, MTV. The advances that Madness made in the US over the next two years paralleled MTV's growth from a regional cable channel to a full-fledged national network, a process that culminated, in 1983, with a Top 10 berth for 'Our House' that was almost wholly built upon the band's ability to match the Nutty Boy sound with a wealth of captivating images.

Amid all this, the group did still attend to the serious business of music, of course. Their performance at Elvis Costello's post-Christmas bash at the Birmingham NEC, sharing the bill with the Selecter and UB40, was nothing short of sensational, even as UB40 themselves stretched towards a career-best intensity.

Still, the group's elevation to these heights was the cause for some disquiet: later in the year, Madness made the surprising decision to record a session for BBC DJ Richard Skinner's evening show, at a time when acts of their stature rarely deemed the effort worthwhile. And, as it transpired, they agreed with that summation. "Madness were more like dullness and don't give a shitness," recalls producer Dale Griffin. "Maybe they just get tired of being Nutty Boys day and night. Plus they were doing just fine – they didn't need to do any half-baked BBC sessions."

If *Dance Craze* had any lasting significance for Madness, it was providing the catalyst for their own flick, *Take It Or Leave It*. Filming began just weeks after *Dance Craze* opened and the completed picture, an enjoyable document of the group's early adventures, was in the theatres by October 1981. There, too, however, the timing was skewed by events. When *Dance Craze* hit the cinema circuit, the Specials were still around to remind movie-goers what this Ska stuff was all about. By the time *Take It Or Leave It* came along, even that last luxury had been withdrawn.

Announcing their intention to take six months off, the Specials splintered in December, bowing out with a John Peel session that was remarkable for its indifference to their own career. Accompanied by Rico and Dick Cuthell, the Specials performed just one song from *More Specials*, 'Stereotypes', before reprising Rico's rearrangement of 'Sea Cruise' and introducing a new song, 'Raquel', described by Roddy Radiation as "a Punky-Ska dig at Miss Welch."

The members scattered. Returning to a part-time project he had launched in the weeks after the Seaside tour, Radiation stepped out at the helm of a new band formed with brother Mark, and fellow former Wild Boys/UK Subs drummer Pete Davies. The Tearjerkers (no relation to the Irish act who gigged around the UK a year or two previous) dug deep into the soul of Radiation's beloved rockabilly – at a time when the now-rampant Stray Cats and Polecats were pushing what looked like a full-scale revival into the chart, only the Tearjerkers' part-time status prevented them following the leaders to glory.

Neville Staples, Lynval Golding and Terry Hall stayed in touch long enough to write and record a few demos for the next Specials album, but Staples was just as devoted to the Jah Baddis sound system that he was setting up with his girlfriend, the Bodysnatchers/Belle Stars' Stella Barker.

The pair formed a record label of their own, Shack Records, and promptly signed 21 Guns, a combo formed by two former Specials' roadies, Trevor Evans and Johnny Rex. Other recruits included rapper Eddie Peters, and the sometime-novelty group Lieutenant Pigeon, Coventry-based chart-toppers nine years earlier with the maddeningly catchy 'Mouldy Old Dough'.

According to Pigeon's Rob Woodward, "the association with Neville proved quite interesting. Knowing the style of music associated with 2-Tone, we were pleasantly surprised when he approached us, although attention to the single was disappointingly muted – a few local radio airplays and the odd Radio 2 spot, before it faded into oblivion." However, the group did retain a relationship with the 2-Tone hierarchy. Various members of the shattered Selecter used Pigeon's own studio to record demos, with Woodward himself adding piano to a couple of them.

Brad Bradbury, too, formed his own label, Race Records, launching it with the first single by Team 23, the combo that had gallantly filled in for the Swinging Cats on the last dates of the Specials' autumn tour. Night Doctor, a Reggae band formed by former Upsetters trombonist Vin "Don D Junior" Gordon, were next, while Race also released the first single by the People, the post 2-Tone supergroup formed by Selecter's Desmond Brown and Charley Anderson, with original Specials drummer Silverton Hutchinson. The single was produced by Lynval Golding.

Bradbury also joined Jerry Dammers and Sir Horace (whose despair at the Specials' situation had seen him turn to the Exegesis cult for support) in Rico's backing unit, as the veteran Ska-man toured the UK and Europe to promote his own latest 2-Tone release, *That Man Is Forward*.

But Dammers turned down Debbie Harry's invitation for the Specials to accompany her on a planned cover of the Paragons' 'The Tide Is High' (her regular band, Blondie, took their place and scored a UK #1), and only the group's political conscience prevented them from lying entirely fallow.

Although they didn't acknowledge it at the time, the Specials had been seriously stung by Rock Against Racism's accusations that they were not doing as much as they could for 'the cause' – stung, but helpless, too. Roddy Radiation explains: "I'm sure we could have done more, but we were burned out from constant touring." Besides, "due to internal conflict, and the sudden success of the 2-Tone movement, we found it hard to address all the world's problems! Our own problems were challenging enough."

It was time to redress that imbalance. In January, 1981, the Specials joined the Beat for three shows in Northern Ireland and Eire, raising money for various childrens' and anti-nuke charities. Unfortunately, their attempts to leave Ireland with the proceeds, somewhere in the region of £8,000, were foiled when airport officials consulted their country's controls on the movement of currency – and learned that the Specials had just driven a bus through them. The entire amount was confiscated, and the charities didn't see a penny.

Most of the band's other 1981 shows were anti-racist events. Only once, at the end of May, did the Specials play for any other reason, when they returned to London to headline a free concert for the army of die-hard protestors who, close to a month before, had set out from Liverpool with the TUC People's March for Jobs – a parade that, in total, was estimated to have involved over a million as it made its way down the country.

In April, with the Brixton riot fresh in the memory, the Specials journeyed to Leamington Spa for a secret gig in aid of the local Anti-Racist and Anti-Fascist Committee. The city was still in shock following the horrific murder, weeks earlier, of an elderly Asian woman, doused in petrol and then set ablaze by her attackers. Two months later, the Specials would headline another benefit – this time in their hometown – to raise money for the family of Samtam Gill, a recently murdered Asian student.

Concerts alone would not combat such absolute evils – nor even keep up with them. According to official police statistics, no less than 31 black Britons had been murdered in racist attacks since 1975, but that was simply the 31 that they acknowledged. How many other killings had been written off as 'unrelated' was another statistic entirely, one which did not take into account the number of attacks that could easily have resulted in deaths had the blow been a little harder, the knife slashed in a little higher, the petrol bomb exploded a little later at night.

Other reports highlighted the threats and coercion to which Britain's immigrant population was subject as a part of daily life – again, little of which ever reached a police blotter.

The only hope the acts who played these events could nurture was that publicity might somehow heighten awareness of the problem, encourage vigilance, and maybe sway a would-be racist or two. Sometimes even that seemed a vain hope. The Coventry benefit had no sooner been announced than the still-battered, but slowly regrouping National Front declared that its intention of marching through the city that same afternoon, warming up for the confrontation with an unofficial show of force in the city centre the weekend before. In the course of two days in mid-June, police arrested over 80 people as the two sides, blacks and Nazis, came together.

The weekend of the concert itself passed surprisingly peacefully, and both sides declared a victory of sorts. The Front's march was banned by the local authorities. But the fear that the Nazis might turn up regardless was enough to keep many prospective concert-goers away from the Butt's Athletic Stadium, where the Specials headlined over a stellar bill of Hazel O'Connor, the ex-Dexy's soul band the Bureau, the still Moddish Reluctant Stereotypes and the People.

June blazed on – literally. As if gearing up for some final apocalypse, a hailstorm of graffiti, stonings and fire fell on both immigrant and left wing properties and organisations. In Walthamstow, north London, four members of an Asian family perished when their home was set ablaze. Offices of both the Labour Party and the Runnymede Trust, an organisation dedicated to Britain's multi-ethnic complexion, were torched; socialist bookshops were attacked; a north London community centre was razed. In Watford, residents awaiting the Multi-Cultural Carnival were deluged with totally spurious, but effectively alarmist civil defense-style leaflets, advising them of what to do if (but, it was insinuated, more likely when) rioting broke out – "do not go out after dark; ensure that any elderly neighbours are safe; keep buckets of water and sand available: use only sand on petrol fires."

But, if the end of world really was just around the corner, the media had only one request – let it be sunny for the Royal Wedding. Oh, and if we could have a sneak peek at Diana's dress, that'd be nice.

After months of speculation, Prince Charles and Lady Diana Spencer had announced their engagement on February 24, 1981. The big day was set for July 29. The whole world would be watching as Britain did what she'd always done best – put on a show fit for the future Queen. A race war could take place any time. But Royal Weddings are something you remember forever. And there was less than one month to go.

CHAPTER EIGHTEEN

On July 3, 1981, the 4-Skins, the Business and the Last Resort, three Oi! groups who'd been gigging alongside one another for much of the year, arrived in Southall for a show at the Hamborough Tavern. It was, so far as they were concerned, just one more gig – a little off the beaten track, admittedly, but one that was chosen for sound logistical reasons.

True, the area had a large immigrant population that might not take too kindly to such an event – as did some of the Oi! crowd's other occasional haunts. "But think about it," cautions Business vocalist Micky Fitz. "Those were the areas which the bands came from as well. It's very difficult to say to Sparrer or the 4-Skins, 'Why are you playing there?' 'Because I bloody live there, that's why.'" Like the Ruts before them, the 4-Skins were a local band; again like the Ruts, they had played numerous times around the town in the past.

There was no advance indication that the night would be any different to all those other occasions. Not at first. According to Business guitarist Steve Kent, "We didn't get [to Southall] until 8 o'clock. We got as far as the road [that] the Hamborough Tavern was in; there was a big traffic jam, so we asked an Asian woman what was going on and she said there was an accident."

The van drove on. There was a moment when things looked a little awry, as a gang of about fifty Asian kids steamed towards the vehicle, but they wound the windows up and carried on towards the Hamborough Tavern. "We went into the pub, which was packed, and went straight on stage."

What they didn't know was, while all the Oi! fans were inside the pub, outside the street was filling with Asians, turning out, they later said, to repel what the local grapevine had been insisting all week was a full-scale Skinhead riot scheduled for later in the evening. There'd already been one 'racist' incident at a local chip shop, although details of the provocation were to remain sketchy (according to singer Max Splodge, "they probably asked the geezer how many rupees a packet of chips cost"), but the agitation was by no means one sided. On the streets outside, Skinhead latecomers were being deliberatly ambushed and sent packing – one minibus-load was even said to have been menaced by Asian swordsmen. Several more lone Skins were forced off buses by other youths, long before Southall came in sight. But the first the crowds inside the Hamborough Tavern knew any of this was when the first bricks came sailing through the windows.

4-Skins bassist Hoxton Tom recalled, "We went on about half past nine and, for a while, it seemed like it was going to be a good gig. There were right and left wing Skins dancing, a couple of black Skinheads and several girls. They were all dancing about happily and there was no trouble." And then the band – and the evening – broke into 'Chaos'.

According to journalist Gary Bushell, "The press said the peaceful Asian community had risen spontaneously to repulse right-wing invaders who had terrorised the town." In fact, he believed that "the young Asians were definitely on the offensive. The sheer quantity of petrol bombs [they] used indicated they'd been stockpiling them for some days before."

The petrol bombs flew in as the Skinheads streamed out of the venue. By the time an even-halfway effective number of police were on the scene, the venue was engulfed in flames, the streets around the pub were barricaded, and a hijacked van was rolling, blazing medieval fireship style, across the tavern's forecourt.

Attempts by the musicians to mediate through the auspices of the Southall Youth Movement were repulsed. So, in turn, were the police. As the Skinheads beat their own retreat, the rioters turned their attention on the lawmen. In a melee that was later estimated to have involved no more than 700 combatants (500 Asians, 200 Skinheads), 61 policemen and 28 civilians were injured, 23 were arrested.

Predictably, the following morning's newspapers made much of this latest so-called race riot, with the blame for the carnage spread between the bands, their audience and the Oi! creed itself. Events of the past six months had shown that the local community's fears of imminent racial assault were unlikely pulled out of thin air. The most pacifist Skinhead might, if pressed, admit that, just as a handful of football hooligans had successfully tarred every supporter with the thuggee brush, so a minority of genuinely racist Skinheads had managed to daub the entire movement with a similar slur. The Southall community's reaction to the Hamborough Tavern gig might have been vastly out of proportion with the actual threat but it was totally understandable.

But Southall wasn't the only neighbourhood to burn that night – and this time, there wasn't an Oi! act in sight. Toxteth, Liverpool 8, also blew up on

July 3, after police stopped and arrested one Leroy Alphonse Cooper, on Selbourne Street. That, in itself, was nothing new. No less than their Brixton brethren in blue, Merseyside police had done little to foster a friendly relationship with the city's black population. Even without the cover of a Operation Swamp 81-style operation, stop-and-search was routine.

This time, however, the arrest did not go off according to plan. The policemen found themselves surrounded by an angry crowd, all demanding to know what Cooper had done. Punches were thrown and three officers were injured. They called for reinforcements; naturally, the crowd began to swell. For anyone making a study of the manner in which the 1981 riots kicked off, Toxteth is the text-book case.

The pitched street battles and fires that turned the night into day did not end at dawn. For four days of street fighting and five more of unrest and sporadic violence, Toxteth became – to employ a cliché hideously misused by the cheap-thrills media – a war zone, one that conjured an image as powerful as any witnessed during the Blitz. Ablaze in the heart of Toxteth centre, the historic old Rialto ballroom was surmounted by a large copper cupola. Peering up through the clouds of smoke and CS gas, you could see it glowing hellish bright as the building burned beneath it.

Pitched battles on Upper Parliament Street saw rioters confronting police with scaffolding, charging their ranks aboard commandeered milk floats. When the smoke finally cleared, the damage was unbelievable. Over 100 buildings were lost, over a thousand police were injured, more than 500 rioters were arrested. Yet, despite the carnage, there was only one death – a man struck and killed by a police Land Rover.

Neither, once it had kicked off, was the violence confined to Toxteth. Across Liverpool, other neighbourhoods rose up, some in solidarity, others to protest their own grievances against authorities that had left Liverpool to rot through the industrial and economic recession of the 1970s and early 80s. Others still, it must be admitted, rioted simply because they could. It wasn't the world's funniest joke but more than one comedian observed that enough television sets had been looted during the riots to ensure that no one need miss the Royal Wedding.

The Specials were in Leeds that weekend, preparing for what was shaping up to be the largest event staged by Rock Against Racism in two years, the Northern Carnival Against Racism. It was their second gig in a week – the previous weekend, they'd played a free concert at Rotherham's Herring Thorpe Playing Fields. Although that drew a large crowd, however, Leeds was simply enormous, 30,000 people turning out for an all-day festival which even a nearby National Front demonstration could not spoil.

The previous evening's events added a grimmer sense of determination to the carnival. Suggestions, rife in both the national and, sadly, the left-wing media, that 'Nazi Skinheads' were at the root of the Southall riot were instantly countered from all over the country. The previous month, it was quickly pointed out, the city of Sheffield saw a 500-strong parade of both black and white Skinheads protesting unemployment and police harassment beneath the banner 'Jobs Not Jails'. The Business, the Partisans, Blitz and Infa-Riot were already planning the long-winded but nonetheless sincere Oi Against Racism and Political Extremism But Still Against The System tour.

Even the 4-Skins, stunned by events at Southall, had put their customary political antipathy aside, to announce their own first ever anti-racist gig, only to break up before they got the chance, shattered by the intensity of the post-Hamborough fall-out. (They reformed later in the year.)

The audience at the Leeds Carnival, too, seemed unphased by the media's rush to find a scapegoat. Skinhead poet Seething Wells was not alone when he directed peoples' eyes towards the thousands of Skins gathered at the Leeds carnival to proclaim their own fierce opposition to the politics of the right. The event passed off peacefully and successfully, but the Specials' set had a significance beyond the performance itself. Roddy Radiation regrets, "by the time of the Leeds carnival, we were a band in name only. The fun had gone."

How ironic, then, that, as the Specials faded away, everything they'd worked towards, everything they represented, and everything they stood for should be given such livid illumination by the events of the next three weeks.

On June 5, 2-Tone released its first new single in six months, the Specials' 'Ghost Town'. It was recorded in Leamington in April, during the Specials' visit to that town for the Anti-Racist Committee show, but the recording session was only the culmination of what Terry Hall described as "months in the [rehearsal] studio," a period scarred by arguments, divisions and point-blank refusals. Dammers himself walked out of the rehearsals on several occasions, furious when someone or other rejected one of his ideas.

The situation was complicated by the nature of the song itself. According to Radiation, "Jerry had it all just about sorted in his head." Dammers agrees: "'Ghost Town' wasn't a free-for-all jam session," he told *The Guardian* in 2002. "Every little bit was worked out and composed." He claimed to have started work on the song "at least" a year earlier, setting out to create a composite of everything the Specials had ever done, or were likely to. He knew how hard his bandmates were bucking against his dictatorship. If he could only prove to them that he knew what he was doing, by delivering the greatest record any of them had ever dreamed of making, maybe things would go back to normal.

The mutiny, however, had gone too far. Staples took to answering

Dammers' demands with an ironically subservient 'Yes, massa...'; Radiation once snapped a bitter 'Jawohl, mein Fuehrer.' Things did get done, but at such a snail's pace that there were times when it felt as though the song would never be completed – because, even if it was, there would be somebody waiting to sabotage it.

Dammers recalled one occasion when, recording the horn section, with its discordant jazz aroma, Golding suddenly burst into the control room complaining that it sounded completely wrong. Another time, he said, Radiation started kicking at the control room wall, as though trying to smash his way through to the studio room. It required Dammers' fervent entreaties, his insistence that they were making "the greatest record that's ever been made in the history of anything," to prevent the exasperated engineer from throwing them all out of the studio.

Only when it was all over could Hall acknowledge, "It seemed to take forever, [but] it was a fantastic process making that record. It was [so] odd-sounding..." Built on an arrangement that was part-Weimar cabaret, part-intro to Reggae star Keith Hudson's brooding 'Jonah' and part ghostly incantation, 'Ghost Town' was a haunting, haunted lament for a town, a country, a lifestyle that had been closed down by poverty, unemployment, fear and the government.

Dammers explained the genesis of the song's bitter lyric: "The country was falling apart. You travelled from town to town and what was happening was terrible. In Liverpool, all the shops were shuttered up, everything was closing down. Margaret Thatcher had apparently gone mad, she was closing down all the industries, throwing millions of people on the dole. We could actually see it by touring around. You could see that frustration and anger in the audience. In Glasgow, there were these little old ladies on the streets selling all their household goods, their cups and saucers. It was unbelievable. It was clear that something was very, very wrong."

At first, the record seemed to fall on deaf ears. Radio initially steered as clear of it as it could, and two long weeks elapsed before 'Ghost Town' entered the British chart. Having done so, however, it proved unstoppable.

#21 on June 20, the following week it lay at #6 and, when the Specials took the stage at Leeds, it was #2, sandwiched between Michael Jackson's 'One Day In Your Life' and Bad Manners' raucous belly-dance through 'The Can Can' – their sixth successive hit. The following Tuesday – on the same day that 250 youths rampaged through the north London suburb of Wood Green, smashing shop windows and fighting the police; the same day that Merseyside's top cop, Kenneth Oxford, did his bit for race relations by declaring that most black Liverpudlians were "the product of liaisons between white prostitutes and black sailors" – 'Ghost Town' reached the top of the chart, physically, spiritually and now unavoidably the soundtrack to the cruellest summer that modern Britain had ever endured.

Oxford's outburst was astonishing. Apparently intending to reassure those who feared Enoch Powell's prophecies had come to pass, he declared that Toxteth-based "thieves and vagabonds" alone were responsible for kicking off the riots; that "irresponsible parents" were to blame for allowing their offspring out on the streets to fuel the carnage. "I have no doubt at all," he insisted, "that this is *not* a racial issue."

The sick thing was, in the last declaration at least, he was correct. Or, at least, he was not *in*correct.

Amid the snowballing economic uncertainty and social confusion that hallmarked 1970s Britain, in a society where street crime, inflation, job insecurity, labour disputes and corruption at every level of the establishment had become the only true certainty for millions of people, race relations became an issue not because society itself was necessarily racist, but because all people, in a crisis, tend to cling together for support.

Areas such as Southall, Brixton, Handsworth, Toxteth and St Paul's have all been described as ghettos. Rightfully so. But aren't their rich white neighbours similarly ghetto-ised in their country homes and chateaus; aren't the middle-classes caged within their suburbs and dormitory towns; and so on across the societal scale? Don't each of those groups react with suspicion when outsiders start moving in? 'There goes the neighbourhood' was heard as often in Hackney when the yuppies moved in, as it was in Notting Hill when the first West Indian immigrants arrived.

It can be argued that Britain is an inherently intolerant country. One needs only look to the race riots of the late 1950s – or those of the late 1990s – to understand that blacks might consider themselves no more welcome during the reign of Queen Elizabeth II than they were 400 years earlier. The present queen's Virgin namesake once loudly complained that "several blackamoors have lately been brought into this realm, of which kind of people there are already too many here."

Compared to the experiences of other westernised nations, Britain's most serious racial problems are sporadic and readily extinguished – as Rock Against Racism and the Anti-Nazi League themselves proved. Crushed at the polls in 1979, the National Front was all but extinct within three years, a victory that allowed the ANL itself to formally disband during 1982. The Front's political aims would rise again, of course, but for every action there's a reaction, for ever poison there's an antidote. It's called Society. If we all agreed with each other, we'd probably go mad with boredom.

Of course there were racists in positions of authority, and those positions were abused, and worse, by the men who assumed them. But those same positions were also filled by criminals, liars, thieves and cheats, all of whom took similar pleasure from the powers they wielded, and all of whom bore equal responsibility for the living hell into which great slices of British society was plunged.

Unemployment, inflation, police brutality, hospital waiting lists, on and on goes the litany of sins – released in November 1979, already a halcyon age that seemed so far away, the title track to the Adverts' *Cast Of Thousands* sophomore album closed on a screaming catalog of everyday agonies, each one dressed as a tabloid headline, but each concealing a reality that was too vile to contemplate in any other form: "rape, runaway wives, other people's lives... earthquakes, floods, bodies in the mud... hospital cases, British weapons to foreign places..." and, most horrific of all, "all the human torches catching fire, especially for you." The band's original sleeve design depicted the Buddhist monk who immolated himself in protest at the Vietnam War in 1964, only for their label, RCA, to turn it down on the grounds of public taste. How sad that other guardians of national morale and morality were not so squeamish when it came to propigating outrages of their own.

For the whites who stood on the frontline during the greatest political confrontations of the late 1970s, the greatest evil that they could perceive was the threat of the National Front. But, for the people who had the most to fear from the Fascists, the Front itself was, indeed, just a front for an evil that had already arrived – the system. At Red Lion Square, Lewisham and Southall, white protestors believed they were fighting for the rights of the blacks. At Toxteth, Brixton and St Paul's, black rioters knew that they were fighting for the rights of everyone.

So yes, Thatcher and Oxford and so on were right: race had nothing to do with it. It was hopelessness, not hatred, that was burning up Britain – the government *was* leaving the youth on the shelf. People *were* getting angry. The same week 'Ghost Town' topped the British chart, and the Jam's bitter, brutal "Funeral Pyre" ignited its own flames of discontent, UB40 released their own new single: 'One In Ten' was titled for the number of British workers who were out of a job that summer. The media, always ready with a snatch of snappy alliteration, called them 'Maggie's Millions.' Now they were striking back.

On July 8, following the latest arrest of a young black man, over 1,000 protesters stormed the police station at Toxteth's tinderbox twin, Moss Side in Manchester, to ignite two days of rioting. The following day, more than 300 police were mobilised to combat street disturbances in Woolwich, south London. That weekend, as Brixton went up in smoke again, street-fighting broke out in – deep breath – Battersea, Dalston, Southall, Streatham and Walthamstow in London, in Birmingham's Handsworth district, in Chapeltown in Leeds and Highfields in Leicester, and in town and city centres the length of the land: Aldershot, Bedford, Blackburn, Chester, Derby, Edinburgh, Ellesmere Port, High Wycombe, Huddersfield, Luton, Newcastle, Nottingham, Portsmouth, Preston, Reading, Sheffield, Southampton, Stockport and Wolverhampton.

The scene was the same in every one. The sirens were sounding by supper-time, their incendiary howl accompanied by the tinkle of shattered plate glass and the first crackles of flame. Long before the evening newscast broke in to announce what was happening, anybody who cared to find out was already on the high street, the nervous ones watching from corners or cars, the more courageous dipping in and out of the open windows that looked as inviting as the ground at the back of the proverbial lorry.

There was a peculiar order to the looting. Most people concentrated on the chainstores, the nationals that the mob believed could absorb the losses with barely a glance – if you can pay rent on 50 different branches, you can afford to lose the contents of one of them. TVs flew out, music centres, cassette players. Later, you found yourself wondering precisely what that fat bloke intended doing with the broken half of a neon sign that he was weaving triumphantly around the rest of the crowd, but maybe he didn't intend *doing* anything. It was a souvenir, a memento, a trophy that would probably wind up mounted on his living room wall, between the flying ducks and the reproduction *Haywain*, so when the grandkids asked him what he did in the war, he could point to it and tell them.

Because it was a war. Although the same things had happened before, you couldn't help but shake the impression that they wouldn't need to happen again.

Rudie ran riot. Blacks with whites with Asians with everyone, an entire generation united by frustration and rage and anger and, most of all, impotence. It was as if the whole country had taken to the streets to *take back* the streets, rising up against the Charles and Dianas and Thatcher and her henchmen; against the faceless bureaucrats who talked of economy, then spent 40 million a year to keep Concorde in the air; who talked of tightening belts, while they let out their own trousers.

Not all of the disturbances were related to specific grievances. Some really were outbreaks of mindless vandalism and violence, taking advantage of police nerves that were already stretched to breaking point. But the authorities were taking no chances.

Thatcher's planned tour of what was left of Toxteth was cancelled because her safety could not be guaranteed. In London, a blanket ban was placed on all political marches and demonstrations for the rest of month – among the casualties of the order, as if to demonstrate the regime's even-handedness, were a proposed National Front march through Chelsea, and a funeral procession for the victims of the previous month's arson attack in Walthamstow.

'Ghost Town' played over it all. It was at #1 when the government 'requested' both the BBC and the independent networks to observe a *de facto* media blackout on any future potential 'flashpoints', to avoid attracting further troublemakers to the scene, and to head off the possibility of copy-cat rioting. It was still at #1 when that request was immediately put to the test as police swooped on a number of addresses in Brixton in search of an alleged petrol bomb factory. They never found one, but the crowds came anyway, to expel the invaders once more from their streets.

It played as police clashed with a thousand motorcyclists in the Lake District paradise of Keswick on July 25, and it played as windows shattered and off-licences were looted on the day of the Royal Wedding itself. Today, we can look back at 'Ghost Town' in the unyielding knowledge that no record before or since has ever nailed a moment so accurately, so comprehensively zapped a zeitgeist.

According to former Adverts vocalist TV Smith, whose own impression of that vivid summer, 'Wheels Out Of Gear', was written as the cities burned: "The first time I heard 'Ghost Town', we were on tour – Birmingham, Manchester, Leeds, all the places that blew up that summer – and it was almost like being in a movie. You'd be looking out of the window at these grey, depressing towns, all closed down and boarded-up. 'Ghost Town' would start playing on the radio, then you'd look at the newspaper and have Maggie saying how great everything was. It was obvious that something was going to happen.

TV Smith / Author's collection

"Music didn't cause the riots, of course. But songs like 'Ghost Town' helped make people aware that that there really was something wrong with the country, and when you realise something is wrong you want to do something about it."

With symmetry that would have been chilling if it wasn't so perfect, the Specials' lament for a club, a town, an entire country, which had been closed and left to rats and ruin, wound up topping the British chart for three long, fiery weeks. And, really, the Specials *had* to break up almost immediately afterwards, because they could never, ever, have followed it up.

No one could. Nothing could.

EPILOGUE

No album was ever scheduled to accompany 'Ghost Town', no follow-up single had been recorded. A handful of songs were in the can, but there were no plans, and even less agreement, on what to do with them. Dammers had one new song called 'War Crimes' that was sketched out, but would not be completed for another two years; another, 'Sweet Revenge', remains unreleased.

Hall, Golding and Staples had completed a demo called 'The Lunatics Have Taken Over The Asylum,' a lopingly percussive chant that, in later years, would find itself fingered among the forebears of western pop's fascination with "World Music," at the same time as its lyric zeroed even tighter in on the villains who presided over the ghost town, and now seemed poised to vaporise it. "When the madman flicks the switch..." warned Hall's most plaintive lilt, "the nuclear will go for me."

But, when Dammers tried to take over the song and graft his own ideas onto it, the trio withdrew it from contention. "I loved the idea of talking to Jerry about making a third album," Hall reflected twenty years later. "But it would have meant that the group would have split in a big way, just making it." It would be better all round, he determined, if they just split. Even as the Leeds carnival audience was still making its way out of the park, Lynval Golding took Roddy Radiation to one side "and told me the end was close."

Their tattered state notwithstanding, the Specials would play a handful of British concerts in the immediate aftermath of 'Ghost Town', heading out on the road with the Night Doctor as support. But a major show scheduled for Dublin's Dalymount Park on July 26 was cancelled as the band continued to squabble with the Irish authorities over the confiscated proceeds from January's charity shows, and, though the Specials did undertake their long-delayed second American tour, it was a shorter trip than last time and considerably less eventful. With no album to push beyond the year-old *More Specials*, and little interest in anything beyond getting home again, the

Specials turned in a series of enjoyable, but seldom-more-than competent shows, then imploded.

On August 23, the Specials joined the Police, the Go-Gos and headliner Iggy Pop for a show in Oakville, near Toronto, Canada. The gig itself was a success but, backstage, all hope for a tentative peace was demolished when Dammers and manager Rick Rogers fell into a fight. Fuelled by drink, exhaustion and anything else that may have been floating around the backstage area, the pair tore into one another. When Dammers told Rogers he was fired, the manager took him at his word. The Specials returned home in pieces, and stayed that way.

Terry Hall, Neville Staples and Lynval Golding had already told their bandmates they were quitting the Specials – according to Radiation, they were backstage at *Top Of The Pops*, with 'Ghost Town' still at #1, when the bombshell dropped. On October 11, 1981, they made the same announcement to the press. Their new group, the Fun Boy 3, would debut at the end of the month with the song that they had snatched back from the Specials, 'The Lunatics Have Taken Over The Asylum'. It immediately fulfilled its original destiny. For every listener who instantly recognised Hall's plaintive vocal, it became the follow-up that 'Ghost Town' never had.

The split was not amicable. While Dammers restricted his public outbursts to a simple confession of disappointment, tempered only by happiness that "they stayed in the band long enough to record 'Ghost Town'," Hall admitted it was the six month lay-off at the start of the year that sounded the death knell for the band. "That period was supposedly six months off to write songs. But we didn't want to write songs. We just wanted to go into the studio and do it."

Roddy Radiation agreed. "The Specials were made up of very different people with very different musical tastes and life styles. This conflict made the band an interesting and unpredictable musical experience." The enforced holiday, however, only served to remind them just how different they all were. "I think, instead of a break, everyone started to enjoy their own projects. This led to the split." The bleak atmosphere that permeated the band's camp through this period remains Radiation's least favourite memory of the entire Specials era. "No-one spoke and now we could barely look each other in the eye."

"It was good for maybe six months to a year," Terry Hall mused a lifetime later, telling *Uncut*: "It was the idea of making a record and releasing a record, and then people buying [the] record that was good. The best memory was a feeling of being a part of something and that felt pretty important and vital. I was part of a movement I helped create." But, when those feelings faded, so did the excitement. "Everything just seemed so heavy. With every gig you'd play there'd be a riot and it got too cartoony for me."

'The Lunatics Have Taken Over The Asylum' entered the Top 40 on November 28, 1981, three days after Lord Scarman published his report on the Brixton riots of the previous April, spelling out his belief that the responsibility lay in the lap of those who professed to have control of the country.

According to his findings, the unrest that scarred Brixton – and, by proxy, every other city which burned that summer – was directly caused by the social and economic problems rife in Britain's inner cities. Race, or at least, "the racial disadvantage that is a fact of British life," did play a part in that crisis, but so did unemployment, poor housing and an absolute lack of understanding between the police and the local community.

In response, Scarman called for a new emphasis on community policing and recommended that more people from ethnic minorities be recruited to the force. He also advised the government to end racial disadvantage, and to tackle the disproportionately high level of unemployment among young blacks – a rate that stood as high as 50 percent in Brixton.

His condemnation may not have been as unequivocal as some observers might have wished. His demands for improvement may not have been quite so emphatic. But, simply by admitting there were problems, and ruthlessly highlighting what those problems were, the Scarman Report set in motion a process that would dampen the fires that blazed through the 2-Tone years to smouldering embers that might some day be extinguished.

The lunatics still had control. But now they knew that they were being watched.

WHATEVER HAPPENED TO THOSE HEROES?

THE ANGELIC UPSTARTS

Signing to EMI following their departure from Warners in early 1980, the Upstarts started well, but were clearly eyeing a more mainstream niche than they currently occupied. 'Last Night Another Soldier' was a (still-timely) swipe at military wastefulness and gave the band their biggest hit since the year-old 'Teenage Warning'. A string of singles later, in October 1981, they unleashed one of their best records yet, the still-triumphant 'Different Strokes' collaboration with Dennis Bovell and Roy Young. Hopes they might pursue this direction, however, were stymied as the band's deliberate shift away from their core constituency saw them making, instead, convincing sounds on the Heavy Metal circuit, the Upstarts were never to isolate a new audience of their own. By late 1982, Mensi and guitarist Mond alone remained of the original quartet.

From EMI the band moved to Anagram, picking up some attention for the recruitment of former Roxy Music drummer Paul Thompson. They continued recording and touring into the early 1990s, before finally breaking up. Mensi reformed the band later in the decade, announcing their return with the extraordinarily admirable *Sons Of Spartacus* album.

STEVE ASHLEY

Despite having cut several critically acclaimed albums earlier in the 1970s, by the time of his involvement with CND, Ashley had been out of the limelight for almost five years. A comeback now saw him release two albums, *Demo Tapes 1* and *2*, for CND itself, the first "full of agitation and the second full of support for agitators." A new single, "Down The Pub," was recorded in seven different languages and debuted, unaccompanied, in front of 250,000 people at the next major CND rally, in Hyde Park. A new Steve Ashley Band came together but, after a decade of gigging and occasional recording,

Ashley dropped out of sight again in 1992. He resurfaced again in 1999, first alongside reissues of his first two albums, and then with a brand new album, 2001's *Everyday Lives*.

BAD MANNERS

With the exception of Madness and the Beat, Bad Manners became the most successful, and longest-lived, chart band in the 2-Tone era. All four of their albums and a dozen singles charted between 1980-83. Disagreements with their label over a TV-advertised compilation, *The Height Of Bad Manners*, saw the band drop from view during 1983, turning their attention to the United States instead.

There, the group found an audience that still skanked like it was 1979. They were feted by the Columbia Records' imprint, Portrait, and the group's fifth album, *Mental Notes*, became their first to receive a major US push – but the experience left a sour taste. Walking out on the deal, the band returned home and sat out the remainder of their contract, still gigging but unable to record. Personnel changes and a massive tax bill furthered their woes. By 1987, the band seemed set to fall apart.

Somehow they rallied. Bloodvessel had been gigging with a new band, Buster's All Stars and, in 1988, this combo merged with what remained of Bad Manners – Martin Stewart, Chris Kane, Louis Alphonso and Alan Sayagg – to cut the first new album in four years, *Eat the Beat*. *Return of the Ugly* and *Fat Sounds* followed, released on Bloodvessel's latest plaything, a revitalisation of the old, classic Blue Beat label. (Longsy D and Skaville UK, both spin-offs from Bad Manners, also enjoyed some success with the label.)

In 1992, longterm member Martin Stewart and recent recruit Nicky Welsh departed to join the reformed Selecter (Sayagg also quit, due to health problems), but Bad Manners marched on. Bloodvessel himself departed for a short time in the late 90s and Louis Cook, the only other surviving founder, left in 1998. But Bad Manners live on, the guardians of the Ska sounds for which they are known and a treasure trove of other period memories: 2001's *Millennium Knees-Up* album included versions of 'March of the Mods' and 'Come On, Eileen'.

THE BEAT

The Beat broke up in 1983 following the release of their third album, *Special Beat Service*. Andy Cox and Dave Steele joined forces with former Akrylyx vocalist Roland Gift in the Fine Young Cannibals. Dave Wakeling and Ranking Roger, together with the Specials' Sir Horace linked up as General Public, one of the key British bands on the 1980s American college rock scene (their *All The Rage* album sold over half a million copies in the US; British audiences completely ignored it). Roger was also a key component of the Special Beat, a band whose very name summed up the group's ingredients. That same year, Everett and Saxa formed the International Beat along with Neil Deathridge and regular guest appearances from Ranking Roger and Micky Billingham. Both bands broke up during the early 1990s.

Wakeling, now resident in California, continued gigging under his own steam through the 1990s, with occasional returns to the Beat (English Beat in America)/General Public alias for live purposes – 1999 even saw the band sign up for an 80s revival tour, in the company of the Human League. That outing fell through – the Beat wound up travelling with Hootie and the Blowfish instead, with Wakeling telling *Rolling Stone*, '[Head Hootie] Darius [Rucker] started to play "Save It For Later" and then he made this huge speech about the English Beat, about how influential we were and what an honor and privilege it was to share the stage.'

Wakeling, Ranking Roger, Everett, Saxa, Neil and Dave "Blockhead" Wright next reunited in 2003, for a much-celebrated Beat Reunion at London's Royal Festival Hallm and Wakeling admitted, 'there seems to be plenty of magic and connection left to share.' However, when next the Beat hit the road in early 2004, Wakeling was again absent – his place at the front of the stage taken instead by Ranking Roger's son, Matt "Ranking Junior."

THE COCKNEY REJECTS

Like the Angelic Upstarts, the Rejects began losing patience with their Skinhead following in 1982, stepping out of the slipstream of so many faster-rising (and somewhat less principled) new bands and turning instead towards a more Heavy Metallic-friendly sound. Shortening their name to the Rejects threw no one off the scent, however, and a new audience never materialised. The band broke up in 1985, following one final album, produced by Pete Way of UFO, *Rock The Wild Side* (even the title puts you off!). They reformed briefly in 1990, but disbanded following just one album, *Lethal*.

The band – now featuring founders Stinky Turner and Mick Geggus, plus Red Alert's Tony Van Frater and Les Cobb – reunited again in the mid-1990s.

JERRY DAMMERS

Since breaking away from the Special AKA set-up in 1985, Dammers threw himself into such organisations as Artists Against Apartheid and the Red Wedge anti-Conservatives campaign. A member of the shortlived post-Madness band *The* Madness, he also contributed to the group's Starvation charity project, but has otherwise remained silent on the recording front. Today, Dammers is most frequently seen behind a DJ booth or mixing desk.

His production credits over the past 15 years include Robert Wyatt's *The Wind Of Change* and Junior Delgado's acclaimed *Fearless* album.

DEXY'S MIDNIGHT RUNNERS

Having abandoned their Mod phase, Dexy's resurfaced in a whole new guise. Citing Rowland's increasing autocracy, founder member Al Archer and latter-day arrivals Andy Growcott and Mick Talbot (ex-Merton Parkas) quit to form the Bureau (Talbot later surfaced in Paul Weller's Style Council). At the same time, Dexy's themselves dismissed their old smart suits and mod sharpness in favour of a rural gypsy look, exacerbated by the recruitment of violin trio Emerald Express: Helen O'Hara, Steve Brennan and Roger MacDuff. The realigned band debuted with the self-affirming 'Celtic Soul Brothers' but it was their sophomore single which was the charm. In June 1982, 'Come On Eileen' topped charts around the world and, the following month, the album *Too Rye Aye* came close to repeating the feat.

Repeating the ructions that tore the band in the wake of 'Geno', however, dissension ripped the band apart. While the singles 'Jackie Wilson Said' and 'Let's Get This Straight From The Start' ensured that Dexy's remained chart contenders, in mid-1983 Kevin Rowland once again shattered the band.

More than two years passed before he re-emerged with a new line-up, comprised largely of session musicians. The ensuing *Don't Stand Me Down* album, since acclaimed their best yet, was ridiculed by the media. When 'Because Of You' did hit, it was too late. By October 1986, Dexy's had broken up yet again.

Rowland released a solo album in 1988, credited, somewhat sadly, to Kevin Rowland Of Dexy's Midnight Runners. Neither *The Wanderer* nor its accompanying singles registered on the charts and the singer faded away, drifting into depression and drug dependency before declaring bankruptcy in 1991.

He began working on a new album with Dexy's co-founder Jimmy Patterson and, in March 1993, made his first TV appearance since 1985 on British television's *Saturday Zoo*. In 1994, he entered rehab. It was 1996 before he considered a comeback again. His demos immediately attracted Creation label head Alan McGee, who offered him a deal. Rowland took it, then set about making an album quite unlike any he had discussed with Creation, an all-covers set based around the songs which Rowland said had helped him through his recovery. *My Beauty* was distinguished by the 45-year-old Rowland's decision to make his public comeback in topless drag. "It's saying I have sexuality, I am a sexual being," he reasoned. "I am here and I can be sexy."

Undaunted by the barely concealed sniggering of the UK press, Rowland announced his live return on the largest stage he could find, at the Reading and Leeds festivals in August 1999, performing a confrontational three-song/15-minute set in a white mini dress which afforded him several opportunities to flash his crotch. "It's borderline psychologically disturbed stuff," mused the *NME*. "Good or bad hardly seemed to matter." *My Beauty* is said to have sold less than 700 copies.

Helming a new version of Dexy's, Rowland resurfaced in less controversial style during 2003.

TERRY HALL

The Fun Boy Three's romping 'Lunatics' was followed by further hits 'It Ain't What You Do, It's The Way That You Do It', 'Really Saying Something' (both recorded with Bananarama), 'The Telephone Always Rings', 'Summertime', 'The More I See', the truly sublime 'Tunnel Of Love' and, finally, 'Our Lips Are Sealed': two years (and two albums) worth of music that finally came to a halt in mid-1983.

Hall bounced back from the collapse of the Fun Boy 3 with a new band, the Colour Field. They made their debut on *The Tube* with a fiery rendition of the song of the same name but, sadly, never lived up to that initial promise. Since then, Hall has remained a contented bit player, surfacing periodically with another excellent recording, but rarely sustaining anything more than short bursts of activity.

"Sometimes it seems like there's a huge gap between records," he told *The Independent* on the occasion of his latest album, a brilliant collaboration with Fun-Da-Mental's Mushtaq, in July 2003. "To me, it seems like 10 minutes. Because I'm spending that time listening to music, doing my homework. It's like an architect drawing up plans for a building. It can take years. It isn't a race. I've never bought into being part of that pop-music, disposable thing. I want to make records until I'm told I can't."

Elsewhere, in a surprisingly eclectic CV, the late 1990s saw him teaming up with the Dub Pistols and trip-hop maven Tricky for, among other things, a positively scarifying version of 'Ghost Town'. When Jerry Dammers was asked whether he felt jealous that Tricky had chosen to work with Hall, his response was a gem: "No, because I've already worked with Terry Hall on a version of 'Ghost Town'."

JUDGE DREAD

Dread is dead. The single most important figure in the history of British Ska, the 250lb former debt collector who kept the music alive and kicking through the fallow years of the Seventies, died from a heart attack on March 13, 1998, aged 53. The hits had long since dried up. Record deals were hard to come by but Dread continued gigging until the end. Following a Canterbury Penny Club gig backed by Arthur Kay's reformed Originator, Dread's last words were "Let's hear it for the band." A true hero, and modest to boot.

MADNESS

Doubts that Madness' creativity could survive an abrupt lurch towards the mainstream were dispelled by four successive Top 10 singles through 1981, 'Embarrassment', the instrumental 'Return Of The Los Palmas Seven', 'Grey Day' and 'Shut Up.' A trip to Compass Point Studios in the Bahamas yielded a third album, *Seven* (#5 UK), just in time for Christmas. 1982 brought a hit rendering of soul balladeer Labi Siffre's 'It Must Be Love' on which Siffre himself conferred approval by appearing in the accompanying video. The follow-up, 'Cardiac Arrest', became the first Madness single since their debut not to make the Top 10. It marked no sort of artistic decline. Summer 1982 brought the band a remarkable triple crown: their new single, 'House Of Fun', the *Complete Madness* greatest hits album and a video collection of the same name all topped their respective charts.

Two new songs, 'Drivin' In My Car' and 'Our House', pursued the Nutty sound into classic Kinks territory, heralding the achievements of their next album, *Rise And Fall*. 'Our House' became the band's American breakthrough, two months after winning an Ivor Novello award for Best Pop Song of 1982.

Madness powered on. Taken from 1984's *Keep Moving* album, 'Wings Of A Dove', 'The Sun And The Rain' and the contrivedly Cockney 'Michael Caine' kept the band hot. The news that Barso intended quitting for a new life in the Netherlands did not, initially, slow the momentum. 'One Better Day' in June 1984 was the group's final single for Stiff before they relocated to their own Zarjazz label (the name was lifted from the *2000 AD* comic). Surely it was tempting fate to title their next single 'Yesterday's Men'? Suddenly, it seemed that they might be.

Although Zarjazz got off to a good start with first signing, former Undertones vocalist Feargal Sharkey's rendition of Madness' own 'Listen To Your Father', Smash and Suggs' Fink Brothers alias flopped with 'Mutants In Mega City'. A Ska Stars for Africa-type benefit single, 'Starvation Tam Tam Pour L'Ethiope' made a mockery of its makers' pedigree: UB40, General Public and the Special AKA all joined Madness under the Starvation banner.

Madness' first self-released album, *Mad Not Mad*, was poorly received. Although the group returned to the Nutty Sound of old for 'Uncle Sam', the magic wasn't there. A cover of Scritti Politti's 'Sweetest Girl' fared even worse and the band began to prepare for the end. In July 1986, Madness played their final show at the Docklands festival in Hartlepool and in

September, the break-up was made public. Their final single, 'Waiting For The Ghost Train', was accompanied by a second hits collection, *Utter Madness,* in December 1986.

After 18 months' silence, Suggs, Chrissy Boy, Kix and Smash reunited as The Madness, with Specials founder Jerry Dammers and former Attractions Steve Nieve and Bruce Thomas. The eponymous album was poorly received. Of the singles, 'I Pronounce You' enjoyed a modicum of success but 'What's That' was a complete flop. The group broke up soon after.

Foreman and Thompson reconvened as the Nutty Boys and released the *Crunch* album in May 1990. The same year, Suggs resurfaced alongside Morrissey on one cut, 'Piccadilly Palare', from the ex-Smith's *Bona Drag* compilation album, while Bedders played bass on the same singer's *Kill Uncle* album. The chart-topping appearance of a third Madness compilation, *Divine Madness*, in early 1992 sparked a flurry of renewed interest in the group. With reissues of 'It Must be Love,' 'House Of Fun' and 'My Girl' enjoying new success a decade after their original release, the classic Madness line-up returned to headline their own Madstock Festival in London.

A live recording from that show, *Madstock*, appeared in November; a movie followed in the new year, while the reconstituted combo's first studio recording in six years, a cover of Jimmy Cliff's 'The Harder They Come', was a welcome Christmas hit.

1993 saw Madness stage a string of sold-out Christmas concerts at Wembley Arena; 1994 brought a second Madstock festival. Since then, the band have become live perennials, have returned to the studio and have even branched into West End theatre.

RODDY RADIATION

Radiation announced his departure from the Specials a week after the Fun Boys, turning his full attention to the Tearjerkers. Their first single, 'Desire', was released by Chiswick Records the following year, after Dammers and 2-Tone turned it down: "I asked Jerry at a party about releasing it on 2-Tone, and he headbutted a wall," laughs Radiation.

Following the Tearjerkers' demise in 1987, Radiation formed

the Bonediggers, before reuniting with various former bandmates in the reformed Specials in 1996. Since that time, he has worked solo, releasing the excellent *Skabilly Rebel* anthology in 2002, collecting recordings made with the Tearjerkers, the Bonediggers, the Raiders and, of course, the reunited Specials.

TOM ROBINSON

Although the group was already defunct, a final Tom Robinson Band single was recorded with session men: was co-written by Robinson and Elton John, 'Never Gonna Fall In Love Again' initially received a lot of airplay. "It was dropped," Robinson later grumbled, "when somebody noticed the (distinctly gay) lyrics." Robinson then joined Sector 27, releasing an eponymous debut album before breaking up when their management company went bankrupt in 1981.

Robinson relocated to Germany, moving first to Hamburg, then East Berlin. There he devised Cabaret 79, a touring revue which spawned the album *North By Northwest*. He returned to the UK in 1983 to make his comeback, returning to the charts with the much-loved 'War Baby'. The single was followed by an album *Hope And Glory* in September 1984 after which the singer lapsed into relative obscurity: his *Still Loving You* album scored in Italy alone. A new cabaret revue, *A Private View*, played successfully at the 1986 Edinburgh Fringe Festival, then fell from view.

The most newsworthy event, then, came when the British tabloid *Sunday People* discovered that the man who performed 'Glad To Be Gay' with such passion a decade previous, had suddenly discovered bisexuality and married life. Headlines such as 'Britain's #1 Gay In Love With Girl Biker' dominated the press for several weeks, although the exposure didn't translate into sales. A duet with Kiki Dee, 'Feels So Good', in January, 1987, went nowhere; a collaboration with Level 42 guitarist Jakko Jaksysk spawned the well-received, but ultimately unsuccessful *We Never Had It So Good*. (The pair also composed the theme to TV's *Hard Cases*.)

An attempted TRB reunion in 1990 failed, Robinson admitted, "for exactly the same reasons we split up the first time." Robinson returned to his solo career. Following the 1992 live album *Living In A Boom Time*, he hooked up with fellow punk veteran TV Smith (ex-Adverts) for a series of tours showcasing both musicians' careers and new material, Smith's 1994 *The Immortal Rich* and Robinson's *Love Over Rage*.

Still recording, Robinson has nevertheless begun cutting back on musical and personal appearances to concentrate on his career as a regular BBC radio presenter.

THE RUTS

Regrouping following Malcolm Owen's death, the Ruts re-emerged as Ruts DC (*Da Capo*, or 'new beginning'). Virgin pieced together a posthumous second album of out-takes and non-album cuts, *Grin And Bear It*. Having recorded several albums' worth of earthshaking dub, Ruts DC broke up in 1983, after which all three members moved into session work. Dave Ruffy subsequently played alongside Aztec Camera, Kirsty MacColl and Joe Strummer, among many others.

THE SELECTER

After the break-up, the members scattered. While Desmond Brown and Charley Anderson's The People enjoyed flickerings of interest during 1981, they broke up after issuing the 'Music Man' single. Brown more-or-less drifted out of the spotlight.

Anderson and Charley Bembridge then formed a new group, the Century Steel Band; Bembridge also joined Anderson, Pauline Black, Roddy Radiation, Arthur Henderson in the Glasshouse Band, an organisation intended to promote music in Coventry schools, offering an alternative to the dole queues. With £25,000 in funding from the local council, the Glasshouse Band would prosper. Anderson alone stayed the course.

Neol Davies and Compton Amanor also moved into education during the 1980s, periodically resurfacing in new bands. In the mid-80s, Davies formed The Radio Beats; more recently, he joined with Sir Horace Gentleman in Box of Blues.

Signing to Chrysalis in her own right in 1982, Pauline Black had hopes for a solo career. An album was recorded but left unreleased and she moved into acting and television work. Occasionally resurfacing on the live scene (she appeared at the Jo-Boxers' Victoria Park free concert in 1983, while her mid-80s Supernaturals toured with the Communards), Black rejuvenated the Selecter in 1992, alongside Bad Manners' Martin Stewart and Nicky Welsh.

Intended largely for American consumption, where Selecter had been swept up in the so-called Third Wave of Ska, *The Happy Album* (1994), *Pucker* (1995) and *Cruel Britannia* (1998) were by no means the best records loosely associated with 2-Tone. But they showed that the band was still fully capable of rising to the occasion. At the time of writing (summer 2003), the group continues touring.

SPECIAL AKA

Following the defections of late 1981, the future of the Specials called into question by legal complications dictating that the remaining trio (Dammers, Bradbury and Gentleman) could not continue working as "the Specials". They opted to revert to the group's 'real' name, Special AKA. Recruiting former Bodysnatchers Rhoda Dakar and Nicky Summers, cornet player Dick Cuthell and a local, Coventry guitarist, John Shipley, they began work on the group's next single, 'The Boiler'.

A harrowing epic of rape, the song was an old Bodysnatchers number, which the girls had never taken past the demo stage – despite Dammers' enthusiasm. Now he was to mastermind a nightmare-inducing version of an already a harrowing number for release in the New Year. With uncanny timing, a High Court Judge earned widespread condemnation the same week after finding a rapist not guilty on the grounds that his victim was 'asking for it' (the same incident provoked Punk poet Attila the Stockbroker's 'Contributory Negligence').

Whereas 'Ghost Town' caught the mood of the day, 'The Boiler' seemed doomed to failure. London's Capital Radio aired it just once: their switchboard was jammed by complaints. The BBC simply ignored the record but did invite Dakar to participate in a few phone-ins.

Despite, or perhaps because of, such exposure, 'The Boiler' crept to #35 on the chart. The team quickly announced that the follow-up would be called 'Female Chauvinist Pig'. Alas, that release never saw the light of day. Apart from appearing with Rico on his *Jama* album, the Special AKA lapsed into a silence that would consume the best part of the year.

The band resurfaced shortly before Christmas with a new single, reprising the unfinished 'War Crimes' (while retaining Roddy Radiation's original guitar part). A hard-hitting condemnation of the Israeli armed forces' conduct during the recent invasion and occupation of Lebanon, which compared the so-called refugee camps the Israelis were establishing to the concentration camps of Nazi Germany, the single received little or no airplay and missed the chart altogether – the first record issued under the Specials aegis to do so. at the same time as staggering beneath the condemnations of anti-Semitism that regularly confuse criticism of Israeli state policy with a deep-seated hatred of the Jewish race.

It would be another nine months before the Special AKA returned to the chart, when 'Racist Friend' scraped to #60 in September 1983. Six months later, they met with memorable success, when the anthemic 'Free Nelson Mandela' climbed to #9 and established itself as the worldwide anthem of the growing demand for the jailed African National Congress leader to be released by the South African authorities.

Skipping ahead another six years to 1990, there can be few more memorable moments in the entire 2-Tone story than the evening in Trafalgar Square, London, when thousands of Mandela's supporters gathered outside the South African embassy to celebrate, at long last, his release. With one voice, the words of 'Free Nelson Mandela' filled the February air not only in central London, but elsewhere, too, as television beamed the celebrations around the world.

The Special AKA released one further single, the chart-scorning 'What I Like Most About You Is Your Girlfriend'. The band did feature amid the skanking cast of thousands that joined Madness beneath the charitable Starvation banner but, when Dammers retired from active recording, the group folded with him.

SPECIAL BEAT

After the break-up of the Fun Boy 3, Lynval Golding and Neville Staples practically disappeared – Golding was involved for a time with Charley Anderson's Glasshouse Band, taking special interest in one of that organisation's new acts, After Tonight. John Bradbury also faded from public view following the demise of JB's All Stars, the sometimes-16-strong soul revue that he formed in 1982, cutting three singles for RCA as well as the historic last-ever 2-Tone 45, 'Alphabet Army'.

He resurfaced as producer of the brave but beleaguered Loafers' *Contagious* album in 1989. When Bradbury, Golding and Staples reunited in the early 1990s, joining forces with Sir Horace Gentleman and Ranking Roger, fresh from General Public (Roger also cut an excellent solo album), Graham Hamilton from the Fine Young Cannibals and two members of the Loafers, Sean Flowerdew and Tony 'Finny' Finn, joined them.

Special Beat was originally conceived as a touring party – with the emphasis firmly on the word 'party.' The group was adopted by the American Ska community as it prepared for its own break-out – they were the highlight of 1993's Skavoovie tour and gigged regularly thereafter. In the studio, Special Beat's triumph stretched little further than a magnificent remake of Prince Buster's 'Time Is Longer Than Rope'. A live album recorded in Coventry captures the ensuing delirium, musicians and audience joined as one, surging through a repertoire which was non-stop skanking action from raucous start to roaring finish.

In 1995, bowing to the inevitable, they reformed as the Specials, they were touring the Ska strongholds of Japan, inspiring that nation's youth to its own new excesses.

THE SPECIALS

Reforming in 1995, the Special Beat contingent of Staples, Golding, Bradbury and Gentleman was buoyed by the return of Roddy Radiation and the arrival of Selecter's H. The group's first task was to record an album with Ska legend Desmond Dekker, quickly followed by a Japanese tour. Nobody viewed the reunion as a permanent arrangement but the Japanese tour was followed by a clutch of European festivals. With a new single, 'Hypocrite', returning an unadorned Specials name to the UK chart for the first time since 'Ghost Town', the group released the all-covers album *Today's Specials* in 1996 on the eve of a tremendously successful US tour.

The absence of Hall and Dammers passed unnoticed by most. When the Specials played WBCN's Christmas Rave in 1997, the *Boston Globe* enthused, "The new material was consistent with their skanking gems of the late 1970s"; when they played KROQ's Acoustic Christmas party, the *LA Times* added, "The Specials... show the depths possible in this genre."

A second album, *Guilty Til Proved Innocent*, followed in 1998. Radiation's assessment: "It had some original tunes, some of which I consider as good, if not better, than the Specials Mark One. But the press backlash and the fact that the old stuff was $5 or more cheaper meant it never got a proper hearing."

The line-up was no more stable than in the past. The guitarist continues: "Even though we were older, it seemed we were no wiser. Differences in direction and the usual petty squabbles split the band." By the end of 1998, the Specials had faded away. At the time of writing (summer 2003), a well-designed website (thespecials.com) is all there is to keep fans informed of all the former members' activities: Neville Staples leads his new 13-piece combo around in support of his *Special Skank Au Go Go* album; Sir Horace links with the Selecter's Neol Davies in Box of Blues; and Roddy Radiation celebrates 20 years of post-Specials activities with *Skabilly Rebel*.

2-TONE

Two new bands were signed during 1982, Leicester's Apollinaires and Norwich's Higsons, but neither proved anything more than the label's continued commitment to unearthing new talent – certainly the 2-Tone connection was of little use to either act and, in some respects, worked against them. For all the Specials' stylistic manoeuvrings, 2-Tone was still widely regarded as a Ska-based label. Neither the Apollinaires or the Higsons fit even the loosest definition of that fare. Both quickly faded: the Apollinaires split, the Higsons launched a label of their own, one infinitely better-suited to their needs.

2-Tone remained in operation through the Special AKA's last flurry of success; it finally folded during 1985, following the failure of three last singles by the Friday Club, John Bradbury's newly launched JB's All-Stars and the AKA's valedictory 'What I Like Most About You Is Your Girlfriend'. Since then, Walt Jabasco has only been spotted when there's a new compilation to promote.

He lives on regardless, in the soul of everyone who grew up alongside 2-Tone in the first place, and in the hearts of the millions who have discovered the label since. The so-called Third Wave of Ska that swept the United States during the mid-1990s and made international superstars of No Doubt and the Mighty Mighty Bosstones, was directly indebted to 2-Tone. Bucket, founder of the Moon Ska label and the New York band the Toasters, insisted that it was wrong to call it a revival: "You have to keep generating to a new audience, and Ska music has just had that ability. Every so often, it just brings up a whole new core audience. That has a lot to do with the fact that the music itself is so vital."

The Bosstones' Dicky Barrett agreed. "When a lot of the bands formed, during the mid-1980s, we're talking a distance from the English 2-Tone movement of about four years, no more than that. So it was kind of 'It's not over; keep it alive.' It wasn't a Ska resurgence or anything. It was the tail end, guys hanging out, saying, 'The spirit is still alive.' When you have something you love so much, you want it to keep going."

UB40

Asked, in 1980, which of the year's up and coming bands seemed most likely to succeed across a period of years... even decades... few people would have selected UB40. No disrespect intended, of course, but compared with all the other groups vying for the top at the time, UB40 truly offered little to become excited about. A quarter of a century later, UB40 aren't simply established as the most successful Reggae act outside of Bob Marley, they are also among the most successful bands in British chart history – as of early 2004, only a handful of acts, doughty pre-punk veterans one-and-all, have racked up more UK hits than UB40.

That this tally includes some truly cloying music is a matter of record, although only 1985's 'I Got You Babe,' a chart-topping duet with Chrissie Hynde, is truly, *truly* ghastly. But the group has also been responsible for some genuinely exhilarating records, including some painstakingly faithful covers of classic ska- and rocksteady-era Jamaican hits ('Red Red Wine' topped the chart in 1983), and a clutch of magnificent originals. The political edge that marked out the band's earliest music has softened, of course. But the music that gave those politics such power remains firmly in place.

DISCOGRAPHY 1979-81

A selectively exhaustive, chronological discography of 2-Tone, Ska, Mod, Oi and related singles and LPs released during the period covered by the main text. Discographies for bands whose careers overlap this period are necessarily incomplete.

1979

MARCH
(LEYTON) BUZZARDS: Saturday Night Beneath The Plastic Palm Trees/Through With You (Chrysalis CHS 2288)

APRIL
ANGELIC UPSTARTS: I'm An Upstart/Leave Me Alone (WB K17354)

MAY
ARTHUR KAY"'S ORIGINALS: Ska Wars/Warska (Red Admiral 001)
THE JOLT: *Maybe Tonight* EP (Polydor 2229 215)
THE RUTS: In A Rut/H-Eyes (People Unite SJP 795)
THE SPECIALS: Gangsters/The Selecter (by The Selecter) (2-Tone TT 1)
SPEEDBALL: No Survivors/Is Somebody There (Dirty Dick 1)
SQUIRE: Get Ready To Go/Doing The Flail (by Coming Shortly) (ROK 1)

JUNE
(LEYTON) BUZZARDS: *From Jellied Eels To Record Deals* (Chrysalis CHR 1213)
RUTS: Babylon's Burning/Society (Virgin VS 271)
SECRET AFFAIR: Time For Action/Soho Strut (I Spy SEE 1)

JULY
ANGELIC UPSTARTS: Teenage Warning/The Young Ones (WB K17426)
COCKNEY REJECTS: *Flares & Slippers EP* (Small Wonder 19)
MERTON PARKAS: You Need Wheels/I Don't Want To Know You (Beggars BEG 22)

THE MOD: MOD/MOD 2 (Vertigo 6059 233)
THE SELECTER: The Selecter/Gangsters (the Specials) (2-Tone TT 2)
various: *Mods Mayday 79* (Bridgehouse BHLP 003)

AUGUST
ANGELIC UPSTARTS: *Teenage Warning* (WB K56717)
BACK TO ZERO: Your Side Of Heaven/Back To Back (Fiction FICS 004)
THE CHORDS: Now It's Gone/Don't Go Back (Polydor 2059 141)
THE DONKEYS: What I Want/Four Letters (Rhesus GO APE 3)
MADNESS: The Prince/Madness (2-Tone TT 3)
PURPLE HEARTS: Millions Like Us/Beat That (Fiction FICS 003)
THE RUTS: Something That I Said/Give Youth A Chance (Virgin VS 285)
TEENBEATS: I Van't Control Myself/I'll Never Win (Safari SAFE 17)

SEPTEMBER
MERTON PARKAS: *Face In The Crowd* (Beggars BEGA 11)
MERTON PARKAS: Plastic Smile/Man With The Disguise (Beggars BEG 25)
THE RUTS: *The Crack* (Virgin V2132)
SQUIRE: Walking Down The Kings Road/It's A Mod Mod World (I Spy SEE 2)
Various: *Quadrophenia (soundtrack)* ((Polydor 2625 037)

OCTOBER
ANGELIC UPSTARTS: Never 'Ad Nothing/Nowhere Left To Hide (WB K17476)
THE CROOKS: Modern Boys/The Beat Goes On

(Blueprint BLU 2002)
JUDGE DREAD: Lovers Rock/Ska fever (Korova SIR 4028)
MADNESS: *One Step Beyond* (Stiff SEEZ 17)
MADNESS: One Step Beyond/Mistakes (Stiff BUY 56)
PURPLE HEARTS: Frustration/Extraordinary Sensation (Fiction FICS 007)
SECRET AFFAIR: Let Your Heart Dance/Sorry Wrong Number (I Spy SEE 3)
THE SELECTER: On My Radio/Too Much Pressure (2-Tone TT 4)
THE SPECIALS: A Message To You (Rudy)/Nite Club (2-Tone TT 5)
THE SPECIALS: *The Specials* (2-Tone LTT 5001)
THE TEENBEATS: Strength Of The Nation/If I'm Gone Tomorrow (Safari SAFE 19)

NOVEMBER
THE CIRCLES: Opening Up/Billy (Graduate GRAD 4)
COCKNEY REJECTS: I'm Not A Fool/East End (EMI 5008)
DEXY'S MIDNIGHT RUNNERS: Dance Stance/I'm Just Looking (Oddball/Parlophone R6028)
KIDZ NEXT DOOR: What's It All About/The Kids Next Door (WB K17492)
THE LAMBRETTAS: Go Steady/Listen Listen/Cortinas (Rocket XPRES 23)
LONG TALL SHORTY: By Your Love/1970s Boy Wonder (WB K17491)
LOW NUMBERS: Keep In Touch/Nine All Out (WB K17493)
MERTON PARKAS: Give It To Me Now/Gi's It (Beggars BEG 30)
THE RUTS: Jah War/I Ain't Sofisticated (Virgin VS 298)
SECRET AFFAIR: *The Glory Boys* (I Spy 1)
SQUIRE: The Face Of Youth Today/I Know A Girl (I Spy SEE 4)
WALKIE TALKIES: Rich And Nasty/Summer In Russia (Sire SIR 4023)

DECEMBER
THE BEAT: Tears Of A Clown/Ranking Full Stop (2-Tone TT 6)
THE GANGSTERS: Rudi The Red Nose Reindeer/White Christmas (Big Bear BB 25)
MADNESS: My Girl/Stepping Into Line (Stiff BUY 62)

1980
JANUARY
ANGELIC UPSTARTS: Out Of Control/Shotgun Solution (WB K17558)
CAIRO: I Like Bluebeat/Version (Absurd 7)

THE CHORDS: Maybe Tomorrow/I Don't Wanna Know (Polydor POSP 101)
ELVIS COSTELLO: I Can't Stand Up/Girls Talk (2-Tone TT 7)
THE LAMBRETTAS: Poison Ivy/Runaround (Rocket XPRES 25)
ROCKERS EXPRESS (JUDGE DREAD): Phoenix City/Chinese Brush (Korova KOW 002)
THE SAME: Movements/Wild About You (Blueprint 2008)
THE SELECTER: Three Minute Hero/James Bond (2-Tone TT 8)
THE SPECIALS: *The Special AKA Live EP* (2-Tone TT 7)
THE STILETTOS: This is The Way/Who Can It Be (Ariola ARO 200)
THE TIGERS: Kidding Stops/Big Expense Small Income (Strike KIK 1)

FEBRUARY
THE ACCIDENTS: Blood Splattered With Guitars/Curtains For You (Hook 1)
AKRYLYKZ: Spyderman/Smart Boy (Red Rhino RED 2)
BAD MANNERS: Ne Ne Na Na Na Na Nu Nu/Holiday (Magnet MAG 164)
THE BEAT: Hands Off She's Mine/Twist And Crawl (Go Feet FEET 1)
CHARLIE PARKAS: Ballad Of Robin Hood/Space Invaders (Paranoid Plastics 001)
COCKNEY REJECTS: Bad Man/The New Song (EMI 5035)
THE ODDS: Saturday Night/Not Another Love Song (Red Rhino RED 1)
PURPLE HEARTS: Jimmy/What Am I Gonna Do (Fiction FICS 009)
SECRET AFFAIR: My World/So Cool (I Spy SEE 5)
THE SELECTER: *Too Much Pressure* (2-Tone TT 5)

MARCH
AKRYLYKZ: Smart Boy/Spyderman (Polydor POSP 128)
ANGELIC UPSTARTS: We Gotta get Out/Unsung Heroes part 2 (WB K17586)
THE BODYSNATCHERS: Let's Do Rocksteady/Ruder Than You (2-Tone TT 9)
COCKNEY REJECTS: *Greatest Hits Vol 1* (RZ ZONO 101)
THE CROOKS: *Just Released* (Blueprint BLUP 5002)
DEXY'S MIDNIGHT RUNNERS: Geno/Breaking Down The Walls (Parlophone R6033)
GRADUATE: Elvis Should Play Ska/Julie Julie (Precision PAR 100)

MADNESS: *Work Rest And Play EP* (Stiff BUY 71)
THE SELECTER: Missing Words/Carry Go Bring
Come (2-Tone TT 10)
SEVENTEEN: Don't Let Go/Bank Holiday Weekend
(Vendetta VD 001)
SMART ALEC: Scooter Boys/Soho (B&C BCS 20)
T & THE UNKNOWN: My Generation/Woodstock
Rock (Carrere CAR 142)
WHITE HEAT: Nervous Breakdown/Sammy Sex
(Vallium 1)

APRIL
ANGELIC UPSTARTS: *We Gotta Get Out Of This
Place* (WB K56906)
ARTHUR KAY'S ORIGINALS: Please Play My
Record/Sooty Is A Rudie (Red Admiral 002)
BAD MANNERS: *Ska'n'B* (Magnet MAG 5033)
THE BEAT: Mirror In The Bathroom/Jackpot (Go
Feet FEET 2)
THE CHORDS: Something's Missing/This Is What
They Want (Polydor POSP 146)
COCKNEY REJECTS: Greatest Cockney Rip-off/Hate
Of The City (RZ Z2)
THE MEDIA: Back On The Beach Again/South Coast
City Rockers (Brain Booster 4)
RELUCTANT STEREOTYPES: She Has Changed/Ben
Shirtman (WEA K 18201)
THE RUTS: Staring At The Rude Boys/Love In Vain
(VS 327)
SOUTH COAST SKA STARS: South Coast
Rumble/Head On (Safari SAFE 27)
THE SPIDERS: Mony Mony/Who's The Other One
(Red 004)

MAY
LAUREL AITKEN (& THE RUTS): Rudi Got
Married/Honey Come Back To Me (I Spy SEE 6)
THE BEAT: *I Just Can't Stop It* (Go Feet BEAT 1)
BOFF/BOSS: Rude Boys Are Back In Town/Live Fast
Die Laughing (RAK 315)
THE CHORDS: *So Far Away* (Polydor POLS 1019)
COCKNEY REJECTS: I'm Forever Blowing
Bubbles/West Side Boys (RZ Z4)
THE DETAILS: Keep On Running/Run Ins (Energy
NRG 2)
THE LAMBRETTAS: Daaance/Feel the Beat (Rocket
XPRES 33)
THE NAME: Forget Art, Let's Dance/Misfits (DinDisc
DIN 14)
PURPLE HEARTS: *Beat That!* (Fiction FIX 002)
THE RENT BOYS: Kick Down The Door/Feeling Ice
(WEA K18230)
THE SPECIALS: Rat Race/Rude Boys Outa Jail (2-
Tone TT 11)

THE SUSSED: I've Ghot Me A Parka/Myself Myself
And I Repeated (Graduate GRAD 7)
various: *Uppers On The South Downs* (Safari UPP
1)

JUNE
LAUREL AITKEN: Big Fat Man/It's Too Late (I Spy SEE
7)
AKRYLYKZ: JD/Ska'd For Life (Polydor 2059 253)
BAD MANNERS: Lip Up Fatty/Night Bus To Dalston
(Magnet MAG 175)
DEXY'S MIDNIGHT RUNNERS: There There My
Dear/The Horse (Parlophone R6038)
JUDGE DREAD: *One Eyed Lodger* EP (Creole CR 202)
THE LAMBRETTAS: *Beat Boys In The Jet Age*
(Rocket TRAIN 10)
THE SKA-DOWS: Apache/The Tune That Time
Forgot (Cheapskate CHEAP 1)
SQUIRE: My Mind Goes Round In Circles/Does
Stephanie Know (Stage One 2)
THE TIGERS: Promises Promises/Ska Trekkin'
(Strike KIK 3)

JULY
ANGELIC UPSTARTS: Last Night Another
Soldier/Man Who Came In From The Beano (RZ7)
THE BLADES: Hot For You/The Reunion (Energy
NRG 3)
THE BODYSNATCHERS: Easy Life/Too Expefienced
(2-Tone TT 12)
CAIRO: Movie Stars/Cuthbert's Birthday Treat
(Absurd 12)
THE CHORDS: The British Way Of Life/The way It's
Got To Be (Polydor 2059 258)
COCKNEY REJECTS: We Can Do Anything/15 Nights
(RZ Z6)
DEXY'S MIDNIGHT RUNNERS: *Searching For The
Young Soul Rebels* (Parlophone PCS 7213)
THE GANGSTERS: Wooly Bully/We Are The
Gangsters (Big Bear BB 28)
RELUCTANT STEREOTYPES: Confused
Action/School Life (WEA K 18355)
THE SCENE: I've Had Enough/Show 'em Now
(Inferno BEAT 2)
STEVE SHARP: We Are The Mods/He wants To Be A
Mod (Happy Face MM 122)

AUGUST
THE ARMY: Shuffle Shuffle/Trendy (Map MAP 1)
THE BEAT: Best Friend/Stand Down Margaret (Go
Feet FEET 3)
BOSS: When The Chips Are Down/War War War
(RAK 320)
THE CIRCLES: Angry Voices/Summer Nights

(Vertigo ANGRY 1)
THE DC 10s: Bermuda/I Can See Through Walls
(Certain Euphoria ACE 451)
EDDIE FLOYD: The Beat/London (I Spy SEE 9)
MERTON PARKAS: Put Me In The Picture/In The
Midnight Hour (Beggars BEG 43)
THE RUTS: West One/The Crack (Virgin VS 370)
SECRET AFFAIR: Sound Of Confusion/Take It Or
Leave It (I Spy SEE 8)
THE SELECTER: The Whisper/Train To Skaville
(Chrysalis CHSS 1)
THE UPSET: Hurt/Lift Off (Upset 1)

SEPTEMBER
BAD MANNERS: Special Brew/Ivor The Engine
(Magnet MAG 180)
JUDGE DREAD: *Reggae And Ska* (RCA PPL 28408 –
Germany)
MADNESS: *Absolutely* (Stiff SEEZ 29)
MADNESS: Baggy Trousers/The Business (Stiff BUY
84)
RELUCTANT STEREOTYPES: Plans For
Today/Subway (WEA K18721)
SECRET AFFAIR: *Behind Closed Doors* (I Spy 2)
THE SKA-DOWS: Telstar/Yes yes Yes (Cheapskate
CHEAP 4)
SPECIALS: *More Specials* (2-Tone LTT 5003)
SPECIALS: Stereotypes (part one)/International Jet
Set (2-Tone TT 13)
SWINGING CATS: Away/Mantovani (2-Tone TT 14)

OCTOBER
AK BAND: Pink Slippers/Skegway (BOB BOB 1)
THE CHORDS: In My Street/I'll Keep Holding On
(Polydor POSP 185)
COCKNEY REJECTS: *Greatest Hits Vol 2* (RZ ZONO
102)
COCKNEY REJECTS: We Are The Firm/War On The
Terraces (RZ Z10)
RICO: Sea Cruise/Carolina (2-Tone TT 15)
THE RUTS: *Grin And Bear It* (Virgin V2188)
WHITE HEAT: Finished With The Fashions/Ordinary
Joe (Vallium 2)

NOVEMBER
ANGELIC UPSTARTS: England/Stick's Diary (RZ
Z12)
BAD MANNERS: *Loonee Tunes* (Magnet
THE BEAT: Too Nice To Talk To/Psychedelic Rockers
(Go Feet FEET 4)
DEXY'S MIDNIGHT RUNNERS: Keep It Part Two/One
Way Love (Parlophone R6042)
MADNESS: Embarrassment/Crying Shame (Stiff

BUY 102)
THE NEGATIVES; Electric Waltz/Money Talks
(Aardvark STEAL 1)
THE SMALL HOURS: *The Kid* EP (Automatic
K17708)

DECEMBER
BAD MANNERS: Lorraine/ (Magnet 181)
THE BLADES: Ghost Of A Chance/Real Emotion
(Energy NRG 5)
PURPLE HEARTS: My Life's A Jigsaw/Just To Please
You (Safari SAFE 30)
THE SPECIALS: Do Nothing/Maggie's Farm (2-Tone
TT 16)

1981
JANUARY
ANGELIC UPSTARTS: Kids On The Street/The Sun
Never Shines (RZ Z16)
FIRST STEPS: Anywhere Else But Here/I Got The
News (English Rose ERIII)
MADNESS: Return Of Las Palmas 7/That's The
Way... (Stiff BUY 108)

FEBRUARY
NIGHT DOCTOR: Just Enough/Hit And Miss Affair
(Race 1)
THE SELECTER: Celebrate The Bullet/Last Tango
(Chrysalis CHSS 2)
THE SKA CITY ROCKERS: Time Is Tight/Roadrunner
(Inferno BEAT 1)
TEAM 23: Whatever Moves You/Move Into Rhythm
(Race 2)
Various: *Original Soundtrack: Dance Craze* (2-Tone
TT 5004)

MARCH
THE ARMY: Kick It Down/Mr Average (Map MAP 3)
BAD MANNERS: Just A Feeling/ (Magnet 187)
COCKNEY REJECTS: Easy Life/Motorhead/Hang 'em
High (RZ Z20)
DEXY'S MIDNIGHT RUNNERS: Plan B/Soul Finger
(Parlophone R6046)
THE LAMBRETTAS: Good Times/Lamba Samba
(Rocket XPRES 48)
RELUCTANT STEREOTYPES: Nightmares/Factory
Wit (WEA K18721)
RICO: *That Man Is Forward* (2-Tone 5005)
THE SELECTER: *Celebrate The Bullet* (Chrysalis
CHR 1036)

APRIL

THE BEAT: Drowning/All Out To Get You (Go Feet FEET 6)

COCKNEY REJECTS: *Greatest Hits Vol 3* (RZ ZEM 101)

THE LAMBRETTAS: *Ambience* (Rocket TRAIN 14)

THE LAMBRETTAS: Anything You Want/Ambience (XPRESS 48)

MADNESS: Grey Day/Memories (Stiff BUY 112)

THE TIMES: Red With Purple Flashes/Biff Bang Pow (Whaam! 002)

MAY

ANGELIC UPSTARTS: I Understand/Never Come Back (RZ Z22)

THE BEAT: *Wha'ppen?* (Go Feet BEAT 3)

THE CHORDS: One More Minute/Who's Killing Who (Polydor POSP 270)

GIFTED CHILDREN: Painting By Numbers/Lichtenstein Girl (Whaam! 001)

THE HEARTBEATS: Go/One Of The People (Nothing Shaking 1)

THE SKA-DOWS: Yes Yes Yes/Twice (Cheapskate CHEAP 25)

Various: *Strength Through Oi!* (Sounds SKIN 1)

JUNE

ANGELIC UPSTARTS: *2 Million Voices* (RZ ZONO 1004)

BAD MANNERS: Can Can/ (Magnet MAG 190)

THE BEAT: Doors Of Your Heart/Get A Job (Go Feet FEET 9)

COCKNEY REJECTS: On The Streets Again/London (RZ Z21)

BOB MANTON: There's No Trees In Brixton Prison/Brixton Walkabout (Mainstreet 101)

THE SPECIALS: Ghost Town/Why/Friday Night Saturday Morning (2-Tone TT 17)

FURTHER LISTENING

JUDGE DREAD: *The Legendary Judge Dread* (Snapper SMD CD 333)

LEYTON BUZZARDS: *The Punk Collection* (Captain Oi! AHOY CD 225)

MADNESS: *The Business – The Definitive Singles* (Virgin MADBOX 1)

RODDY RADIATION: *Skabilly Anthology* (SBR 01)

THE COVENTRY AUTOMATICS: *Dawning Of A New Era* (Receiver RR 178)

THE RUTS: *Something That I Said: The Best Of* (Caroline 1251)

THE SELECTER/THE SPECIALS: *BBC Radio 1 Live In Concert* (Windsong WINCD 030)

THE SPECIALS: *In The Studio* (2-Tone TT 5008)

THE SPECIALS: *Live At The Moonlight Club* (2-Tone CCD 5011)

TOM ROBINSON BAND: *Power In The Darkness* (EMI EMC 3226)

UB40: *Signing Off* (Graduate GRAD LP 2)

UB40: *The Singles Album* (Graduate GRAD LP 3)

Various: *100% British Ska* (Captain Mod MODSKA 7)

Various: *A Checkered Past: The 2-Tone Collection* (Chrysalis 7243 8 27677 2 5)

Various: *The Beat Goes On* (IRS X2 13086)

Various: *Mod City* (Angel Air SJPCD 097)

Other Titles available from Helter Skelter

Coming Soon

Save What You Can: The Day of The Triffids and the Long Night of David McComb

Finely crafted biography of cult Australian group and their ill-fated frontman who was simply the greatest lyricist of his generation.

Charismatic frontman McComb's finely crafted tales of misfits and troubled outsiders and lost souls, merged Dylan with Carver and a Perth sensibility to brilliant effect, while his sprawling melodies set against "Evil" Graham Lee's slide guitar created an achingly beautiful sound best exemplified by critics' favourites, Born Sandy Devotional and Calenture. In spite of rave critical plaudits, the Triffids' sales were mediocre and in 1990 the band split and returned to Australia. McComb put out one excellent solo album in 1994 before the sense of ominous foreboding that lurked throughout his music was proved prescient when he collapsed and was rushed to hospital to undergo a full heart transplant. Months later he was back in hospital with even more agonising intestinal surgery. McComb made a partial recovery, but the medication he was taking kept him in a permanent state of drowsiness. On Saturday January 30th, 1999, he fell asleep at the wheel of his car. Though McComb survived the crash and discharged himself from hospital, he died suddenly three days later.

Paperback   ISBN 1-900924-21-8   234 X 156mm   16pp b/w photos
UK £14.99   US $19.95

Action Time Vision: The Story of Sniffin Glue, Alternative TV and Punk Rock
By Mark Perry

The legendary founder-editor of Sniffin' Glue – the definitive punk fanzine – gives his own account of the punk years. An eyewitness account of the key gigs; an insider's history of the bands and personalities; the full story of the hugely influential fanzine and the ups and downs of Perry's own recording career with Alternative TV.

Paperback   ISBN 1-900924-89-7   234 X 156mm   16pp b/w photos
UK £14.99   US $21.95   Coming – Spring 2005

The Who By Numbers
By Alan Parker and Steve Grantley

Detailed album-by-album, song-by-song commentary on the songs of one of rock's most important and enduring acts, by Sid Vicious biographer and Lennon expert Parker, teamed with Stiff Little Fingers drummer, Grantley.

Paperback   ISBN 1-900924-91-9   234 X 156mm   16pp b/w photos
UK £14.99   US $19.95

David Bowie: The Shirts He Wears
by Jonathan Richards

A Bowie book with a difference, this is a study of Bowie as a cultural icon that draws together his music, artworks and fashion to paint a fascinating portrait of one of rock's most important figures.

Paperback   ISBN 1-900924-25-0   234 X 156mm   16pp b/w photos
UK £14.99   US $19.95

John Martyn
by Chris Nickson

First ever biography of the pioneering guitarist best-known for his still-revered 70s album *Solid Air*. Draws on interviews with many friends and associates.

Paperback   ISBN 1-900924-86-2   234 X 156mm   16pp b/w photos
UK £14.99   US $19.95

Kicking Against The Pricks: An Armchair Guide to Nick Cave
by Amy Hanson

Nick Cave is the only artist to emerge from the post–punk era whose music and career can truly be compared with legends such as Bob Dylan or Van Morrison, with a string of acclaimed albums including *Junkyard*, *Tender Prey* and *The Boatman's Call*.

Cave left Australia to become part of a maelstrom unleashed to awestruck London audiences in the late seventies: the Birthday Party. Miraculously, Cave survived that band's excesses and formed the Bad Seeds, challenging his audience and the Godfather-of-Goth tag: as a bluesman with a gun in one hand, a Bible in the other; a vamp-ish torch singer with echoes of Vegas-era Elvis and a sensitive writer of love songs. *Kicking Against The Pricks* chronicles in depth these diverse personalities and the musical landscapes that Cave has inhabited, with a penetrating commentary on all his themes and influences. Cave's memorable collaborations and forays into other media are covered too: duets with Kylie Minogue, PJ Harvey and Shane MacGowan, the acclaimed novel *And The Ass Saw The Angel*, film appearances such as Wim Wenders' *Wings of Desire*, and his stint as Meltdown 2000 curator. Ultimately, it reveals Cave as the compelling and always-relevant musical force he is.

Paperback   ISBN 1-900924-96-X   234 X 156mm   16pp b/w photos
UK £14.99   US $19.95

John Lydon's Metal Box: The Story of Public Image Ltd
by Phil Strongman

In between fronting rock's most iconoclastic group, the Sex Pistols, and re-emerging in the 21st century as a reality TV hero on *I'm A Celebrity*, Lydon led the post-punk pioneers Public Image Ltd who tore up the rulebook and merged disco funk and industrial punk to create coruscating soundscapes with catchy tunes – from "Death Disco" and "Flowers of Romance" to "Rise" and "This Is Not A Love Song" – and caused riots at their gigs. An essential chapter in the growth of post punk music and one that reveals Lydon as always forward-thinking and always compelling.

Paperback   ISBN 1-900924-66-8   234 X 156mm   16pp b/w photos
UK £14.99   US $19.95

Music in Dreamland: The Story of Be Bop Deluxe and Bill Nelson
by Paul Sutton-Reeves

Draws on hours of new interviews with Bill Nelson and other members of the band, as well as admirers such as David Sylvian, Stone Roses producer John Leckie, Steve Harley and Reeves Gabrel. Cover artwork especially designed by Bill Nelson himself.

Paperback   ISBN 1-900924-08-8   234 X 156mm   16pp b/w photos
UK £14.99   US $19.95

Wheels Out of Gear: Two Tone, The Specials and a World on Fire
By Dave Thompson

When the punks embraced reggae it led to a late 1970s Ska revival that began in Coventry with Jerry Dammers' Two Tone record label and his band, The Specials. Original 60s rude boy fashions – mohair suits, dark glasses and the ubiquitous pork pie hats – along with Dammers' black & white themed logo were the emblems for a hugely popular scene that also comprised hitmaking groups such as Madness, The Beat and The Selector.

Paperback   ISBN 1-900924-84-6   234 X 156mm   256pp, 16pp b/w photos
UK £12.99   US $19.95

Electric Pioneer: An Armchair Guide to Gary Numan
By Paul Goodwin

From selling 10 million records in 2 years, both with Tubeway Army and solo, to more low key and idiosyncratic releases through subsequent decades, Gary Numan has built up an impressive body of work and retained a hugely devoted cult following. *Electric Pioneer* is the first ever guide to his recorded output, documenting every single and album and featuring sections on his live shows, memorabilia and DVD releases.

Paperback   ISBN 1-900924-95-1   234 X 156mm   256pp, 16pp b/w photos
UK £14.99   US $19.95

Al Stewart: Lights, Camera, Action – A Life in Pictures
By Neville Judd

Best known for his 70s classic "The Year of The Cat," Al Stewart continues to record and tour and retains a large and loyal international fanbase. This is a unique collection of rare and unpublished photographs, documenting Al's public and private life from early days in 1950s Scotland, through to his success in Hollywood and beyond.

Luxury Paperback ISBN 1-900924-90-0 192pp   310 X 227mm
All pages photos, 16pp of colour
UK £25.00   US $35.00

'77 – The Year of Punk and New Wave
by Henry Bech Poulsen

As, 1967 was to the Haight-Ashbury scene, so 1977 was to punk: a year in which classic singles and albums by all the key bands made it the only musical movement that counted, and before its energy and potential was diluted and dampened by the forces of conservatism and commercialism. '77 tells the story of what every punk and new wave band achieved in that heady year – from The Pistols, Clash and Damned to The Lurkers, The Adverts and The Rezillos, and everyone in between.

Paperback   ISBN 1-900924-92-7   245 X 174mm   512pp Illustrated throughout UK £16.99   US $25.00

Linda Ronstadt: A Musical Life
By Peter Lewry

Ronstadt's early backing band became The Eagles and she has had success with songs by Neil Young, Jackson Browne and Hank Williams. After a US number 1 single and grammy winning country rock albums in the 1970s, she has continued to challenge preconceptions with albums of Nelson Riddle-produced standards, a record of mariachi songs and a collaboration with Dolly Parton and Emmylou Harris. This is her first ever biography.

Paperback   ISBN 1-900924-50-1   234 X 156mm   256 pp 16pp b/w photos UK £16.99   US $25.00

Sex Pistols: Only Anarchists are Pretty
Mick O'Shea

Drawing both on years of research and on creative conjecture, this book, written as a novel, portrays the early years of the Sex Pistols. Giving a fictionalised fly-on-the-wall account of the arguments, in-jokes, gigs, pub sessions and creative tension, it documents the day-to-day life of the ultimate punk band before the Bill Grundy incident and Malcolm Mclaren-orchestrated tabloid outrage turned their lives into a media circus.

Paperback   ISBN 1-900924-93-5   234mm X 156mm 256pp 8pp b/w photos UK £12.99   US $19.95

True Faith: An Armchair Guide to New Order
By Dave Thompson

Formed from the ashes of Joy Division after their ill fated singer Ian Curtis hung himself, few could have predicted that New Order would become one of the seminal groups of the 80s, making a series of albums that would compare well with anything Joy Division had produced, and embracing club culture a good ten years before most of their contemporaries.

From the bestselling 12 inch single "Blue Monday" to later hits like "Bizarre Love Triangle" [featured in the *Trainspotting* movie] and their spectacular world cup song "World In Motion" the band have continued making innovative, critically revered records that have also enjoyed massive commercial success.

This book is the first to treat New Order's musical career as a separate achievement, rather than a postscript to Joy Division's and the first to analyse in depth what makes their music so great.

Paperback   ISBN 1-900924-94-3 8   234mm X 156mm 256pp 8pp b/w photos UK £12.99   US $19.95

Currently Available from Helter Skelter Publishing

Steve Marriott: All Too Beautiful
by Paolo Hewitt and John Hellier £20.00

Marriott was the prime mover behind 60s chart-toppers The Small Faces. Longing to be treated as a serious musician he formed Humble Pie with Peter Frampton, where his blistering rock 'n' blues guitar playing soon saw him take centre stage in the US live favourites. After years in seclusion, Marriott's plans for a comeback in 1991 were tragically cut short when he died in a housefire. He continues to be a key influence for generations of musicians from Paul Weller to Oasis and Blur.

"One of the best books I've read about the backwaters of rock music." *Daily Mail*

"A riveting account of the singer's life, crammed with entertaining stories of rebellion and debauchery and insightful historical background... Compulsive reading." *The Express*

"Revealing... sympathetic, long overdue." ****Uncut*

"We won't see the like of him again and *All Too Beautiful* captures him perfectly. A right riveting read as they say." Gary Crowley, BBC London.

"Hewitt's portrayal makes compelling reading."**** *Mojo*

Hardback   ISBN 1-900924-44-7   234mm X 156mm 352pp 32pp b/w photos
UK £20   US $29.95

Bob Dylan: Like The Night (Revisited)
by CP Lee

Fully revised and updated edition of the hugely acclaimed document of Dylan's pivotal 1966 show at the Manchester Free Trade Hall where fans called him Judas for turning his back on folk music in favour of rock 'n' roll. The album of the concert was released in the same year as the book's first outing and has since become a definitive source.

"A terrific tome that gets up close to its subject and breathes new life into it... For any fan of Dylan this is quite simply essential." *Time Out*

"Putting it all vividly in the context of the time, he writes expertly about that one electrifying, widely-bootlegged night." *Mojo*

"CP Lee's book flushed 'Judas' out into the open." *The Independent*

"An atmospheric and enjoyable account." *Uncut* (Top 10 of the year)

Paperback   ISBN 1-900924-33-1   198mm X 129mm 224pp 16pp b/w photos
UK £9.99   US $17.95

Everybody Dance
Chic and the Politics of Disco
By Daryl Easlea

Everybody Dance puts the rise and fall of Bernard Edwards and Nile Rodgers, the emblematic disco duo behind era-defining records 'Le Freak', 'Good Times' and 'Lost In Music', at the heart of a changing landscape, taking in socio-political and cultural events such as the Civil Rights struggle, the Black Panthers and the US oil crisis. There are drugs, bankruptcy, up-tight artists, fights, and Muppets but, most importantly an in-depth appraisal of a group whose legacy remains hugely underrated.

Paperback   ISBN 1-900924-56-0   234mm X 156mm 256pp 8pp b/w photos
UK £14.00   US $19.95

This Is a Modern Life
by Enamel Verguren

Lavishly illustrated guide to the mod revival that was sparked by the 1979 release of *Quadrophenia*. This Is a Modern Life concentrates on the 1980s, but takes in 20 years of a Mod life in London and throughout the world, from 1979 to 1999, with interviews of people directly involved, loads of flyers and posters and a considerable amount of great photos.

"Good stuff ... A nice nostalgic book full of flyers, pics and colourful stories." *Loaded*

Paperback ISBN 1-900924-77-3 264mm X 180mm 224pp photos throughout
UK £14.99 US $19.95

Smashing Pumpkins: Tales of A Scorched Earth
by Amy Hanson

Initially contemporaries of Nirvana, Billy Corgan's Smashing Pumpkins outgrew and outlived the grunge scene and with hugely acclaimed commercial triumphs like *Siamese Dream* and *Mellon Collie and The Infinite Sadness*. Though drugs and other problems led to the band's final demise, Corgan's recent return with Zwan is a reminder of how awesome the Pumpkins were in their prime. Seattle-based Hanson has followed the band for years and this is the first in-depth biography of their rise and fall.

"Extremely well-written ... A thrilling and captivating read." *Classic Rock*

"Sex, bust-ups, heavy metal, heroin death and a quadruple-platinum dream-pop double album... The first ever 'serious' Pumpkins biography." *NME*

"A fascinating story ... Hanson has done her research." *Q*

Paperback ISBN 1-900924-68-4 234mm X 156mm 256pp 8pp b/w photos
UK £12.99 US $18.95

Be Glad: An Incredible String Band Compendium
Edited by Adrian Whittaker

The ISB pioneered 'world music' on '60s albums like *The Hangman's Beautiful Daughter* – Paul McCartney's favourite album of 1967! – experimented with theatre, film and lifestyle and inspired Led Zeppelin. *Be Glad* features interviews with all the ISB key players, as well as a wealth of background information, reminiscence, critical evaluations and arcane trivia, this is a book that will delight any reader with more than a passing interest in the ISB.

Paperback ISBN 1-900924-64-1 234mm X 156mm 288pp
b/w photos throughout
UK £14.99 US $22.95

ISIS: A Bob Dylan Anthology
Ed Derek Barker

ISIS is the best-selling, longest lasting, most highly acclaimed Dylan fanzine. This ultimate Dylan anthology draws on unpublished interviews and research by the *ISIS* team together with the best articles culled from the pages of the definitive Bob magazine. From Bob's earliest days in New York City to the more recent legs of the Never Ending Tour, the *ISIS* archive has exclusive interview material – often rare or previously unpublished – with many of the key players in Dylan's career: friends, musicians and other collaborators, such as playwright Jacques Levy and folk hero Martin Carthy.

Fully revised and expanded edition features additional previously unpublished articles and further rare photos;

"Astounding ... Fascinating... If you're more than mildly interested in Bob Dylan then this is an essential purchase." *Record Collector*

"This book is worth any Dylan specialist's money." Ian MacDonald – **** *Uncut*

Paperback   ISBN 1-900924-82-X   198mm X 129mm 352pp, 16pp b/w photos
UK £9.99   US $17.95

Waiting for the Man: The Story of Drugs and Popular Music
Harry Shapiro
From Marijuana and Jazz, through acid-rock and speed-fuelled punk, to crack-driven rap and Ecstasy and the Dance Generation, this is the definitive history of drugs and pop. It also features in-depth portraits of music's most famous drug addicts: from Charlie Parker to Sid Vicious and from Jim Morrison to Kurt Cobain. Chosen by the BBC as one of the Top Twenty Music Books of All Time. "Wise and witty." *The Guardian*

Paperback   ISBN 1-900924-58-7   198mm X 129mm 320pp
UK £10.99   US $17.95

Jefferson Airplane: Got a Revolution
Jeff Tamarkin
With smash hits "Somebody to Love" and "White Rabbit" and albums like *Surrealistic Pillow*, Jefferson Airplane, the most successful and influential rock band to emerge from San Francisco during the 60s, created the sound of a generation. To the public they were free-loving, good-time hippies, but to their inner circle, Airplane were a paradoxical bunch – constantly at odds with each other. Jefferson Airplane members were each brilliant, individualistic artists who became the living embodiment of the ups and downs of the sex, drugs and rock 'n' roll lifestyle.

Tamarkin has interviewed the former band members, friends, lovers, crew members and fellow musicians to come up with the definitive full-length history of the group.

"A compelling account of a remarkable band." *Record Collector*

"A superb chunk of writing that documents every twist and turn in the ever-evolving life of a great American band." *Record Collector*

Paperback   ISBN 1-900924-78-1   234mm X 156mm 408pp , 16pp b/w photos
UK £14.99   US No rights

Surf's Up: The Beach Boys on Record 1961-1981
Brad Elliott
The ultimate reference work on the recording sessions of one of the most influential and collectable groups.

"factually unimpeachable ... an exhausting, exhilarating 500 pages of discographical and session information about everything anybody connected with the group ever put down or attempted to put down on vinyl." *Goldmine*

Paperback   ISBN 1-900924-79-X   234mm X 156mm 512pp, 16pp b/w photos
UK £25.00   US No rights

Get Back: The Beatles' Let It Be Disaster
Doug Suply and Ray Shweighardt

Reissued to coincide with the release of *Let It Be ... Naked*, this is a singularly candid look at the greatest band in history at their ultimate moment of crisis. It puts the reader in the studio as John cedes power to Yoko; Paul struggles to keep things afloat, Ringo shrugs and George quits the band.

"One of the most poignant Beatles books ever." *Mojo*

Paperback   ISBN 1-900924-83-8   198mm X 129mm 352pp
UK £9.99   No US rights

The Clash: Return of the Last Gang in Town
Marcus Gray

Exhaustively researched definitive biography of the last great rock band that traces their progress from pubs and punk clubs to US stadiums and the Top Ten. This edition is further updated to cover the band's induction into the Rock 'n' Roll Hall of Fame and the tragic death of iconic frontman Joe Strummer.

"A must-have for Clash fans [and] a valuable document for anyone interested in the punk era." *Billboard*

"It's important you read this book." *Record Collector*

Paperback   ISBN 1-900924-62-5   234mm X 156mm 512pp, 8pp b/w photos
UK £14.99   US No rights

Love: Behind The Scenes
By Michael Stuart-Ware

LOVE were one of the legendary bands of the late 60s US West Coast scene. Their masterpiece *Forever Changes* still regularly appears in critics' polls of top albums, while a new-line up of the band has recently toured to mass acclaim. Michael Stuart-Ware was LOVE's drummer during their heyday and shares his inside perspective on the band's recording and performing career and tells how drugs and egos thwarted the potential of one of the great groups of the burgeoning psychedelic era.

Paperback   ISBN 1-900924-59-5   234mm X 156mm 256pp
UK £14.00   US $19.95

A Secret Liverpool: In Search of the La's
By MW Macefield

With timeless single "There She Goes", Lee Mavers' La's overtook The Stone Roses and paved the way for Britpop. However, since 1991, The La's have been silent, while rumours of studio-perfectionism, madness and drug addiction have abounded. The author sets out to discover the truth behind Mavers' lost decade and eventually gains a revelatory audience with Mavers himself.

Paperback   ISBN 1-900924-63-3   234mm X 156mm 192pp
UK £11.00   US $17.95

The Fall: A User's Guide
Dave Thompson

Amelodic, cacophonic and magnificent, The Fall remain the most enduring and prolific of the late-'70s punk and post-punk iconoclasts. *A User's Guide* chronicles the historical and musical background to more than 70 different LPs (plus reissues) and as many singles. The band's history is also documented year-by-year, filling in the gaps between the record releases.

Paperback   ISBN 1-900924-57-9   234mm X 156mm 256pp, 8pp b/w photos
UK £12.99   US $19.95

Pink Floyd: A Saucerful of Secrets
by Nicholas Schaffner

Long overdue reissue of the authoritative and detailed account of one of the most important and popular bands in rock history. From the psychedelic explorations of the Syd Barrett-era to 70s superstardom with *Dark Side of the Moon*, and on to triumph of *The Wall*, before internecine strife tore the group apart. Schaffner's definitive history also covers the improbable return of Pink Floyd without Roger Waters, and the hugely successful *Momentary Lapse of Reason* album and tour.

Paperback   ISBN 1-900924-52-8   234mm X 156mm 256pp, 8pp b/w photos
UK £14.99   No rights

The Big Wheel
by Bruce Thomas

Thomas was bassist with Elvis Costello at the height of his success. Though names are never named, *The Big Wheel* paints a vivid and hilarious picture of life touring with Costello and co, sharing your life 24-7 with a moody egotistical singer, a crazed drummer and a host of hangers-on. Costello sacked Thomas on its initial publication.

"A top notch anecdotalist who can time a twist to make you laugh out loud." *Q*

Paperback   ISBN 1-900924-53-6   234mm X 156mm 192pp
UK £10.99 $17.95

Hit Men: Powerbrokers and Fast Money Inside The Music Business
By Fredric Dannen

Hit Men exposes the seamy and sleazy dealings of America's glitziest record companies: payola, corruption, drugs, Mafia involvement, and excess.

"This is quite possibly the best book ever written about the business side of the music industry." *Music Week*

"This is simply the greatest book about the business end of the music industry." *Q******

"So heavily awash with cocaine, corruption and unethical behaviour that it makes the occasional examples of chart-rigging and playlist tampering in Britain during the same period seem charmingly inept." *The Guardian*.

Paperback   ISBN 1-900924-54-4   234mm X 156mm 512pp, 8pp b/w photos
UK £14.99   No rights

I'm With The Band: Confessions of A Groupie
By Pamela Des Barres

Frank and engaging memoir of affairs with Keith Moon, Noel Redding and Jim Morrison, travels with Led Zeppelin as Jimmy Page's girlfriend, and friendships with Robert Plant, Gram Parsons, and Frank Zappa.

"Long overdue reprint of a classic 60s memoir – one of the few music books to talk openly about sex." *Mojo*

"One of the most likeable and sparky-first hand accounts." *Q*****

"Miss Pamela, the most beautiful and famous of the groupies. Her memoir of her life with rock stars is funny, bittersweet, and tender-hearted." Stephen Davis, author of *Hammer of the Gods*

Paperback   ISBN 1-900924-55-2   234mm X 156mm 256pp, 16pp b/w photos
UK £14.99 $19.95

Psychedelic Furs: Beautiful Chaos
by Dave Thompson

Psychedelic Furs were the ultimate post-punk band – combining the chaos and vocal rasp of the Sex Pistols with a Bowie-esque glamour. The Furs hit the big time when John Hughes wrote a movie based on their early single "Pretty in Pink". Poised to join U2 and Simple Minds in the premier league, they withdrew behind their shades, remaining a cult act, but one with a hugely devoted following.

Paperback   ISBN 1-900924-47-1   234mm X 156mm 256pp, 16pp b/w photos
UK £14.99 $19.95

Marillion: Separated Out
by Jon Collins

From the chart hit days of Fish and "Kayleigh" to the Steve Hogarth incarnation, Marillion have continued to make groundbreaking rock music. Collins tells the full story, drawing on interviews with band members, associates, and the experiences of some of the band's most dedicated fans.

Paperback   ISBN 1-900924-49-8   234mm X 156mm 288pp, illustrated throughout
UK £14.99 $19.95

Rainbow Rising
by Roy Davies

The full story of guitar legend Ritchie Blackmore's post-Purple progress with one of the great 70s rock bands. After quitting Deep Purple at the height of their success, Blackmore combined with Ronnie James Dio to make epic rock albums like *Rising* and *Long Live Rock 'n' Roll* before streamlining the sound and enjoying hit singles like "Since You've Been Gone" and "All Night Long." Rainbow were less celebrated than Deep Purple, but they feature much of Blackmore's finest writing and playing, and were one of the best live acts of the era. They are much missed.

Paperback   ISBN 1-900924-31-5   234mm X 156mm 256pp,
illustrated throughout
UK £14.99 $19.95

Back to the Beach: A Brian Wilson and the Beach Boys Reader
REVISED EDITION
Ed Kingsley Abbott

Revised and expanded edition of the Beach Boys compendium *Mojo* magazine deemed an "essential purchase." This collection includes all of the best articles, interviews and reviews from the Beach Boys' four decades of music, including definitive pieces by Timothy White, Nick Kent and David Leaf. New material reflects on the tragic death of Carl Wilson and documents the rejuvenated Brian's return to the boards. "Rivetting!" **** *Q* "An essential purchase." *Mojo*

Paperback   ISBN 1-900924-46-3   234mm X 156mm 288pp
UK £14.99 $19.95

Harmony in My Head
The Original Buzzcock Steve Diggle's Rock 'n' Roll Odyssey
by Steve Diggle and Terry Rawlings

First-hand account of the punk wars from guitarist and one half of the songwriting duo that gave the world three chord punk-pop classics like "Ever Fallen In Love" and "Promises". Diggle dishes the dirt on punk contemporaries like The Sex Pistols, The Clash and The Jam, as well as sharing poignant memories of his friendship with Kurt Cobain, on whose last ever tour, The Buzzcocks were support act.

"Written with spark and verve, this rattling account of Diggle's time in the Buzzcocks will appeal to those with an interest in punk or just late-1970s Manchester. " *Music Week* "This warts'n'all monologue is a hoot ... Diggle's account of the rise, fall and birth of the greatest Manchester band of the past 50 years is relayed with passion and candour... but it works best as a straightforward sex, drugs and rock'n'roll memoir." – *Uncut* ****

Paperback   ISBN 1-900924-37-4   234mm X 156mm 224pp, 8pp b/w photos
UK £14.99 $19.95

Serge Gainsbourg: A Fistful of Gitanes
by Sylvie Simmons

Rock press legend Simmons' hugely acclaimed biography of the French genius.

"I would recommend A Fistful of Gitanes [as summer reading] which is a highly entertaining biography of the French singer-songwriter and all-round scallywag"- JG Ballard

"A wonderful introduction to one of the most overlooked songwriters of the 20th century" (Number 3, top music books of 2001) *The Times*

"The most intriguing music-biz biography of the year" *The Independent*

"Wonderful. Serge would have been so happy" – Jane Birkin

Paperback   ISBN 1-900924-   198mm X 129mm 288pp, 16pp b/w photos
UK £14.99 $19.95

Blues: The British Connection
by Bob Brunning

Former Fleetwood Mac member Bob Brunning's classic account of the impact of Blues in Britain, from its beginnings as the underground music of 50s teenagers like Mick Jagger, Keith Richards and Eric Clapton, to the explosion in the 60s, right through to the vibrant scene of the present day.

"An invaluable reference book and an engaging personal memoir" – Charles Shaar Murray

Paperback   ISBN 1-900924-41-2   234mm X 156mm 352pp, 24pp b/w photos
UK £14.99 $19.95

On The Road With Bob Dylan
by Larry Sloman

In 1975, as Bob Dylan emerged from 8 years of seclusion, he dreamed of putting together a travelling music show that would trek across the country like a psychedelic carnival. The dream became a reality, and On The Road With Bob Dylan is the ultimate behind-the-scenes look at what happened. When Dylan and the Rolling Thunder Revue took to the streets of America, Larry "Ratso" Sloman was with them every step of the way.

"The War and Peace of Rock and Roll." – Bob Dylan

Paperback   ISBN 1-900924-51-X   234mm X 156mm 448pp
UK £14.99 $19.95

Gram Parsons: God's Own Singer
By Jason Walker

Brand new biography of the man who pushed The Byrds into country-rock territory on Sweethearts of The Rodeo, and quit to form the Flying Burrito Brothers. Gram lived hard, drank hard, took every drug going and somehow invented country rock, paving the way for Crosby, Stills & Nash, The Eagles and Neil Young. Parsons' second solo LP, Grievous Angel, is a haunting masterpiece of country soul. By the time it was released, he had been dead for 4 months. He was 26 years old.

"Walker has done an admirable job in taking us as close to the heart and soul of Gram Parsons as any author could." **** Uncut book of the month

Paperback   ISBN 1-900924-27-7   234mm X 156mm 256pp, 8pp b/w photos
UK £12.99 $18.95

Ashley Hutchings: The Guvnor and the Rise of Folk Rock – Fairport Convention, Steeleye Span and the Albion Band
by Geoff Wall and Brian Hinton

As founder of Fairport Convention and Steeleye Span, Ashley Hutchings is the pivotal figure in the history of folk rock. This book draws on hundreds of hours of interviews with Hutchings and other folk-rock artists and paints a vivid picture of the scene that also produced Sandy Denny, Richard Thompson, Nick Drake, John Martyn and Al Stewart.

Paperback   ISBN 1-900924-32-3   234mm X 156mm 288pp,
photos throughout
UK £14.99 $19.95

The Beach Boys' Pet Sounds: The Greatest Album of the Twentieth Century
by Kingsley Abbott

Pet Sounds is the 1966 album that saw The Beach Boys graduate from lightweight pop like "Surfin' USA", *et al*, into a vehicle for the mature compositional genius of Brian Wilson. The album was hugely influential, not least on The Beatles. This the full story of the album's background, its composition and recording, its contemporary reception and its enduring legacy.

Paperback   ISBN 1-900924-30-7   234mm X 156mm 192pp
UK £11.95 $18.95

King Crimson: In The Court of King Crimson
by Sid Smith

King Crimson's 1969 masterpiece *In The Court Of The Crimson King*, was a huge U.S. chart hit. The band followed it with 40 further albums of consistently challenging, distinctive and innovative music. Drawing on hours of new interviews, and encouraged by Crimson supremo Robert Fripp, the author traces the band's turbulent history year by year, track by track.

Paperback   ISBN 1-900924-26-9   234mm X 156mm 288pp, photos throughout
UK £14.99 $19.95

A Journey Through America with the Rolling Stones
by Robert Greenfield UK Price £9.99
Featuring a new foreword by Ian Rankin

This is the definitive account of The Stones' legendary '72 tour.

"Filled with finely-rendered detail ... a fascinating tale of times we shall never see again" *Mojo*

"The Stones on tour in '72 twist and burn through their own myth: from debauched outsiders to the first hints of the corporate business – the lip-smacking chaos between the Stones fan being stabbed by a Hell's Angel at Altamont and the fan owning a Stones credit card." – Paul Morley #2 essential holiday rock reading list, *The Observer*, July 04.

Paperback   ISBN 1-900924-24-2   198mm X 129mm 256pp
UK £14.99 $19.95

The Sharper Word: A Mod Reader
Ed Paolo Hewitt

Hewitt's hugely readable collection documents the clothes, the music, the clubs, the drugs and the faces behind one of the most misunderstood and enduring cultural movements and includes hard to find pieces by Tom Wolfe, bestselling novelist Tony Parsons, poet laureate Andrew Motion, disgraced Tory grandee Jonathan Aitken, Nik Cohn, Colin MacInnes, Mary Quant, and Irish Jack.

"An unparalleled view of the world-conquering British youth cult." *The Guardian*

"An excellent account of the sharpest-dressed subculture." *Loaded*, Book of the Month

Paperback   ISBN 1-900924-34-X   198mm X 129mm 192pp
UK £14.99 $19.95

Backlist

The Nice: Hang On To A Dream by Martyn Hanson
1900924439   256pp   £13.99

Al Stewart: Adventures of a Folk Troubadour by Neville Judd
1900924366   320pp   £25.00

Marc Bolan and T Rex: A Chronology by Cliff McLenahan
1900924420   256pp   £13.99

Razor Edge: Bob Dylan and The Never-ending Tour by Andrew Muir
1900924137   256pp   £12.99

Calling Out Around the World: A Motown Reader Edited by Kingsley Abbott
1900924145   256pp   £13.99

I've Been Everywhere: A Johnny Cash Chronicle by Peter Lewry
1900924226   256pp   £14.99

Sandy Denny: No More Sad Refrains by Clinton Heylin
1900924358   288pp   £13.99

Animal Tracks: The Story of The Animals by Sean Egan
1900924188   256pp   £12.99

Like a Bullet of Light: The Films of Bob Dylan by CP Lee
1900924064   224pp   £12.99

Rock's Wild Things: The Troggs Files by Alan Clayson and J Ryan
1900924196   224pp   £12.99

Dylan's Daemon Lover by Clinton Heylin
1900924153   192pp   £12.00

XTC: Song Stories by XTC and Neville Farmer
190092403X   352pp   £12.99

Born in the USA: Bruce Springsteen by Jim Cullen
1900924056   320pp   £9.99

Bob Dylan by Anthony Scaduto
1900924234   320pp   £10.99

Firefly Publishing: An Association between Helter Skelter and SAF

The Nirvana Recording Sessions
by Rob Jovanovic £20.00
Drawing on years of research, and interviews with many who worked with the band, the author has documented details of every Nirvana recording, from early rehearsals, to the *In Utero* sessions. A fascinating account of the creative process of one of the great bands.

The Music of George Harrison: While My Guitar Gently Weeps
by Simon Leng £20.00
Often in Lennon and McCartney's shadow, Harrison's music can stand on its own merits. Santana biographer Leng takes a studied, track by track, look at both Harrison's contribution to The Beatles, and the solo work that started with the release in 1970 of his epic masterpiece *All Things Must Pass*. "Here Comes The Sun", "Something" – which Sinatra covered and saw as the perfect love song – "All Things Must Pass" and "While My Guitar Gently Weeps" are just a few of Harrison's classic songs.

Originally planned as a celebration of Harrison's music, this is now sadly a commemoration.

The Pretty Things: Growing Old Disgracefully
by Alan Lakey £20
First biography of one of rock's most influential and enduring combos. Trashed hotel rooms, infighting, rip-offs, sex, drugs and some of the most remarkable rock 'n' roll, including land mark albums like the first rock opera, *SF Sorrow*, and *Rolling Stone*'s album of the year, 1970's *Parachute*.

"They invented everything, and were credited with nothing." Arthur Brown, "God of Hellfire"

The Sensational Alex Harvey
By John Neil Murno £20
Part rock band, part vaudeville, 100% commitment, the SAHB were one of the greatest live bands of the era. But behind his showman exterior, Harvey was increasingly beset by alcoholism and tragedy. He succumbed to a heart attack on the way home from a gig in 1982, but he is fondly remembered as a unique entertainer by friends, musicians and legions of fans.

U2: The Complete Encyclopedia by Mark Chatterton £14.99

Poison Heart: Surviving The Ramones by Dee Dee Ramone and Veronica Kofman £9.99

Minstrels In The Gallery: A History Of Jethro Tull by David Rees £12.99

DANCEMUSICSEXROMANCE: Prince – The First Decade by Per Nilsen £12.99

To Hell and Back with Catatonia by Brian Wright £12.99

Soul Sacrifice: The Santana Story by Simon Leng UK Price £12.99

Opening The Musical Box: A Genesis Chronicle by Alan Hewitt UK Price £12.99

Blowin' Free: Thirty Years Of Wishbone Ash by Gary Carter and Mark Chatterton UK Price £12.99

www.helterskelterbooks.com

All Helter Skelter, Firefly and SAF titles are available by mail order from
www.helterskelterbooks.com
Or from our office:
Helter Skelter Publishing Limited
South Bank House
Black Prince Road
London SE1 7SJ

Telephone: +44 (0) 20 7463 2204 or Fax: +44 (0)20 7463 2295
Mail order office hours: Mon-Fri 10:00am – 1:30pm,
By post, enclose a cheque [must be drawn on a British bank],
International Money Order, or credit card number and expiry date.

Postage prices per book worldwide are as follows:

UK & Channel Islands	£1.50
Europe & Eire (air)	£2.95
USA, Canada (air)	£7.50
Australasia, Far East (air)	£9.00

Email: info@helterskelterbooks.com